AA
BRITAIN
FOR
FREE

2

Editor: Robert Baker

Art Editor: P. M. Davies

Gazetteer: compiled by the Publications Research Unit of the Automobile Association

Maps: prepared by the Cartographic Services Unit of the Automobile Association

Cover pictures: *Left : HMS Victory, Portsmouth; Mow Cop, Staffs; St Mary's Church, Fairford, Glos; Botanical Gardens, Oxford; Brecknock Museum, Brecon;*
Right: St Paul's Cathedral, London; Box Hill, Surrey; Pentre Ifan, Newport, Dyfed; Canal boat; The Mall, London.

Head of Advertisement Sales: Christopher Heard tel 0256 20123

Advertisement Production: Karen Weeks tel 0256 20123

Advertisement Sales Representatives: London, East Anglia, East Midlands, Central Southern and South East England: Edward May tel 0256 20123 or 0256 467568 South West, West, West Midlands: Bryan Thompson tel 0272 393296

Wales, North of England, Scotland: Arthur Williams tel 0222 620267

Filmset by: Turnergraphic Ltd, Basingstoke, Hants

Printed and bound by: Purnell (Book Production) Ltd, Paulton, Avon

ISBN 0 86145 330 1   **AA Ref: 59132**

Published by the Automobile Association, Fanum House, Basingstoke, Hampshire RG21 2EA.

Please note that, in line with recent Government policy, some museums and other places of interest may introduce, or may already have introduced, an entry charge since this book was compiled.

CONTENTS

Ancient Monuments, National Trust Properties and The National Gardens Scheme

Ancient Monuments
AM Ancient Monuments in England are in the care of the Historic Buildings and Monuments Commission for England, popularly known as English Heritage, PO Box 43, Ruislip, Middlesex HA4 0XW, with the exception of seven properties in and around London which are administered by the Department of the Environment. Ancient Monuments in Scotland (with the exception of Holyrood House) are the responsibility of the Scottish Development Department, 3 Melville St, Edinburgh EH3 7QD.
Ancient Monuments in Wales are the responsibility of CADW, Brunel House, Fitzalan Rd, Cardiff.
Except where otherwise stated, the standard times of opening for all Ancient Monuments, except Scotland, are as follows:
16 Oct-14 Mar:
    weekdays 9.30-4
    Sunday 2-4
15 Mar-15 Oct:
    weekdays 9.30-6.30
    Sunday 2-6.30
Certain standard times for Ancient Monuments now include Sunday opening from 9.30 between April and September only; these entries have in each case been marked with a † after the word 'open' in the gazetteer. Standard times of opening for all Ancient Monuments in Scotland are as follows:
Apr-Sep:
    weekdays 9.30-7

    Sundays 2-7
Oct-Mar:
    weekdays 9.30-4
    Sundays 2-4
All monuments in England and Wales are closed on 1 January and 24-26 December. Those in Scotland are closed on 25 and 26 December, also 1 and 2 January. Some of the smaller monuments may close for the lunch hour and may be closed for one or two days a week. It is advisable to check before visiting.

The National Trusts
NT Indicates properties in England and Wales administered by the National Trust for Places of Historic Interest or Natural Beauty, 42 Queen Anne's Gate, London SW1H 9AS.
NTS National Trust for Scotland, 5 Charlotte Square, Edinburgh EH2 4DU.

The National Gardens Scheme
NGS National Gardens Scheme, 57 Lower Belgrave St, London SW1W 0LR.
Over 1,700 gardens (some entries are in this book) open to the public, mostly for one or two days a year.
Proceeds for charity. Booklets £1.35 including postage.

Symbols and abbreviations
Other symbols and abbreviations used throughout this publication will be found inside the front cover, whilst an explanation of how to use the gazetteer section appears on page 5.

About this Book

In this book we list hundreds of places to visit and try to provide as much information as possible for the intending visitor.

Gazetteer
The gazetteer is listed in strict alphabetical order throughout. As far as possible, the places of interest situated within one or two miles of a town or village are placed under the nearest town or village heading. However, some establishments are too remote for this to be done and such places are listed under their own name. Should you be in any doubt about a particular place, the comprehensive index at the back of the book will indicate where it can be found.

Atlas
If you are planning a day out or a holiday in a particular area, you might find it useful to refer in the first instance to the atlas at the back of the book where all of the towns and individual establishments that we list are located. A useful key at the front of the atlas section will help you find the area you require. Each gazetteer entry also gives a map reference which includes the atlas page number and grid code.

Opening dates
The dates quoted in the gazetteer are inclusive, so that Apr-Oct indicates that the establishment is open from the beginning of April to the end of October. (For Ancient Monuments see page 4.)

Telephone
Unless otherwise stated the telephone exchange given in the gazetteer is that of the town under which the establishment is listed. Where the exchange for a particular establishment is not that of the town under which it appears the name of the exchange is given after the telephone symbol and before the dialling code and number.
In some areas telephone numbers are likely to be changed by the telephone authorities during the currency of this publication. If you have any difficulty it is advisable to check with the operator.

Donation and Charity Boxes
Some of the places of interest listed in the gazetteer are administered by Charities, Trusts and Associations. They are responsible for carrying out much of the restoration work in order to promote Britain's heritage and rely on public generosity to continue their work. They do not charge for admission, but donations are appreciated.

Care of the Countryside
The gazetteer contains a selection of countryside sites and nature reserves. Many have public footpaths or waymarked trails leading through them, and these should always be followed, since the object of such reserves is that these areas should remain undisturbed. Irreparable damage can be done to reserves by those who, perhaps quite innocently, wander over them at will. Access to some reserves, or parts of reserves, is often limited and these details should always be checked before making a visit.

Please always follow the Country Code:
Enjoy the countryside and respect its life and work
Guard against all risk of fire
Fasten all gates
Keep dogs under close control
Keep to public paths across farmland
Use gates and stiles to cross fences, hedges and walls
Leave livestock, crops and machinery alone
Take your litter home
Help to keep all water clean
Protect wildlife, plants and trees
Take special care on country roads
Make no unnecessary noise

Please note that, in line with recent Government policy, some museums and other places of interest may introduce, or may already have introduced, an entry charge since this book was compiled.

GRANADA

Your welcome to the motorways for fast and friendly service 24 hours a day 365 days a year

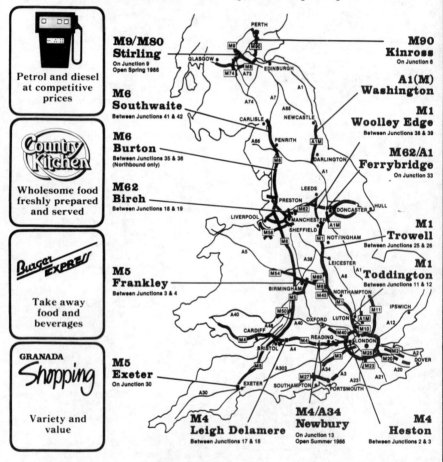

Petrol and diesel at competitive prices

Country Kitchen
Wholesome food freshly prepared and served

Burger Express
Take away food and beverages

GRANADA *Shopping*
Variety and value

M9/M80 Stirling
On Junction 9
Open Spring 1986

M6 Southwaite
Between Junctions 41 & 42

M6 Burton
Between Junctions 35 & 36
(Northbound only)

M62 Birch
Between Junctions 18 & 19

M5 Frankley
Between Junctions 3 & 4

M5 Exeter
On Junction 30

M4 Leigh Delamere
Between Junctions 17 & 18

M4/A34 Newbury
On Junction 13
Open Summer 1986

M90 Kinross
On Junction 6

A1(M) Washington

M1 Woolley Edge
Between Junctions 38 & 39

M62/A1 Ferrybridge
On Junction 33

M1 Trowell
Between Junctions 25 & 26

M1 Toddington
Between Junctions 11 & 12

M4 Heston
Between Junctions 2 & 3

Granada Motorway Service Areas offer a wide range of light refreshments, snacks, take-away food and full meals to suit all tastes and pockets. Shopping and petrol facilities are also available.

Choose Granada–you are very welcome

GAZETTEER

The gazetteer gives locations and details of AA-listed establishments in England, Wales, Scotland and Isle of Man.
Details for islands are shown under individual place-names.
A useful first point of reference is to consult the location maps which show where AA-listed establishments are situated.
(There is no map for the Isles of Scilly.)

ABERBARGOED
Mid Glamorgan   *Map 3 ST19.*
Stuart Crystal
Pengam Glassworks, Angel Ln
Stuart Crystal has been established in Wales since 1966. Here visitors can see the age-old skill of glass cutting and decorating at close hand.

☎ Bargoed (0443) 832705
Open: Tours Mon-Fri, 9.45, 11, 1.30 & 3.15 (ex factory holidays)
Factory shop daily 9-5 (ex Xmas)
⌨

ABERDEEN
Grampian (Aberdeenshire) .
   Map 15 NJ90.
Aberdeen Art Gallery and Museums
Schoolhill
Scottish art from 16th century to present day, with outstanding collection of 20th-century paintings. Water colours, print-room, and art library; contemporary sculpture and decorative arts; special exhibitions and events throughout the year.

☎ (0224) 646333.
Open: Mon-Sat 10-5 (8pm Thu) Sun 2-5. (Closed: Xmas and 1 & 2 Jan.)

⌨ ♿ Shop ✖ (ex guide dogs).

Cruickshank Botanic Garden
University of Aberdeen
Developed at the end of the 19th century, the 10 acres include rock and water gardens, a heather garden, collections of spring bulbs, gentians and Alpine plants. There is also an extensive collection of trees and shrubs.

☎ (0224) 40241 ext 5250 or 5247.
Open: all year Mon-Fri 9-4.30; also Sat & Sun May-Sep 2-4.30
♿

Duthie Park Winter Gardens
Polmuir Road/Riverside Drive
This fine park, with beautifully laid-out gardens occupies an area in the south of the city and on the north bank of the River Dee. It has many exotic plants, flowers, turtles, birds and fish. Of particular interest is a cactus house and a famous 'hill of roses'.

☎ Leisure and Recreation Dept of Aberdeen City Council (0224) 642121.
Open: Dawn-dusk.
♿ ⌨ (✖ in Winter Gardens).

Gordon Highlanders Regimental Museum
Viewfield Road
Situated in the western suburbs, the museum displays the regiment's varied campaigns. There are collections of silver and medals, colours and banners, uniforms and the library has historical material and photographic albums.

☎ (0224) 313387.

Open: Sun & Wed 2-5.
✖

James Dun's House
61 Schoolhill
18th-century house used as a museum with changing exhibitions.

☎ (0224) 646333.
Open: Mon-Sat 10-5
(Closed: Xmas and 1 & 2 Jan.)
Shop ✖ (ex guide dogs).

Kings College
High Street
The college was founded in 1494, but its crown tower is 17th century. The chapel with its richly carved woodwork, dates from the 16th century.

☎ (0224) 40241.
Open: Mon-Fri 9-5, Sat 9-12.30 (ex weddings).
♿ ✖

Marischal College
Broad Street
The college was founded in 1593 but the present building dates from 1844. Forming part of Aberdeen University, it is said to be one of the finest granite buildings in the world with its Mitchell Tower 233 ft high. The College houses the University Anthropological Museum, the Henderson Collection of classical vases, the Grant-Bey Egyptian Collection, a collection of Chinese art (with bronzes of the Shang Yin period), Tang Dynasty horses, and carved jade of the Ming Dynasty.

☎ (0224) 40241.
Open: Mon-Fri 10-5, Sun 2-5.
✖ Shop.

Maritime Museum
Provost Ross's House, Shiprow
This new museum, housed in Aberdeen's oldest surviving building, which is a National

Trust of Scotland property, highlights Aberdeen's maritime history in dramatic and graphic fashion.

☎ (0224) 572215. For group bookings (0224) 646333.
Open: Mon-Sat 10-5 (Closed: Xmas and 1 & 2 Jan).
& (ground floor only) Shop ✻ (ex guide dogs).

Provost Skene's House
Guestrow
A 17th-century house restored as a museum of local history and social life. Furnishings, panelling and plaster ceilings of 17th and 18th century.

☎ (0224) 641086.
Open: Mon-Sat 10-5, (Closed: Xmas and 1 & 2 Jan)
🖻 & (ground floor only) Shop ✻ (ex guide dogs).

St Machar's Cathedral
Chanonry (Old Aberdeen)
Located in Old Aberdeen the partly castellated Cathedral is a magnificent granite building dating from the 14th century. The ceiling is of oak and is painted with emblems of spiritual and temporal monarchs and dates from the 16th century. There are two squat west towers surmounted by spires.

☎ (0224) 45988.
Open: daily 9-5
& ✻

ABERDOUR
Fife (Fife)   Map 11 NT18.
Moray Workshop
High Street
The workshop is housed in a former 18th-century village hospital. Visitors can see the various stages involved in the manufacture of silver and gold jewellery.

☎ (0383) 860248.

Open: Mar-Oct
Mon-Sat 9-5.30.
Shop.

ABERFORD
West Yorkshire   Map 8 SE43.
Lotherton Hall Bird Gardens
The Gardens, close to Leeds, are on a charming rural estate set in beautiful landscaped grounds with waterfalls and ornamental ponds. Here are to be found one of the finest, and developing, collections of species in the country — many of them rare and endangered. Other animals, such as deer, wallabies and chinchillas, also live here.

☎ Leeds (0532) 813723.
Open: Etr-Oct, Tue-Fri 10-4.15; Sat, Sun & BH 11-6 (last admission 5.15).
Admission charged at Lotherton Hall.
🖻 ㅠ &

ABERYSTWYTH
Dyfed   Map 6 SN58.
National Library of Wales
Penglais Hill
One of Britain's six copyright libraries, housed in imposing building of 1911-16, with later additions. Large number of books in all languages, musical publications, prints, drawings and old deeds; specialises in Welsh and Celtic literature. Exhibitions of pictures.

☎ (0970) 3816.
Open: all year Mon-Fri 9.30-6, Sat until 5pm. (Closed BH.) Exhibition Gallery only, open Whitsun & Aug BH.
🖻 & Shop ✻

ACCRINGTON
Lancashire   Map 7 SD72.
Haworth Art Gallery
Haworth Park
Standing in 13½-acre park, the art gallery houses what is

Statue at Lotherton Hall

considered to be one of the finest collections of Tiffany Favrille glass in the world. Also on display are fine collections of 19th-century watercolours and 18th- and 19th-century oil paintings, the most notable being 'The Tempest' by Claude Vernet.

☎ (0254) 33782.
Open: daily 2-5 (closed Fri).
✻

ACHILTIBUIE
Highland (Ross and Cromarty)
                           Map 14 NC00.
The Smokehouse
(3m NW)
Although not allowed into the premises for hygiene reasons, visitors can look through the viewing-gallery windows and see the tradit-

ional craft of curing and smoking of local meat, fish and game being carried out.

☎ (085482) 353.
Open: Mon-Sat 9.30-6.
Shop

ACTON BURNELL
Shropshire   Map 7 SJ50.
Acton Burnell Castle
Ruined 13th-century fortified manor house where the first English Parliament is said to have met in 1283.

Open: at all reasonable times.
(AM)

ALDERSHOT
Hampshire   Map 4 SU85.
Royal Corps of Transport Museum
Buller Barracks
Uniforms and badges of Royal Corps of Transport and predecessors. In addition models and photographs of vehicles used from 1795 to present day.

☎ (0252) 24431 (ext 2417).
Open: Mon-Fri 9-12.30, 2-4.30. 'At Home Day' 12 Jul, Corps Sunday 13 Jul. (Closed BH.)
& Shop ✖

ALLEN BANKS
Northumberland   Map 12 NY76.
(3m W of Haydon Bridge ½m S of A69)
Covering 185 acres, Allen Banks is located in the deep valley of the River Allen shortly before it flows into the River South Tyne. The valley is noted for its deciduous woodland of mature beech and oak inhabited by roe deer and the rare red squirrel. There are attractive riverside trails and in Morralee Wood on the eastern side of the river, a steep climb gives rewarding views.

Open: accessible at all reasonable times.
⊟ NT.

ALTON
Hampshire   Map 4 SU73.
Curtis Museum & Allen Gallery
High St
Contains local collections of geology, botany, zoology, archaeology and history, also craft tools, dolls, toys and games. The Allen Gallery houses a changing programme of temporary exhibitions and the Bignell collection of English ceramics.

☎ (0420) 82802.
Open: Mon-Sat 10-5 (Allen Gallery closed Mon).
⊟ & (ground floor only)
Shop ✖

AMBLESIDE
Cumbria   Map 11 NY30.
Hayes Garden World
(½m S on A591)
The knowledge of six generations of the Hayes family has gone into developing this, one of the most outstanding nurseries in Europe. Beautiful landscaped gardens display an abundance of plants, shrubs and trees, while fascinating tropical plants thrive in the Plant House.

☎ (0966) 33434.
Open: Mon-Fri 9-5.30 (or dusk) Sun & BH 10-5 (or dusk). (Closed 25-26 Dec, 1 Jan.) & ⊏⊐ ⊟ Shop.

AMPTHILL
Bedfordshire   Map 4 TL03.
Houghton House
(N off A418)
Ruined 17th-century mansion with associations with the Countess of Pembroke.

Open: at all reasonable times.
(AM) & (ground floor & gardens only)

ANDERTON
Cheshire   Map 7 SJ67.
Anderton Canal Lift
Designed by Sir E Leader Williams, this unique electric canal lift hoists vessels from the River Weaver Navigation to the Trent and Mersey Canal.
The lift, formerly worked hydraulically, lifts barges 50 ft in just two and a half minutes.

Open: accessible at all reasonable times along canal towpath.

ANDOVER
Hampshire   Map 4 SU34.
Andover Museum
Church Close
The museum is housed in a fine Georgian building; among its displays are locally manufactured agricultural machinery and an aquarium designed to display local fish found in the Test Valley. There is a new natural history gallery.

☎ (0264) 66283.
Open: Tue-Sat 10-5
& (ground floor only) Shop.

ARBORFIELD
Berkshire   Map 4 SU76.
Royal Electrical and Mechanical Engineers' Museum
Isaac Newton Road
The museum tells the story of the REME, whose function is to repair and maintain army vehicles and equipment. Photographs, models and a variety of other related items cover the military and technical aspects of the corps' history.

☎ Arborfield Cross (0734) 760421 Ext 218.
Open: Mon-Fri 9-12.30 & 2-4.30 (4 on Fri) (Closed BH)
& (ground floor only) ✖ Shop.

ARBOR LOW
Derbyshire   *Map 7 SK16.*
Arbor Low Henge
*(off unclass road ¾m E of
A515 at Parsley Hay)*
A particularly fine example of
a henge monument with two
entrances in the containing
bank which is 6 ft high and has
a diameter of 250 ft. There are
some 50 stones many of which
are standing. There is also a
later bronze age barrow on
the site.

Open: accessible at all
reasonable times.
(AM)

ARBROATH
Tayside (Angus)   *Map 12 NO64.*
Arbroath Museum
Signal Tower, Ladyloan
Collection of local history
from prehistoric times to the
industrial revolution. Special
features include the Bellrock
Lighthouse, fishing and wild-
life of Arbroath Cliffs.

☎ (0241) 75598.
Open: Apr-Oct, Mon-Sat
10.30-1, 2-5, Jul & Aug also
Sun 2-5; Nov-Mar, Mon-Fri
2-5, Sat 10.30-1, 2-5.
& (ground floor only) ✖
(ex guide dogs).

ASHBURTON
Devon   *Map 3 SX77.*
Ashburton Museum
1 West Street
Exhibits include local an-
tiquities, weapons, American
Indian antiques, geology
specimens.

☎ (0364) 53278.
Open: May-Sep, Tue, Thu,
Fri, Sat 2.30-5
✖

ASHFORD
Kent   *Map 5 TR04.*
**Intelligence Corps
Museum**
Templer Barracks
Items concerning the Corps

from the two World Wars and
other articles up to the
present day.

☎ (0233) 25254 Ext 208.
Open: Mon-Fri 10-noon, 2-4.
(Closed BH.)
& Shop ✖

ASH VALE
Surrey   *Map 4 SU85.*
RAMC Historical Museum
Keogh Barracks
A collection of some 2,500
items, mainly of military interest but with many unusual
items of general interest.
Exhibits include a horse-
drawn ambulance and a 1942
Austin K2 ambulance. There
are three cases of items relating to the Falklands War
and a display of a patient on
an operating table.

☎ Aldershot (0252) 24431
Ext Keogh 212.
Open: Mon-Fri 8.30-4.
(Closed: Xmas, New Year &
BH.) Weekends & BH by
appointment only.
& Shop ✖

ASTON ROWANT
Oxfordshire   *Map 4 SU79.*
Nature Reserve
*(1½m W of Stokenchurch on
unclass road off A40)*
The Nature Reserve com-
mands an excellent view over
the Oxfordshire Plain and is
located on the scarp slope of
the Chiltern Hills. There are
extensive beech woodlands,
and scattered areas of juni-
per scrub among chalk grass-
lands. In summer, warblers,
nightingales, kestrels and
sparrowhawks can be seen.
Violet helleborine, large
white helleborine and wood
barley are some of the unusual plants found in the
wooded areas.

☎ Kingston Blount
(0844) 51833
or Ickford (08447) 719.

Open: accessible at all
reasonable times.
No picnicking ✖

AULDEARN
Highland (Nairn)   *Map 14 NH95.*
Boath Doocot
*(off A96 at Auldearn, 2m E
of Nairn)*
A 17th-century doocot (as the
Scots call a dovecote) stands
on the site of an ancient castle
where, in 1645, Montrose flew
the standard of Charles I
when he defeated an army of
covenanters. The plan of the
battle is on display.

Open: accessible at all
reasonable times.
(NTS)

AVEBURY
Wiltshire   *Map 4 SU16.*
Stone Circle
The largest stone circle in
Europe, measuring 1,400 ft
across, consists of 100 sarsen
stones, some of them about 20
ft high. Within the main circle
there are traces of a smaller
one. There is an enclosing
bank of chalk, 20 ft high in
places, and a chalk ditch.
Leading away to the south
east is an avenue of stones.

Open: accessible at all
reasonable times.
(AM)

AVIEMORE
Highland (Inverness-shire)
                    Map 14 NH81.
**Craigellachie National
Nature Reserve**
Aviemore Centre
Lying on the western edge of
Aviemore, this 642-acre na-
ture reserve rises to over
1,700 ft. One third of it is
covered by birch woodlands,
the remainder is moorland.
The starting point of the mile-
long nature trail is close to
Loch Puladern and from the
trail there are some im-
pressive views of the Cairn-

gorm Mountains. The birch trees support several species of moth including the great brocade and the angle-striped sallow.

Open: accessible at all reasonable times.

AVON FOREST PARK
Dorset   *Map 4 SU10.*
(1m W of Ringwood off A31)
Three areas of heathland and pine woodland. North Park covers almost 300 acres and contains some fine Maritime, Corsican, and Weymouth Pines. Noble Fir and Redwood are among other interesting trees in the area. Thickly-wooded Matchams View is located close to the River Avon and was flooded many thousands of years ago. South Park includes an open area called Tumuli Hill from where there are good views. Much of this area was destroyed by fire in 1976. There are waymarked walks at all three sites.

☎ Ringwood (04254) 78082.
Open: accessible at all reasonable times.
&. 📮

AXBRIDGE
Somerset   *Map 3 ST45.*
King John's Hunting Lodge
The Square
Restored early Tudor house with old photographs and exhibits of local interest. Town stocks and constables' staves also on show.

Open: Apr-Sep, daily 2-5.
(NT)

AXMINSTER
Devon   *Map 3 SY29.*
Axminster Carpets Ltd
Gamberlake
Visitors can see the complete process of making an Axminster carpet from winding the bobbins, weaving, and add-

ing the latex backing to the finished product.

☎ (0297) 32244.
Open: Mon-Fri 9-12, 1.30-4.30. (Ex Spring Bank Hol week, last week of Jul/first week of Aug).
&. 🏸

AYLESBURY
Buckinghamshire   *Map 4 SP81.*
Bucks County Museum
Church Street
Housed in former grammar school built in 1720 and two 15th-century houses, which were completely altered in the mid 18th century. The displays relate to the geology, natural history, archaeology and history of the county and include costumes, Rural Life Gallery and Aylesbury Gallery.

☎ (0296) 82158 or 88849.
Open: Mon-Fri 10-5, Sat 10-12.30, 1.30-5. (Closed: Sun, Good Fri, Xmas and New Years day.)
Shop 🏸

AYLESFORD
Kent   *Map 5 TQ76.*
Kit's Coty House
(1½m NE off unclass road)
The best-preserved Neolithic burial chamber in Kent, dating from about 3,500 BC. Three upright stones are capped by a fourth. The covering mound of earth has long since disappeared.

Open: accessible at all reasonable times.
(AM)

Priory
The Friars
Restored 13th- to 14th-century Carmelite house with fine cloisters, now conference centre and place of pilgrimage and retreat. Sculpture and ceramics by modern artists and pottery.

☎ Maidstone (0622) 77272.
Open: daily 9-dusk. Guided tours by arrangement. Shop, tea rooms and pottery open: 10.30-12.45 & 2-4.30.
Donations
📮 &. Shop.

AYR
Strathclyde (Ayrshire) *Map 10 NS32.*
Auld Kirk
Off High Street
Robert Burns was baptised in the present church which dates from 1654, when it replaced the 12th-century church of St John. Inside are the Merchants, Trades, and Sailors Lofts. Around the walls are the colours of various Scottish regiments, notably those carried in the Crimean War. Other items of note are the Mort-Safe and Mortification board. Monuments to various Burns characters in churchyard.

☎ (0292) 262938.
Open: By arrangement, with Kirk Office — (times under review)
(donation box)
🏸

Maclaurin Art Gallery & Rozelle House
Rozelle Park
Monument Road
Contemporary and traditional art, decorative and applied. Nature trail in surrounding park with open air sculpture, work by Henry Moore on display. Local history and art exhibitions displayed in mansion house. Small military museum.

☎ Alloway (0292) 45447.
Gallery open: Mon-Sat 11-5, Sun (Apr-Oct only) 2-5. House open: Apr-Oct, Mon-Sat 11-5, Sun 2-5 (Nov-Mar Sat only 2-5).
📮 📮 &. (ground floor only)
🏸

AYSGARTH
North Yorkshire   *Map 7 SE08.*
National Park Centre
Visitor centre with interpretative display, maps, walks, guides and local information available.

☎ (09693) 424.
Open: Apr-Oct daily mid mornings to late afternoons.
&

BACONSTHORPE
Norfolk   *Map 9 TG13.*
Baconsthorpe Castle
A late 15th-century moated and semi-fortified house, incorporating a gate-house, a range of curtain walls and towers.

Open: at all reasonable times.
(AM) &

BADBURY RINGS
Dorset   *Map 3 ST90.*
(off B3082 4m NW of

Wimborne Minster)
A massive iron age hill fort comprising three concentric rings, the centre of which is thickly wooded. Four Roman roads lead from the fort to Dorchester, Old Sarum, Poole Harbour and Bath. Also of interest is the Roman posting station of Vindogladia which lies just outside the fort.

Open: accessible at all reasonable times.

BALLOCH
Strathclyde (Dunbartonshire)
Map 10 NS38.
Balloch Castle Country Park
Situated on the shore of the loch, with large area of grassland suitable for picnics and surrounded by extensive woodlands. Views of the loch from the castle terrace (c 1808). Walled garden. Nature trail. Countryside ranger service.

☎ Alexandria (0389) 58216.
Open: Visitor Centre; Apr, May & Sep Sat, Sun 10-5. Jun-Aug daily 10-5. Country Park 8-dusk, garden 10-9 (4.30 winter).
⊟ &

BAMBURGH
Northumberland   *Map 12 NU13.*
Grace Darling Museum
Radcliffe Road
Pictures, documents and various relics of the heroine, including boat in which she and her father, keeper of Longstone Lighthouse, Farne Islands, rescued nine survivors from the wrecked 'SS Forfarshire' in 1838. Grace and her father rowed to the wreck at considerable risk to themselves.

☎ Seahouses (0665) 720037.
Open: early Apr, May, & Sep-mid Oct daily 11-6 and Jun-Aug daily 11-7.
& Shop ✄

BAMFORD
Derbyshire   *Map 8 SK28.*
High Peak Garden Centre
This well-established garden centre in the heart of the Peak District offers much to attract all visitors, particularly gardeners. It is thoughtfully laid out with trees and shrubs in alphabetical order, a rose garden, rockery with fountain and a display of mature hedges and many other items. The centre is all on one level with good paths making it suitable for disabled visitors.

☎ Hope Valley (0433) 51484.
Open: Mon-Fri 9-5, Sat & Sun 10-5.30.
⌨ (Mar-Sep) ও ✗

BANBURY
Oxfordshire   *Map 4 SP44.*
Banbury Museum
8 Horsefair, Marlborough Road
This small museum exhibits items of local history and archaeology. Changing programme of temporary exhibitions and of local artist's work. Tourist Information Centre.

☎ (0295) 59855.
Open: 31 Mar-4 Oct, Mon-Sat 10-5; 6 Oct-29 Mar, Tue-Sat 10-4.
⌨ ও Shop.

BANCHORY
Grampian (Kincardineshire)
          Map 15 NO69.
Banchory Museum
Council Chambers
Exhibition of local history and items of bygone days.

☎ Peterhead (0779) 77778.
Open: Jun-Sep daily (ex Thu) 2-5.20.
Shop ✗ (ex guide dogs).

Dee Lavender Farm
(Ingasetter Ltd)

North Deeside Road
The Dwarf Munstead variety of lavender grows behind the factory on a five-acre site and is harvested during July and August. A film and short tour of the factory gives visitors the opportunity to see the processing of lavender from distillation to the making of a wide range of cosmetics. Dee Lavender and other Scottish fragrances can also be sampled.

☎ (03302) 2600.
Open: Mon-Fri 9-5
ও ✗ Shop

BANFF
Grampian (Banffshire) *Map 15 NJ66.*
Banff Museum
High Street
Exhibition of British birds set out as an aviary. Local history and costumes also on show.

☎ Peterhead (0779) 77778.
Open: Jun-Sep, daily (ex Thu) 2-5.20.
ও (ground floor only) shop ✗ (ex guide dogs).

BANGOR
Gwynedd   *Map 6 SH57.*
Bangor Museum & Art Gallery (University College of North Wales)
Ffordd Gwynedd
The museum portrays history of North Wales, collections of furniture, crafts, costumes, maps, ceramics, and both Roman and prehistoric antiquities. Exhibitions illustrating history of the Menai Bridges and Conwy Bridge. Attendant always on duty to deal with enquiries. Art Gallery stages exhibitions of sculpture and paintings each year changing at approximately monthly intervals. If there is an exhibition in gallery the Museum may be closed and if the Museum is open the gallery will generally be closed. From Apr-Sep

both will normally be open.

☎ (0248) 351151 Ext 437.
Open: Tue-Sat 12-4.30
✗

BARDSEA
Cumbria   *Map 7 SD37.*
Bardsea Country Park
(½m S on A5087)
Overlooking Morecambe Bay, this strip of the Cumbrian coast combines woodland walks with fine coastal bird-watching country. The best times are in winter, when thousands of birds from northern Europe and Russia move here to feed, or in early spring and early autumn, when migrant birds pass through. At the south end of the country park is the 60-acre Sea Wood. About a mile to the north is Conishead Priory, the grounds of which offer three nature trails.

Open: at all reasonable times. (Conishead Priory nature trails open Apr-Sep, Sat & Sun 2-5, mid Jul-end Aug Wed & Thu 2-5.)
⊓

BARNARD CASTLE
Co Durham   *Map 12 NZ01.*
Egglestone Abbey
(1m SE)
Picturesque remains of Premonstratensian Abbey on right bank of River Tees.

Open: at all reasonable times. (AM) ও

BARR, GREAT
West Midlands   *Map 7 SP09.*
Bishop Asbury Cottage
Newton Road
The boyhood home of Francis Asbury, the founder of Methodism in America. A small, mid 17th-century cottage containing furniture of the period of Asbury's home life.

☎ 021-569 2308.

Open: Mon-Fri 2-4. Other times by arrangement.
🐕

BARROW-IN-FURNESS

Cumbria *Map 7 SD26.*

Furness Museum

Ramsden Square

Museum of Furness district with finds from late Stone Age sites. Also Vickers ship models and Lake District bygones. Various monthly exhibitions.

☎ (0229) 20650.
Open: Mon-Wed & Fri 10-5, Thu 10-1 & Sat 10-4. (Closed: PH.)
🐕

BARRY

South Glamorgan *Map 3 ST16.*

Porthkerry Country Park

(2m W on coast)

Fossil-rich limestone cliffs rising to 150 ft, and a lofty viaduct built in 1898 for the Vale of Glamorgan Railway, are dramatic features of the Park. Other links with the past include the remains of a kiln where lime was burned to make fertiliser, and a 19th-century sawmill overlooked by Mill Wood.

Open: at all reasonable times.
♿ ☕ ⛱ Shop.

BASINGSTOKE

Hampshire *Map 4 SU65.*

Willis Museum and Art Gallery

Old Town Hall, Market Place

The museum has recently moved and is now housed in the handsome Old Town Hall. Temporary displays show what the new museum will eventually look like. Exhibition gallery shows touring exhibitions.

☎ (0256) 465902.
Open: Tue-Sat, 10-5.
Parties by arrangement.
Shop.

BATH

Avon *Map 3 ST76.*

Botanic Gardens (Royal Victoria Park)

Avenues of cherry trees (which blossom in spring) are only one of the thousands of different varieties of plants, trees and shrubs here. They come from all parts of the world, demonstrating what can be grown on local soil. The Gardens form part of some 50 acres of Royal Victoria Park, which offers good views of the Royal Crescent.

☎ (0225) 314213.
Open: daily, 8-sunset.
☕ ♿

Victoria Art Gallery

Bridge Street

The museum contains a varied collection of 18th-to 20th-century British paintings, watercolours and drawings, with the European Old Masters well represented. Also on display is the Carr collection of English glass and watches from the 18th and 19th century. There is a mixed programme of temporary exhibitions.

☎ (0225) 61111.
Open: Mon-Fri 10-6, Sat 10-5. (Closed BH)
🐕

BATLEY

West Yorkshire *Map 8 SE22.*

Art Gallery

Market Place

Permanent collection of British oil paintings, water colours, drawings and sculpture from mid 19th-century onwards. Temporary loan and special exhibitions throughout the year.

☎ (0924) 473141.
Open: Mon-Fri 10-6, Sat 10-4.
Shop 🐕

Bagshaw Museum

Wilton Park

A 19th-century building housing museum of local history, archaeology, geology, ethnography, oriental arts, natural history and folk life. (Best approached from Upper Batley Lane.)

☎ (0924) 472514.
Open: Mon-Sat 10-5, Sun 1-5.
♿ (ground floor and gardens only) Shop 🐕

BEACON FELL

Lancashire *Map 7 SD54.*

Beacon Fell Country Park

(2½m NE of Inglewhite)

Opened in 1970, the Beacon Fell Country Park covers a wooded hilltop to the south-west of the Forest of Bowland. Around the perimeter there are a number of car parks and many woodland paths lead to the summit (873 ft) which commands a good view across the Lancashire coastal plain. The wooded slopes are mostly coniferous and the home for many small mammals and a variety of birds. About half a mile south-east is the Carwags Information Centre which contains a small exhibition.

☎ Chipping (09956) 235 or Preston (0772) 263896.
Open: Country Park; Accessible at any reasonable time.
Information Centre Mar-Oct daily 1-5.
⛱ (☕ most days, pm only)

BEARSDEN

Strathclyde (Dumbartonshire) *Map 11 NS57.*

Roman Bath House

Roman Road

Sited close to the Antonine

Wall, the Bath House was discovered in 1973 and forms part of a larger Roman fort. Excavations have revealed several rooms and a nearby latrine. Many finds were made on site and are now displayed at the Hunterian Museum in the University of Glasgow. The fort was probably in use between 142AD and 158AD.

☎ Glasgow 041-339 8855 Ext 221.
Open: accessible at all reasonable times.

BECCLES
Suffolk   *Map 5 TM49.*
Beccles & District Museum
Newgate
Local industrial, rural and domestic displays, which includes tools of the printing trade, a prominent industry in the town. A new addition is a needlework banner depicting scenes of the town.

☎ (0502) 712628.
Open: Apr-Oct, Wed, Sat, Sun & BH 2.30-5; Nov-Mar, Sun only 2.30-5.
✗

BEDALE
North Yorkshire   *Map 8 SE28.*
Bedale Hall
(on A684 1½m W of A1 at Leeming Bar)
Georgian ballroom and

museum room.

☎ (0677) 23123.
Open: May-Sep, Tue 10-4, other times by appointment.
& (ground floor only) ✗

BEDFORD
Bedfordshire   *Map 4 TL04.*
Bedford Museum
Castle Lane
A local history and natural history museum with 19th-century room sets, displays on agriculture, Bedfordshire geology, archaeology, birds and mammals, fossils and minerals.

☎ (0234) 53323.
Open: all year, Tue-Sat 11-5 & Sun 2-5. (Closed: Mon, ex BH Mon afternoons, Good Fri & Xmas.)
& (lift available on request)
Shop ✗

BEDWYN, GREAT
Wiltshire   *Map 4 SU26.*
Bedwyn Stone Museum
An open air museum that explains the ancient secrets of the freemason and how the carvings trace the behaviour of man in a language vastly different to that taught in school. Finest known sequence of carvings are to be found in the church adjacent.

☎ Marlborough (0672) 870234.

Open: all year.
& garden centre.

BERKHAMSTED
Hertfordshire   *Map 4 SP90.*
Berkhamsted Castle
Remains of an 11th-century motte and bailey castle with later circular keep. Former home of Black Prince and prison of King John of France.

Open: at all reasonable times.
(AM) &

BERWICK-UPON-TWEED
Northumberland   *Map 12 NT95.*
Castle and Town Walls
Remains of 12th-century stronghold incorporating three towers and west wall. Medieval town walls reconstructed during Elizabethan period.

☎ (0289) 7881.
Open: at all reasonable times.
(AM)

BEVERLEY
Humberside   *Map 8 TA03.*
Art Gallery, Museum & Heritage Centre
Champney Road
Local antiquities, Victorian bygones and china, pictures by F W Elwell of Beverley and others, and bust of Sir Winston Churchill by Bryant Baker of New York. Various solo Art Exhibitions. Heritage

Centre recently established.

☎ Hull (0482) 882255.
Open: Mon-Wed & Fri
9.30-12.30, 2-5, Thu 9.30-12,
Sat 9.30-4.
Shop ✗

Lairgate Hall
Dates from 1710-80, now used
as council offices. Interesting
late 18th-century stucco ceiling, marble mantelpiece.
Chinese room with hand-
painted wallpaper.

☎ Hull (0482) 882255.
Open: Mon-Thu, 8.45-5.30,
Fri 9-4.
& ✗

BEXLEY
Gt London   *see page 84.*
Hall Place
*(Near Junction of A2 &
A233)*   *London plan 2 : 38 F2.*
15th-16th-century mansion
Grade I listed building and
ancient monument with

Locks at Bingley

contrasting elevations of
chequered flint and brick.
Ornamental gardens with
topiary in form of 'Queen's
Beasts' roses, rock, water,
herb, peat gardens, con-
servatory houses and
recreation facilities.

☎ Crayford (0322) 526574.
Open: Mon-Sat 10-5, Sun 2-6
(summer); Mon-Sat 10-5,
Sun 2-dusk (winter);
Gardens: Mon-Fri
7.30-dusk, Sat & Sun 9-dusk.
⌨ (weather permitting)
& (gardens only) ✗

BIDDENDEN
Kent   *Map 5 TQ83.*
Baby Carriage Collection
Bettenham Manor
A unique collection of 400
baby carriages (prams) of a
bygone era. Exhibits portray
the history of the pram up to
the present day and include

18th-century stickwagons,
perambulators and mailcarts,
Edwardian bassinettes, Vic-
torias and large coachbuilt
prams of the twenties. The
museum, in a Kentish oast
house, adjoins a 15th-century
moated manor house of historical and architectural
interest and is set in a 15-acre
garden.

☎ (0580) 291343.
Open: all year (ex Xmas
Day) by appointment only.
& (ground floor & garden
only) ✗

Biddenden Vineyards
*Little Whatmans (1½m S off
A262)*
The present vineyard was established in 1969 and has now
reached 18 acres. The varieties planted are mainly of
German origin all of which
produce fruity fragrant
wines. Harvesting usually
commences on 20 October
when visitors can see the
presses in operation. Visitors
are welcome to stroll around
the vines at leisure and to call
at the shop for tasting of the
wines, and cider etc.

☎ (0580) 291726.
Shop open: all year Mon-Sat
11-5 (2pm Nov-Apr) May-
Oct, Sun 12-5.
Parties by arrangement.
Shop.

BINGLEY
West Yorkshire   *Map 7 SE13.*
Bingley Five Rise Locks
*(½m N of Bingley on canal
towpath)*
One of the wonders of the
waterways. The lock staircase is situated on the Leeds
and Liverpool Canal and was
designed and built by John
Longbotham of Halifax during
the 1770s.

**Open: Towpath accessible
at all reasonable times.**

BINHAM
Norfolk   *Map 9 TF93.*
Binham Priory
The Priory, or at least its extensive ruins, dates from the 12th century. The main fragment to survive intact is the western end of the monastic church which is now used as the parish church. Inside, there is a perpendicular, seven-sacrament font and the stalls have misericords.

Open: (Ruins) accessible at all reasonable times.
& (AM)

BIRKENHEAD
Merseyside   *Map 7 SJ38.*
Birkenhead Priory
Priory St
Founded in 1150, the Priory provided accommodation for a prior and 16 Benedictine monks. Most of the buildings were neglected after the Dissolution and only the ruins remain.

☏ 051-652 4177
Open: May-Sep,
Tue-Sat, 10-1, 2-4;
Oct-Apr, Tue-Sat 10-1.
& (ground floor only)

Williamson Art Gallery & Museum
Slatey Road
Exhibits include: major collection of work by English water-colourists and Liverpool school of painters; sculpture; decorative arts; ceramics (English, Continental, Oriental wares); glass, silver and furniture. Also a large collection of paintings by P Wilson Steer, as well as approximately 25 special exhibitions throughout the year. A local history and maritime museum adjoins.

☏ 051-652 4177.
Open: Mon-Wed, Fri & Sat, 10-5; Thu, 10-9; Sun 2-5.
(Closed: Xmas & BH.)
& Shop ✖
See advertisement on page 143

BIRMINGHAM
West Midlands   *Map 7 SP08.*
City Museum & Art Gallery
Chamberlain Square
Fine and applied arts, natural history, archaeology and local history exhibits. There is a fine collection of paintings from the 14th century to the present day, including a most important collection of Pre-Raphaelite work. Applied arts include costume, silver, ceramics and textiles; there are prehistoric, Egyptian, Greek and Roman antiquities, local history exhibits, an important coin collection and the famous Pinto Collection of wooden items. There are frequent lectures, temporary exhibitions, demonstrations and holiday activities for children.

☏ 021-235 2834.
Open: Mon-Sat 10-5,
Sun 2-5.
(Closed: 25-27 Dec.)
⌨ & Shop ✖
(ex guide dogs)

Museum of Science & Industry
Newhall Street (close to Post Office Tower)
Displays from the Industrial Revolution up to the present. Engineering hall was formerly a Victorian plating works and contains machine tools, electrical equipment, working steam, gas and hot air engines. Locomotive hall. Transport section. Science section. Pen room. Music room. World War II Spitfire and Hurricane, and collection of aircraft engines. New James Watt building contains oldest working steam engine in the world, dated 1779. Steam weekends Mar and Oct. Traction Engine Rally 12 May. Engines steamed 1st and 3rd Wed each month.

☏ 021-236 1022.
Open: Mon-Sat 10-5,
Sun 2-5. (Closed: Xmas & New Year's Day.)
& Shop ✖ (ex guide dogs)

Selly Manor & Minworth Greaves
Sycamore Road, Bournville off A38
Two 13th- and early 14th-

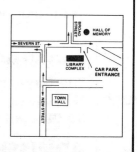

a 14th/16th century half-timbered house
SELLY MANOR
and
MINWORTH GREAVES EXHIBITION HALL
(corner of Maple Road and Sycamore Road, Bournville, Birmingham 30)

Come and spend a couple of hours exploring this fascinating old house in Bournville. Discover how people used to live in days gone by. Walk round the herb garden and look round the Exhibition Hall.

Large parties (not more than 30 please) are invited to book now for a free guided tour, or you can wander round by yourself if you wish.

Exhibitions of various sorts; photography, art, crafts, etc. are held in Minworth Greaves throughout the year.

You can spend from 10 minutes (to whet your appetite) to the full opening time FREE!

Post Cards and Guide Books are on sale.

For further details and bookings for Guided Tours ring the Curator on 021 472 0199 during opening times.

OPENING TIMES
Tuesdays, Wednesdays, Thursdays, Fridays
10.00 a.m. to 5.00 p.m.

ADMISSION FREE

BOURNVILLE
VILLAGE TRUST

century half-timbered houses re-erected in Bournville. Collection of old furniture etc. and herb garden.

☎ 021-472 0199.
Open: mid Jan-mid Dec, Tue-Fri 10-5 (ex BH). Parties & guided tours by arrangement with the curator.
& (ground floor only) ✶

BIRSAY
Orkney Islands   Map 16 HY22.
Earls Palace
(14m N of Stromness on A967)
Located in a windy position on the north-west corner of the Orkney Mainland, this large ruin was the residence of the 16th-century Earls of Orkney. The Palace was constructed around a courtyard with projecting rectangular towers at the corners, except at the northwest.

Open: accessible at all reasonable times.
& (AM)

BLACKBURN
Lancashire   Map 7 SD62.
Lewis Museum of Textile Machinery
Noted for series of period rooms portraying continuous development of textile industry from 18th century onwards. The gallery on the first floor has exhibitions.

☎ (0254) 667130.
Open: Mon-Sat 10-5.
(Closed: Sun, Good Fri, Xmas, New Years day & some BH.)
(Booking 3 weeks in advance will enable a party to see machinery in operation.)
Shop ✶ (ex guide dogs).

Museum & Art Gallery
Library Street
Local history, militaria, coins, ceramics, fine books and manuscripts, paintings, icons, watercolours and Japanese prints. Time tunnel and children's corner.

☎ (0254) 667130.
Open: Mon-Sat 10-5.
(Closed: Sun, Good Fri, Xmas, New Years day & some BH.)
& (ground floor only) shop ✶ (ex guide dogs)

BLACKPOOL
Lancashire   Map 7 SD33.
Grundy Art Gallery
Queen Street
Established 1911, this gallery exhibits a permanent collection of paintings by 19th- and 20th-century artists. Also touring exhibitions, one man shows and group exhibitions.

☎ (0253) 23977.
Open: Mon-Sat 10-5.
(Closed: BH.)
✶

BLANDFORD FORUM
Dorset   Map 3 ST80.
Royal Signals Museum
Blandford Camp
Museum of history of army communications; paintings, uniforms, medals and badges.

☎ (0258) 52581 Ext 248.
Open: Mon-Fri 8.45-4.30.
(Closed: BH.)
✶

BLEAN WOODS
Kent   Map 5 TR16.
(A2 Dunkirk, NE to A291 at Herne Common. Clowes Wood, 1m S of Radfall)
Blean Woods complex combines a variety of woods and heaths. There are many acres of coppice, where trees are cut to the base on a 15-year cycle to produce a cluster of straight poles used for stakes, fencing and tools. Other areas of hazel, chestnut and oak are all rich in wildlife, and noted for interesting bird life including nightjars, redstarts, nightingales, warblers and woodpeckers. There is a forest walk at Clowes Wood. Bluebells may be seen here too.

Open: at all reasonable times. Generally restricted to footpaths on nature reserve and public rights of way.
⋒ (Clowes Wood)

ROYAL SIGNALS MUSEUM BLANDFORD CAMP, DORSET

The museum contains items dealing with the history of army communications dating from the Crimean War to the Falkland Islands Campaign of 1982, as well as the history of the Royal Engineer (Signal Service) and the Royal Corps of Signals.

★ Military vehicles and motorcycles.
★ Early wireless equipment.
★ Uniforms, badges and medals.
★ The Queen's Gurkha Signal display.
★ A horse drawn cable laying wagon.
★ Clandestine radio equipment from World War II.

The display contains early telegraphic and radio equipment dating from the South Africa War, World War I, the campaigns on the North-West Frontier of India, and World War II. There are many colourful uniforms on display as well as the only surviving example of the horse drawn cable laying wagon. An 8th Army Armoured Command Vehicle is shown, in a desert setting, and there are a number of examples of military motor cycles used by Despatch Riders of the Corps. An airborne communications jeep is also in the display.

Admission: FREE. Opening hours: Monday to Friday 0845–1630 hours. Saturday—by appointment.

BOLTON

Gt Manchester   *Map 7 SD71.*
Tonge Moor Textile Museum
Tonge Moor Library, Tonge Moor Road
Includes Arkwright's water-frame (1768), Compton's spinning mule (1779) and Hargreave's spinning jenny.

☎ (0204) 22311 Ext 379.
Open: Mon & Thu 9.30-7.30, Tue & Fri 9.30-5.30, Sat 9.30-12.30.
(Closed: Sun & Wed.)
&. ✻

BO'NESS

Central (West Lothian) *Map 11 NS98.*
Kinneil Museum & Roman Fortlet
Situated in the renovated 17th-century stable block of Kinneil House. The ground floor illustrates the industrial history of Bo'ness. On the upper floor there is an interpretive display on the history and environment of the Kinneil Estate. Kinneil Roman fortlet near the museum.

☎ Falkirk (0324) 24911 Ext 2202.
Open: May-Oct, Mon-Sat 10-12.30, 1.30-5; Nov-Apr, Sat only 10-5.
Shop ✻

BOSCOBEL

Shropshire   *Map 7 SJ80.*
Whiteladies Priory (St Leonards Priory)
Remains of Augustinian nunnery, dating from 1158. Largely destroyed in the Civil War. Guide book available at Boscobel House.

Open: at any reasonable time.
(AM)

BOWES

Co Durham   *Map 12 NY91.*
Bowes Castle
(on A66)

Norman keep built between 1171 and 1187, in angle of Roman fort of 'Lavatrae'.

Open: at any reasonable time.
(AM)

BRADFIELD WOODS

Suffolk   *Map 5 TL95.*
(4½m SE of Bury St Edmunds, off A134 between Sicklesmere and Gedding)
This nature reserve is one of the finest examples in the country of a woodland still managed by the ancient practice of coppicing. The ground is extremely rich, with over 370 species of plant having been identified. The coppicing of woodland also provides suitable habitats for a large variety of wildlife, including woodpeckers, tawny owls and four types of deer.

☎ Bury St Edmunds (0284) 810379.
Open: all reasonable times, along waymarked paths.
Visitor Centre Apr-Sep, Sun 1-5
(dogs on lead)

BRADFORD

West Yorkshire   *Map 7 SE13.*
Bolling Hall
Bolling Hall Road
House dates from 15th century and contains fine furnishings including rare Chippendale bed, heraldic glass and 'ghost room'.

☎ (0274) 723057.
Open: Apr-Sep, Tue-Sun & BH Mon 10-6; Oct-Mar, Tue-Sun 10-5. (Closed: Good Fri, Xmas day & Boxing day.)
Shop ✻

Cartwright Hall
Lister Park
Contains permanent collections of European and British paintings, sculpture, drawings, modern prints and ceramics. Also includes varied and imaginative exhibition programme.

☎ (0274) 493313.
Open: Apr-Sep, Tue-Sun & BH Mon 10-6; Oct-Mar, Tue-Sun 10-5. (Closed: Good Fri, Xmas day & Boxing day.)
⌨ &. Shop ✻

Industrial Museum
Moorside Road, Eccleshill
Features the growth of the worsted textile industry and other exhibits relevant to the era.

☎ (0274) 631756.
Open: Tue-Sun & BH Mon 10-5. (Closed: Good Fri, Xmas day & Boxing day.)
⌨ &. Shop ✻

National Museum of Photography, Film & Television
Prince's View
Incorporates displays, concepts, galleries that explore photography in all its many forms including press, medical/scientific, moving pictures, exhibitions and studios. Displays and voice-over tapes make for realism and visitor participation. In addition the only IMAX Cinema in Britain is housed in the museum.

☎ (0274) 727488.
Open: Tue-Sat 12-8, Sun 2.30-6. (Closed Mon ex BH.)
(Opening times under review.)
IMAX Cinema, admission charge.
⌨ (licensed) &. Shop ✻
(ex guide dogs).

The Colour Museum
82 Grattan Road
The headquarters of the Society of Dyers and Colourists. Housed on two floors, the museum has 'The World of Colour' exhibition

on the first floor, which is designed to increase visitors' awareness and enjoyment of colour as a factor of great importance in their daily lives. 'The Science of Colour' exhibition is housed on the second floor and shows how scientific technology is employed in making and using colouring matters of all kinds, and the methods by which they can be tested and their colours measured.

☎ (0274) 725138.
Open: Tue-Fri 2-5 Sat 10-4 (ex PH).

BRADFORD-ON-AVON

Wiltshire *Map 3 ST86.*

Barton Tithe Barn

14th-century building, once property of Shaftesbury Abbey, since presented to Wiltshire Archaeological Society.

Open: at any reasonable time.
(AM) ♿

BRADGATE PARK & SWITHLAND WOOD ESTATE

Leicestershire *Map 8 SK51.*

(6½m NE of Leicester off B5327)

850-acre country park. Natural parkland, woods, herds of red and fallow deer with Old John Tower (1786). Ruins of Bradgate House, completed c1510 by son of 1st Marquis of Dorset. The birthplace of Lady Jane Grey (1537-54).

☎ **Leicester (0533) 871313 Ext 645 (The Ranger)**
Open: all year to pedestrians during daylight hours. Ruins open Apr-Oct, Wed, Thu & Sat, 2.30-5; Sun 10-12.30. Parties by arrangement Apr-Oct. Registered disabled or permit holders issued by Bradgate Park Trust may drive through the park, Apr-Oct, Thu 2.30-7.30, Sun 9-11 am.

Also **Marion's Cottage**
(visitor centre)
Newtown Linford

Typical Charnwood Forest cottage offering selection of gifts, publications, etc. Exhibition. Adjoins Newton Linford car park.

Open: Apr-Oct, Wed, Thu, Sat & Sun 2-6; Nov-Mar, Sat & Sun 2-5. Also BH Mon & Tue. Parties by arrangement.
⛩ ♿ Shop.

BRAMBER

West Sussex *Map 4 TQ11.*

Bramber Castle

Former home of the Dukes of Norfolk, this ruined Norman stronghold lies on a South Downs ridge with views.

Open daily.
(NT)

BRAMHOPE

West Yorkshire *Map 8 SE24.*

Golden Acre Park

The Park covers 137 acres of mature woodland and gardens, and incorporates an attractive lake, the home of many species of wildfowl. There is a collection of trees and shrubs as well as herbaceous and aquatic plants. Created features include rock gardens, a large Alpine house, a demonstration garden for vegetables and flowers, old shrub roses, rhododendrons and azaleas, an arboretum and a pinetum.

Open: daily, 11-5 (summer); 10-4 (winter).
☕ ⛩ ♿

BRANSGORE

Hampshire *Map 4 SZ19.*

Macpenny's

One-time gravel pits have been converted into this large woodland garden and nurseries, with rare trees, shrubs, rhododendrons, azaleas, camellias and heathers.

☎ **(0425) 72348.**
Open: Mon-Sat 8-5; Sun 2-5 (collection box).
⛩ (NGS)

BRECON

Powys *Map 3 SO02.*

Brecknock Museum

Captain's Walk

Archaeological and local historical exhibits, folk life, decorative arts and natural history.

☎ **(0874) 4121.**
Open: Mon-Sat (incl BH) 10-5.
Shop ♿

BRIDGEND

Mid Glamorgan *Map 3 SS97.*

Newcastle

Small ruined 12th-century and later stronghold, with rectangular tower, richly carved Norman gateway to south side and massive curtain walls enclosing polygonal courtyard.

Open: Apr-Sep, weekdays 10-7, Sun 2-7; Oct-Mar, weekdays 10-dusk, Sun 2-dusk.

BRIDGWATER

Somerset *Map 3 ST23.*

Admiral Blake Museum

Blake Street

The Museum is housed in the birthplace of Admiral Robert Blake (1587-1657). Exhibits include an audio-visual of the Battle of Sedgemoor, industrial history of Bridgwater and its docks and the Archaeology of Bridgwater and District. In the Blake Room there is a diorama of the Battle of Santa Cruz, Blake's greatest victory over the Spaniards. Several of Blake's personal belongings are also on show.

☏ (0278) 456127.
Open: daily 11-5, Wed 11-8.
♿ Shop

BRIERLEY HILL

West Midlands *Map 7 SO98.*

Royal Brierley Crystal

North Street

The company was founded in 1847 and every piece of its crystal is made and cut by hand. The 1½ hour factory tour shows the production of hand-made crystal and includes a visit to the site museum which contains some unique pieces.

☏ (0384) 70161.
Open: Factory tours by appointment only. Mon-Thu 11, 1 & 2.30, Fri 11. (Children under 13 years are unable to join the tour.) Shop Mon-Sat 9-4.30, also Sun in summer season.
☕

BRIGHOUSE

West Yorkshire *Map 7 SE12.*

Brighouse Art Gallery

Halifax Road

Temporary exhibitions throughout the year of local artists work and of other modern works of interest.

☏ (0484) 719222.
Open: Mon-Sat 10-5, Sun 2.30-5. (Closed: Sun, Oct-Mar; Xmas & New Year's day.)
♿ 🐕

BRIGHTON

East Sussex *Map 4 TQ30.*

Booth Museum of Natural History

194 Dyke Road

Contains British birds mounted in natural settings, butterfly gallery, also vertebrate evolution and 'Unnatural History' displays. Geology gallery. Temporary exhibitions; classroom available for use.

☏ (0273) 552586.
Open: Mon-Sat (ex Thu) 10-5, Sun 2-5. (Closed: Good Fri, Xmas & New Year's day).
♿ Shop 🐕

Museum & Art Gallery

Church Street

The collections include Old Master paintings, watercolours, Sussex archaeology, folklife and local history, ethnography and musical instruments. Also the Willett Collection of pottery and porcelain, and display of 20th-century fine and applied art, including Art Nouveau, Art Deco and 19th & 20th-century costume. Also various special exhibitions.

☏ (0273) 603005.
Open: Tue-Sat 10-5.45, Sun 2-5. (Closed: Mon, Good Fri, Xmas & New Year's day.)
☕ (closed Sun) ♿ (ground floor only) Shop 🐕

BRISTOL

Avon *Map 3 ST 57.*

Avon Gorge and Leigh Woods

(off A369, 2m W of Bristol City Centre.) Plan: **A3.**

Leigh Woods is a nature reserve offering many delightful walks through deciduous woodland containing a wide variety of birds. The Avon Gorge, nearby, is two miles long and its fossil-rich limestone cliffs rise to 300 ft. The soil here suits some rare plants and the area is an attraction to botanists. In fact, the rare Bristol Whitebeam, found here, grows nowhere else in the world. The Avon Walkway is a recreational path which follows the southern bank of the River Avon through the Gorge.

Open: accessible at all reasonable times.
NT (part)

Blaise Castle House Museum

Henbury (4m NW of city, off B4057, not on plan)

18th-century mansion, now social history museum, situated in extensive grounds.

☏ (0272) 506789.
Open: Sat-Wed 10-1 & 2-5. (Closed: Xmas day-28 Dec & New Year's day.)
Shop 🐕

Museum at Bridgwater

Bristol Cathedral
College Green. Plan: **D3.**
Dating from the 12th century, the Cathedral was originally a monastic church but gained cathedral status in 1542. The Cathedral has been heavily restored and only the chapter house and adjoining buildings date from the original period. The nave has some unusual features which include the side aisles being as high as the central aisle, and a complex system of vaulting in the central aisle. The Lady Chapel contains some unique 'Stellar' tomb recesses found only in Bristol. The furnishing of stalls and misericords are of note.

☎ (0272) 24879 or 298567.
Open: daily 8-6 (donations).
& (☐ 10.30-3.30) ✝

Bristol Industrial Museum
Prince's Wharf, Prince Street. Plan: **D2.**
A converted dockside transit shed in the heart of Bristol, 400 yards from SS 'Great Britain'. Display of vehicles, horse-drawn and motorised from the Bristol area, locally built aircraft, aero-engines; railway exhibits include full-size industrial locomotive Henbury, steamed around once a month. Various kinds of machinery illustrating local trade and manufacturing. Newly-opened display of history of the port of Bristol.

☎ (0272) 299771 Ext 290.
Open: Sat-Wed 10-1 & 2-5.
(Closed: Xmas day-28 Dec & New Year's day).
& (ground floor only) Shop ✝

City Museum & Art Gallery
Queen's Road. Plan: **C4.**
Regional and world-wide collections, representing ancient history, natural sciences, fine and applied arts.

☎ (0272) 299771.
Open: Mon-Sat 10-5.
(Closed: Good Fri, May Day, Spring BH Mon & Tue, 25-28 Dec & New Year's day)
☐ & Shop ✝

John Wesley's Chapel (The New Room)
Broadmead. Plan: **E4.**
The oldest Methodist Chapel in the world built 1739, rebuilt 1748, in each case by John Wesley. Both chapel and living rooms above are preserved in their original form. John Wesley frequently resided in the rooms, also used as his headquarters.

☎ (0272) 24740.
Open: daily 10-4. (Closed: Sun, Wed & BH.)
& (ground floor & gardens only) Shop ✝

Maritime Heritage Centre

Gas Ferry Road.   Plan : *C2.*
This new museum, which was opened by the Queen on 26 July 1985, is located alongside the SS 'Great Britain' next to the floating harbour in the city. Exhibits include 200 years of Bristol maritime history, paintings, plans, models and relics associated with Hillhouse and Hill Shipbuilders. Centre-piece of the museum is a reconstruction of an early Bristol-built iron vessel, designed by Isambard Kingdom Brunel to dredge the harbour.

☎ (0272) 20680.
Open: daily summer 10-6; winter 10-5. (Closed 24 & 25 Dec)
🕭 🛱 �& (ground floor only) ✕

Red Lodge

Park Row.   Plan : *D3.*

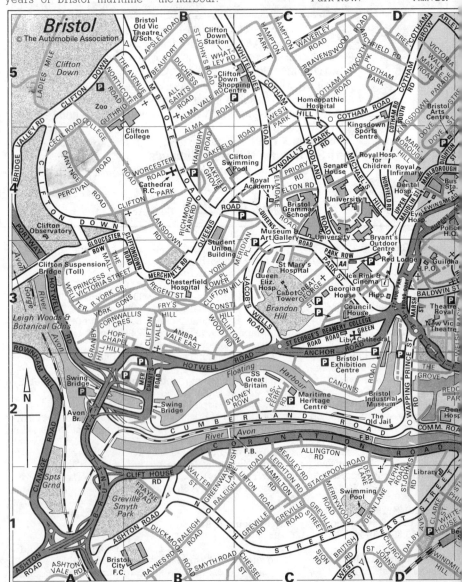

16th-century house altered in the early 18th century, with fine oak carvings and furnishings of both periods.

☏ (0272) 299771 Ext 236.
Open: Mon-Sat 10-1, 2-5. (Closed: Good Fri, May Day, Spring BH Mon & Tue, Xmas & New Year's day.) Shop 🐕

St Mary Redcliffe Church
Redcliffe Way. *Plan :* ***E2.***
One of the largest churches in England and noted for its outstanding example of perpendicular architecture. The earliest part of the church dates from 1180, however much of it was constructed during the 13th century including the impressive hexagonal outer porch. In the 15th century the spire was struck by lightning and wasn't rebuilt until 1873. Rising to 295 ft the spire is a well known Bristol landmark. In 1574, Queen Elizabeth I reputedly described the church as 'the fairest, goodliest and most famous parish church in England'.

☏ (0272) 291487.
Open: daily 8-6, May-Aug Mon-Fri 8-8 (donations)
♿

St Nicholas Church Museum
St Nicholas Street. *Plan :* ***E3.***
The history of Bristol from its beginning until the Reformation including Bristol church art and silver. Changing art exhibitions showing topographical features of the city mainly during the 18th and 19th century and the Hogarth altarpiece originally painted for St Mary Redcliffe. Brass rubbing centre.

☏ (0272) 299771 Ext 243.
Open: Mon-Sat 10-5. (Closed: Good Fri, May day, Spring BH Mon & Tue, 25-28 Dec & New Year's day.)
♿ (ground floor only) Shop
🐕

The Georgian House
7 Gt George St. *Plan :* ***C3.***
Georgian house with 18th-century furniture and fittings.

☏ (0272) 299771 Ext 237
Open: Mon-Sat 10-1, 2-5 (Closed: Good Fri, May day, Spring BH Mon & Tue, Xmas & New Year's day)
🐕

University Botanic Gardens

North Road.   Plan : **A3.**
The mature Gardens contain a wide range of plants, some labelled with their history. Many of the plants are tropical and include a collection from New Zealand. There is a small collection of regional fauna representing different British ecological situations. An arrowed route shows the way around the garden and staff are willing to answer questions.

☎ (0272) 733682.
Open: Mon-Fri 8.30-5
&

BRIXHAM
Devon   Map 3 SX95.
Berry Head Country Park
Gillard Road
Occupying an exposed limestone promontory at the southern end of Tor Bay, the Country Park is rich in limestone-loving wild flowers such as rockrose and orchids. On the cliffs there is a wide variety of sea birds including guillemots, kittiwakes, shags, cormorants and several species of gull. Part of the area has been designated a nature reserve. There are slight traces of a iron age promontory fort and in the past centuries a large area has been quarried.

☎ Torquay (0803) 26244.
Open: accessible at all reasonable times.
& (⌂ Apr-Sep daily 10-6)

BRIXWORTH
Northamptonshire   Map 4 SP77.
All Saints Church
Northern edge of village (signed from A508)
This is one of the best-preserved Saxon churches in the country and dates from the 7th century. The building incorporates many Roman tiles and was monastic until 870. In the 14th century a belfry and spire were added to the Saxon tower.

☎ (0604) 880286.
Open: 9-sunset (donations)
✸

BROOK
Kent   Map 5 TR04.
Wye College Museum of Agriculture
(4m ENE of Ashford on unclass road)
An exhibition of old farm implements and machinery housed in a fine 14th-century tithe barn. Display of hop cultivation in old oast house.

☎ Wye (0233) 812401.
Open: May-Sep, Wed 2-5, Sat in Aug.
Parties by arrangement in writing to:
Hon. Curator, Museum, Wye College, Wye, Ashford, Kent TN25 5AH.
& (ground floor only) ✸

BROUGHTON
Borders (Peeblesshire) Map 11 NT13.
Broughton Place
Built on the site of a much older house and designed by Sir Basil Spence in 1938 in the style of a 17th-century Scottish tower house. The drawing room and main hall are open to the public and contain paintings and crafts by living British artists for sale. The gardens, open for part of the summer, afford fine views of the Tweeddale hills.

☎ (08994) 234.
Gallery open: Apr-Sep daily 10.30-6 (ex Wed)
Donation for garden
& Shop ✸

BRUAR
Tayside (Perthshire)   Map 14 NN86.
Clan Donnachaidh (Robertson) Museum
Documents, books and pictures associated with the Clan Donnachaidh, one of whose early chiefs fought for King Robert the Bruce. Craft display.

☎ Calvine (079683) 264.
Open: Etr-mid Oct, Mon-Sat 10-1 & 2-5.30, Sun 2-5.30. Other times by arrangement.
& Shop

BRYN-CELLI-DDU
Gwynedd   Map 6 SH57.
Bryn-Celli-Ddu Burial Chamber
(3m W of Menai Bridge off A4080)
Excavated in 1865, and again 1925-29, prehistoric circular cairn covering passage grave with polygonal chamber.

Open: accessible at all reasonable times.
(AM)

BUCKHAVEN
Fife (Fife)   Map 11 NT39.
Museum
Above Buckhaven Library, College Street
A small museum depicting life in Buckhaven in the heyday of its fishing industry. The museum includes old photographs, model boats, local history and a reconstruction of a fisherman's kitchen.

☎ (0592) 712192.
Open: all year Mon 2-7; Tue 10-12.30, 2-5;
Thu 10-12.30, 2-7; Fri 2-5; Sat 10-12.30.
✸ Shop.

BUCKIE
Grampian (Banffshire)   Map 15 NJ46.
Buckie Museum & Peter Anson Gallery
Maritime museum with displays relating to the fishing industry including exhibits on coopering, navigation, lifeboats and fishing methods.

Selections from the Peter Anson watercolour collection of fishing vessels are on display.

☎ Forres (0309) 73701.
Open: Mon-Fri 10-8;
Sat 10-12.
& Shop ✗

BUCKLAND
Gloucestershire   *Map 4 SP03.*
Buckland Rectory
(off A46)
England's oldest rectory, associated with John Wesley; medieval house with 15th-century great hall which has an open timber roof and contemporary glass. Also earlier half-timbered house and spiral stone staircase.

☎ Broadway (0386) 852479.
Open: May-Sep, Mon 11-4, Aug Mon & Fri, 11-4.
& (ground floor & gardens only)

BURGH CASTLE
Norfolk   *Map 5 TG40.*
The Castle
(off A143)
Massive walls from former 3rd-century Roman fort, guarded by six pear-shaped bastions. Irish missionary St Fursey founded a monastery here, and the Normans also used the castle site.

Open: accessible at any reasonable time.
(AM)

BURGHEAD
Grampian (Moray)   *Map 15 NJ16.*
Burghead Museum
16-18 Grant Street
Local history and temporary exhibitions.

☎ Forres (0309) 73701.
Open: Tue 1.30-5, Thu 5-8.30, Sat 10-noon.
& ✗

BURNHAM MARKET
Norfolk   *Map 9 TF84.*
Carmelite Friary
(¼m NE on unclass road)
Gatehouse and remains of Carmelite Friary founded in 1241 with some original windows and interesting flint and stone panelling. The adjoining farmhouse incorporates a 14th-century doorway and a large buttress.

☎ Norwich (0603) 611122
Ext 481.
Open: all year. Gatehouse and remains of Carmelite Friary, accessible at all times.

BURNLEY
Lancashire   *Map 7 SD83.*
The Weavers' Triangle
off Manchester Road
The Triangle is a region where the Leeds to Liverpool canal passes through an area of warehouses, cotton-spin-

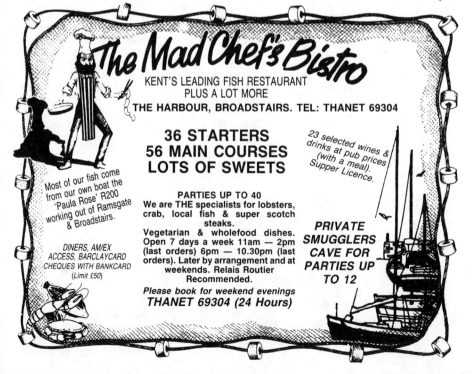

ning and weaving mills, iron foundries and workers' houses. Descriptive signs are attached to some of the more impressive features along the towpath. The Toll House museum in Manchester Road has a display on the development of the cotton industry and the Weavers' Triangle.

☏ (0282) 24213.
Open: Weavers' Triangle — Accessible at all reasonable times along towpath.
Toll House Museum — Apr-Sep, Wed & Sun 2-4 (organised walks available, charge payable).

Towneley Hall Art Gallery & Museum of Local Crafts & Industries
14th-century house with later modifications. Collection of oil paintings, early English water colours, period furniture, ivories, 18th-century glassware, archaeology and natural history. Nature trails. Loan exhibitions Apr-Sep.

☏ (0282) 24213.
Open: Mon-Fri 10-5.30 (5.15 winter), Sun 12-5. (Closed: Sat & over Xmas period.)
🖙 (in grounds) 🗻
占 (ground floor only) Shop & Garden Centre ✘

BURTON AGNES
Humberside   Map 8 TA16.
Norman Manor House
Dates from 1170 and preserves original Norman piers and groined roof of a lower

chamber. Upper room and an old donkey wheel.

Open: see page 4.
(AM)

BURY
Gt Manchester   Map 7 SD81.
Bury Art Gallery & Museum
Moss Street
Contains a fine collection of 19th-century British paintings including works by Turner, Constable and Landseer. The museum outlines the social history of the town. Temporary exhibitions.

☏ 061-761 4021.
Open: Mon-Fri 10-6, Sat 10-5. (Closed Sun & BH.)
占 Shop ✘

BURY ST EDMUNDS
Suffolk   Map 5 TL86.
Abbey Gardens & Ruins
Beautifully laid-out formal gardens form the centrepiece of the Abbey grounds and lead down to the 13th-century Abbots Bridge. A riverside path leads past a hexagonal dovecot to the ruins; little remains of the great Abbey which was once an important place of

Bury St Edmunds: Abbey Gate

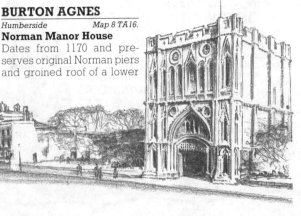

pilgrimage and held the Shrine of St Edmund. Stripped of its facing stone after the Dissolution of the Monasteries, there are Tudor, Georgian and Victorian houses built into it, giving it the appearance of a folly.

☏ (0284) 64667 (May-Sep) 63233 (Oct-Apr).
Open: daily, 7.30-dusk.

Angel Corner & The Gershom-Parkington Collection
Angel Hill
Queen Anne house containing Gershom-Parkington fine collection of clocks and watches.

☏ (0284) 63233 Ext 227.
Open: Mon-Sat 10-1, 2-5 (4pm Nov-Feb). (Closed: Sun, Good Fri, Etr Sat, May BH, Xmas & New Year.)
Donation.
✘ (NT)

Cathedral Church of St James
Of particular interest is the attractive hammerbeam roof with its painted angels holding shields with the insignia of St James, St Edmund and St George. The statue of St Edmund outside the south side is a bronze by the modern sculptress Elizabeth Frink. The tower, an outstanding example of Norman architecture, originally served as one of the gateways to the abbey precincts.

☏ (0284) 4933.
Open: daily May-Sep 8-8, Oct-Mar 8-5.30 (donation box)
✘

Suffolk Regiment Museum
The Keep, Gibraltar Barracks, Out Risbygate
Exhibits include uniforms,

weapons, medals, campaign souvenirs, documents and photographs.

☎ (0284) 2394.
Open: all year, Mon-Fri
10-12 & 2-4.
Shop ✖

CADEBY
Leicestershire   Map 4 SK40.
Cadeby Light Railway
in grounds of Cadeby Rectory
Probably the smallest of Britain's narrow-gauge railways. Engine normally running is a 1919 steam saddle tank locomotive. Other exhibits include a 1927 Foster Traction Engine and two steam rollers from 1903 onwards. Exhibition model railway in 4mm scale representing the Great Western Railway in South Devon of about 1935. There is a Brass Rubbing Centre in Cadeby Church (50 facsimiles).

☎ Market Bosworth
(0455) 290462.
Open: all year on second Sat of each month 2-5.30.
⊓ & (ground floor & gardens only) Shop

CAERNARFON
Gwynedd   Map 6 SH46.
Segontium Roman Fort and Museum
Branch archaeological gallery of the National Museum of Wales. Remains of Roman fort of 'Segontium' and also a museum of excavated relics.

☎ (0286) 5625.
Open: Mar, Apr & Oct Mon-Sat 9.30-5.30, Sun 2-5.30; May-Sep Mon-Sat 9.30-6, Sun 2-6; Nov-Feb Mon-Sat 9.30-4, Sun 2-4.
(Closed: 24-26 Dec, 1 Jan, Good Fri & May Day.)
Shop ✖ (AM)

CAERWENT
Gwent   Map 3 ST49.
Roman Town
(beside A48)
Complete circuit of town wall (in use from 1st-to 4th centuries) together with excavated areas of houses, shops and temple.

Open: accessible at any time.
(AM)

CAISTER-ON-SEA
Norfolk   Map 9 TG51.
Roman Town
South gateway, town wall built of flint with brick bonding courses, part of what may have been a seaman's hostel.

Open: at all reasonable times.
(AM)

CALLANDER
Central (Perthshire)   Map 11 NN60.
Kilmahog Woollen Mill
A former woollen mill, famous for hand-woven blankets and tweed. An old water wheel has been preserved in working order. Showroom open for sale of woollens, tweeds and tartans.

☎ (0877) 30268.
Open: mid Mar-mid Nov daily 9-5 & mid Nov-mid Mar daily 10-4. (Closed: Jan.)
🖵 Shop.

CALLANISH
*Isle of Lewis, Western Isles
(Ross & Cromarty)   Map 13 NB23.*
Callanish Standing Stones
Unique collection of megaliths comprising an avenue 27 ft in width, with 19 standing stones, terminating in a 37 ft-wide circle containing 13 additional stones. Other stones, burial cairns and circles may be seen in the near vicinity.

Open: accessible at all times.
(AM)

CAMBRIDGE
Cambridgeshire   Map 5 TL45.
Ancient university city on the River Cam. Many of the colleges line the East bank, overlooking the Back; sweeping lawns set with willow trees, on the opposite side of the river transformed from rough marshland by Richard Bently (Master of Trinity College from 1669 to 1734). The colleges are open to the public on most days during daylight though there are some restrictions during term time.

(All free except Queens College, small admission charge.)

Clare College
These beautiful college gardens overlook the river and portray in their two acres many of English gardening's 20th-century ideas.

☎ (0223) 358681.
Open: afternoons 2-4

Fitzwilliam Museum
Trumpington Street
Houses an extensive art and archaeological collection including Egyptian, Greek and Roman antiquities, European paintings, manuscripts, Renaissance objets d'art and armour plus exhibitions.

☎ (0223) 69501.
Open: Tue-Sat Lower gallery (porcelain, ceramics etc) 10-2. Upper gallery (paintings & drawings) 2-5. Sun (both gallerys) 2.15-5 plus Etr Mon, Spring & Summer BH. (Closed: Good Fri, May Day & 24 Dec-1 Jan.)
🖵 (Tue-Sat 10.30-4) & Shop
✖ (ex guide dogs)

Kettles Yard

The house is converted from four 17th- and 18th-century cottages and has an extension with an adjoining exhibition gallery. A large collection of 20th-century paintings and sculptures are on display and there is a continuous programme of modern art exhibitions, lectures, films and videos. A fascinating place to visit.

☎ (0223) 352124.
Open: House, daily 2-4; Exhibition gallery Mon-Sat, 12.30-5.30; Sun 2-5.30 during exhibitions. Closed 24 Dec-4 Jan.

Kings College Chapel

One of the finest Gothic churches in England, the stained glass windows show the story of the New Testament beginning in the northwest corner and ending in the south-west corner. They are the most complete set of Renaissance windows to survive in this country. The intricately-carved screen and choir stalls are fine examples of Renaissance craftsmanship.

Open: weekdays 9-3.45; Sun 2-3 & 4.30-5.45. University holidays; weekdays 9-5; Sun 10.30-5.30. The chapel may be closed at certain times.

Museum of Archaeology

Downing Street
New archaeology gallery covering man's development from the earliest times to Civilisation throughout the world, and local archaeology up to the 19th-century.

☎ (0223) 359714.
Open: Mon-Fri 2-4, Sat 10-12.30. (Closed 24 Dec-2 Jan & 1 wk Etr.)
& (ground floor only) ✖

Scott Polar Research Institute

Lensfield Road
Contains relics and equipment relating to arctic and antarctic expeditions with special emphasis on those of Captain Scott. Includes Eskimo and general polar art collections and information on current scientific exploration.

☎ (0223) 66499.
Open: Mon-Sat 2.30-4. (Closed: Some BH's.)
Shop ✖

University Botanic Garden

1 Brookside, Bateman Street
Originally founded in 1762 and now covering 40 acres with fine botanical collections.

☎ (0223) 350101.
Open: Mon-Sat 8-6.30 (dusk in winter). Sun, for non-keyholders May-Sep 2.30-6.30. For keyholders open all year 10-6.30. Glasshouses 11-12.30 & 2-4. (For Sunday keys-particulars from Director.)
🚗 & Shop ✖ (ex guide dogs) no bicycles
See advert Three Horseshoes Madingley, 3m W, page 95

CANTERBURY

Kent   Map 5 TR15.

Canterbury Cathedral

Canterbury Cathedral has been regarded as the mother church of British Christianity since the 12th century. The famous and dramatic murder of Thomas Beckett took place here in 1170; from then on the Cathedral became the setting for the shrine of the martyr, attracting thousands of pilgrims. Dating from 1100, the crypt is the oldest part of the building, the nave is 15th century and Bell Harry tower, which dominates the exterior, dates from the 16th century.

☎ (0227) 463135.
Open: daily, 8.45-6. Donations. &

Howe Barracks (Queens Regimental Museum)

Contains exhibits of all the former county regiments of Kent, Surrey, Sussex and Middlesex from which the

Canterbury Cathedral

Queen's Regiment was formed on 31 Dec 1966.

☎ (0227) 457411 Ext 259.
Open: all year Mon-Fri 10-12.30 & 2-4. Shop ✗

Royal Museum, Art Gallery and Buffs Regimental Museum
High Street
The archaeology of east Kent, Anglo-Saxon glass and jewellery, English and Continental porcelain, paintings include works by local artist Sidney Cooper, engravings and photographs; collections of medals, uniforms, weapons and trophies of the Royal East Kent Regiment. Canterbury festival exhibitions Sep/Oct plus monthly-changing exhibitions.

☎ (0227) 452747.
Open: Mon-Sat 10-5 Shop ✗
See advert The White Lion Selling, 6m W, page 126

CAPEL DEWI
Dyfed   Map 2 SN44.
Y Felin Wlan (Rock Mills)
This is one of the few remaining water-wheels in the country. Built in 1890 by the grandfather of the present owner, it has been in continuous operation since then. The water is supplied from the River Clettwr, a tributary of the Teifi.

☎ Llandysul (055932) 2356.
Open: Mon-Fri 8.30-5.30 Shop.

CARDIFF
South Glamorgan   Map 3 ST17.
National Museum of Wales (Main Building)
Cathays Park
Collections and exhibitions in archaeology, geology, botany, zoology, industry and art.

☎ (0222) 397951.
Open: Tue-Sat 10-5, Sun 2.30-5. (Closed: 24-26 Dec, New Year's day, Good Fri & May day.)
⌨ ♿ Shop ✗

Welsh Industrial and Maritime Museum
Bute Street
A branch museum of the National Museum of Wales. Working exhibits tell the story of motive power and the roles played by a variety of machines over two centuries of intense industrial production and progress in Wales. Collection of boats, road and railway vehicles.

☎ (0222) 481919.
Open: Tue-Sat 10-5, Sun 2.30-5. (Closed: Good Fri, May day, 24-26 Dec & New Year's day.)
♿ Book shop ✗

CARLISLE
Cumbria   Map 12 NY45.
Guildhall
Greenmarket
Renovated, half-timbered early 15th-century Guildhall with exposed timberwork and wattle and daub walls. Once the meeting place of Carlisle's eight trade guilds and retains much of the atmosphere of the period. Displays feature many items relating to these guilds, and other reminders of life in medieval Carlisle.

☎ (0228) 34781.
Open: mid May-mid Sep, Tue-Sat 12-4.
Shop ✗

Museum and Art Gallery
Castle Street
At Tullie House — a fine Jacobean House (1689), with Victorian extensions are comprehensive collections featuring the Archaeology and Natural History of Cumbria, English porcelain, costume, toys and musical instruments.

☎ (0228) 34781.
Open: Apr-Sep, Mon-Fri 9-6.45, Sat 9-5. Also Sun (Jun-Aug only) 2.30-5; Oct-Mar Mon-Sat 9-5.
♿ (ground floor only) Shop ✗

CARLOWAY
Isle of Lewis, Western Isles
(Ross & Cromarty)   Map 13 NB24.
Dun Carloway Broch
Well preserved broch of late prehistoric, about 30ft in height, one of the finest in the Western Isles.

Open: see page 4.
(AM)

CARNASSERIE CASTLE
Strathclyde (Argyll)   Map 10 NM80.
(1½m N of Kilmartin off A816)
Built in the 16th century by John Carswell, first Protestant Bishop of the Isles. It was taken and partly destroyed in Argyll's rebellion of 1685, and consists of a towerhouse with a courtyard built on to it.

Open: see page 4.
(AM)

CARRAWBROUGH
Northumberland   Map 12 NY87.
Roman Wall (Mithraic Temple)
(on B6318)
Remains of Mithraic temple measuring only 35 ft by 15 ft, dating from 3rd century but with later alterations. On line of Roman Wall near fort of 'Procolitia'. Excavations in 1950 revealed three dedicatory altars to Mithras and figure of the Mother Goddess.

Open: at all reasonable times.
(AM)

CASTLE TIORAM
Highland (Inverness-shire)
*   Map 13 NM67.*
(3½m NW of Acharacle off A861)
A ruined but picturesque, 14th-century castle. It stands on a small grassy island connected to the mainland by a ribbon of sand which is covered in high spring tides. The Castle once belonged to the MacDonalds of Clanranald and was set alight in 1715 by the then chief, fearing it might be captured by his enemies, the Campbells.

Open: accessible at all reasonable times.

CAWTHORNE
South Yorkshire   Map 8 SE20.
Cannon Hall
(on A635)
Built circa 1765, mainly by John Carr of York, the museum set in 70 acres of parkland is owned by Barnsley Metropolitan Borough Council. Also Regimental Museum of the 13th/18th Royal Hussars (Queen Mary's Own). The Harvey Collection of Dutch and Flemish paintings (formerly the National Loan Collection) is now on permanent display.

☎ Barnsley (0226) 790270.
Open: Mon-Sat 10.30-5 & Sun 2.30-5. (Closed: Good Fri & 25-27 Dec.)
& (ground floor only) 🐾

CERNE ABBAS
Dorset   Map 3 ST60.
Cerne Giant
(on footpath ¼m NE of village)
The Cerne Giant can be seen clearly from the A352. It is an 18 ft high turf-cut figure on a chalk hillside of a naked man bearing a club. It was associated with ancient fertility rites and is believed to date from Roman times.

Open: accessible at all reasonable times.
(NT)

CERRIGYDRUDION
Clwyd   Map 6 SH94.
Llyn Brenig Information Centre & Estate
A 2,400 acre estate with a unique archaeological trail and 'round the lake' walk of ten miles for which a completion certificate is available. Nature trail, and Nature Reserve includes a number of rare plants and birds. Access to bird hide, best viewing Dec-Feb. There are special fishing platforms, and an open day for disabled anglers. The Centre includes a bi-lingual exhibition on geology, archaeology, history and natural history.

☎ (049082) 463.
Open: daily Apr-17 Oct 8-6; Nov-Mar Mon-Fri 8-4.
(Access in the winter may be limited by snow; cross-country skiing is then available.)
Charge for fishing, canoeing & sailing.
🖙 (wknds Apr-Jun & Sep, daily Jul-Aug) & Souvenir & fishing tackle shop (Apr-17 Oct)

CHEDDLETON
Staffordshire   Map 7 SJ95.
Flint Mill
beside Caldon Canal, Leek Road
Two mills are preserved here with their low-breast wheels, one in working order. The original 17th-century south watermill ground corn but the 18th-century north mill was built to grind flint for the pottery industry. Museum collection includes examples of motive power (100hp Robey steam engine and model Newcomen engine) and transport (restored 70 ft horse-drawn narrow boat 'Vienna' moored on the Caldon Canal) and a haystack boiler of about 1770.

☎ Barlaston (078139) 2561.
Open: Sat & Sun afternoons. Application in advance for weekday visits to Mr Underwood, 4 Cherry Hill Avenue, Meir, Stoke-on-Trent.
& (ground floor only)

CHELMSFORD
Essex   Map 5 TL70.
Chelmsford and Essex Museum
Oaklands Park, Moulsham Street
Prehistoric and Roman Essex, coins, costumes, paintings, British birds and mammals, glass, ceramics, geology and local industries display. Also Victorian room, Tunstill collection of glass and temporary exhibition programme. Incorporates Essex Regiment Museum brought here from Warley. Special events & exhibitions planned for 150th anniversary.

☎ (0245) 353066, Essex Regiment Museum (0245) 260614.

Open: Mon-Sat 10-5, Sun 2-5. (Closed: Good Fri, 25-26 Dec & 1 Jan plus other days as may be advertised). ё (ground floor only) Shop ✱

CHELTENHAM
Gloucestershire   Map 3 SO92.
Art Gallery & Museum
Clarence Street
Contains nationally important Arts and Crafts Movement collection; notable 17th-century Dutch and 17th-20th century British paintings. Also in this museum are a large collection of English and Oriental ceramics, pewter, social history and archaeological material relating to the area. Temporary exhibitions are held throughout the year.

☎ (0242) 37431.
Open: Mon-Sat 10-5.30. (Closed Sun & BH)
ё Shop ✱

Gustav Holst Museum
4 Clarence Road, Pittville
The composer's birthplace containing rooms with period furnishings and working Victorian kitchen. There is also a display of Holst personalia and reference collection.

☎ (0242) 524846.
Open: Tue-Fri noon-5.30, Sat 11-5.30. (Closed BH)
Shop ✱

CHEPSTOW
Gwent   Map 3 ST59.
Stuart Crystal
Bridge Street
Visitors can view craftsmen applying decoration to handmade crystal; included in the tour is a museum section displaying past and present Stuart crystal produced over 150 years. A video of the techniques used in present day manufacture can also be seen.

☎ (02912) 70135.
Open: factory tours daily 10, 11, noon & 1.30, 2.30, 3.30, 4.30. Shop daily 9-8 May-Sep; 9-5 Oct-Apr
ё ⊓

CHERTSEY
Surrey   Map 4 TQ06.
Chertsey Museum
33 Windsor Street
A late Georgian house, The Cedars, containing Matthews collection of costumes and accessories, local history collection, including a 10th-century Viking sword, silver, glass, dolls and collection of Meissen porcelain figures. Also various exhibitions throughout the year and the 'Black Cherry Fair' in July.

☎ (09328) 65764.
Open: Tue & Thu 2-5, Wed, Fri & Sat 10-1 & 2-5. (Closed Xmas.)
⊓ ё (ground floor & garden only) Bookshop.

CHESTER
Cheshire   Map 7 SJ46.
Grosvenor Museum
27 Grosvenor Street
Chester having been an important Roman centre, the museum has one of the finest collections of Roman remains in Britain, including special Roman Army gallery and many inscribed and sculptured stones excavated in Chester. Natural History gallery and art gallery. Temporary exhibitions are held.

☎ (0244) 21616 and 313858.
Open: Mon-Sat 10.30-5, Sun 2-5. (Closed: Good Fri & Xmas.)
ё (ground floor only) Shop ✱

CHESTERFIELD
Derbyshire   Map 8 SK37.
Peacock Information and Heritage Centre
Low Pavement
A medieval timber framed building, thought to have been a guildhall. First floor is now used as an exhibition room. Audio visual on history of Chesterfield available for showing on request. Special medieval market in July.

☎ (0246) 207777/8.
Open: Mon-Sat. Information centre 9-5.30; Heritage centre noon-5.
⊓ ё (ground floor only) Shop.

CHICHESTER

West Sussex   *Map 4 SU80.*

District Museum
29 Little London
Housed in a former 18th-century corn store with displays of local history, archaeology and geology. Temporary exhibitions programme.

☎ (0243) 784683.
Open: all year, Tue-Sat 10-5.30.
& (ground floor only) Shop ✗ (ex guide dogs). Parties by arrangement.

Guildhall Museum
Priory Park
Branch of District Museum in medieval Greyfriars church, later used as City Guildhall, containing archaeological finds from district. The small public park contains mound of Norman Castle.

☎ (0243) 784683.
Open: Jun-Sep, Tue-Sat 1-5; Park open daily.
& Shop ✗

CHRISTCHURCH

Dorset   *Map 4 SZ19.*

Christchurch Castle and Norman House
Rare example of ruined Norman house c.1160; stands in bailey of 11th-century house.

Open: at all reasonable times.
(AM)

CHURCH CROOKHAM

Hampshire   *Map 4 SU85.*

Gurkha Museum
Queen Elizabeth's Barracks
Contains a record of the Gurkha's service to the Crown from 1815.

☎ Fleet (02514) 3541 Ext 63.
Open: all year, Mon-Fri 9.30-4.30, Apr-Oct Sat & BH 9.30-4.30. Other times by request.
& Shop ✗

CLAPHAM

North Yorkshire   *Map 7 SD76.*

Yorkshire Dales National Park Centre
Visitor Centre with interpretative display on 'The Limestone Dales'. Audiovisual theatre. Maps, walks, guides and local information available.

☎ (04685) 419.
Open: daily Apr-Oct mid morning-late afternoon.
⊓

CLAVA CAIRNS

Highland (Inverness-shire)
Map 14 NH74.
(6m E of Inverness)
Situated on the south bank of the River Nairn, this group of burial cairns has three concentric rings of great stones.

Open: at all reasonable times.
(AM)

CLAWDD-NEWYDD

Clwyd   *Map 6 SJ05.*

Bod Petrual Visitor Centre
(on B5105 3m W)
On the southern edge of Clocaenog Forest, with waymarked walks. The centre is in a converted keepers cottage and has an exhibition on the history and ecology of the forest.

☎ (08245) 208.
Open: Visitor Centre, daily Apr-Sep 9-6.
⊓

CLUN

Shropshire   *Map 7 SO28.*

Clun Town Trust Museum
Situated in the town hall, the original court house to Clun Castle; court was moved to market square in 1780. Flint tools, maps of earthworks, etc., domestic and family relics. There are also exhibits of local geological and mineralogical interest.

☎ (05884) 247.
Open: Etr-Nov, Tue-Sat 2-5 and BH weekends Sat, Mon & Tue 11-1 & 2-5.
Other times by request, and parties by arrangement only. Enquiries *Mrs F Hudson, Florida Villa.*
(Donations)

COLCHESTER

Essex   *Map 5 TL92.*

Hollytrees Museum
High Street
Fine Georgian house, dating from 1718, with collection of costume, toys, etc.

☎ (0206) 712481.
Open: Mon-Sat 10-1, 2-5 (4pm Sat, Oct-Mar). (Closed: Good Fri & 25-27 Dec.)
Shop ✗

Museum of Social History
Holy Trinity Church, Trinity Street
Historical displays of country life and crafts, with some bicycles, etc.

☎ (0206) 712481.
Open: Mon-Sat 10-1 & 2-5 (4pm Sat, Oct-Mar). (Closed: Good Fri & 25-27 Dec.)
& Shop ✗

Natural History Museum
All Saints Church, High Street
Formerly 15th-century All Saints Church, with the flint tower. Features the Natural History of Essex with special reference to the area.

☎ (0206) 712481.
Open: Mon-Sat 10-1 & 2-5 (4pm Sat, Oct-Mar). (Closed: Good Fri & 25-27 Dec.)
& Shop ✗

COLLIESTON

Grampian (Aberdeenshire)
Map 15 NK03.

Slains Castle
(1m NE)

On show at Colchester's
Museum of Social History

Spectacular but fragmentary Keep on a rocky headland, home of the Hays of Erroll for three centuries. Nearby are two cannons salvaged from the Spanish galleon *Santa Caterina*, wrecked in 1594. A coastal path from Collieston leads to the castle.

Open: accessible at all reasonable times.
(AM)

COLONSAY
Strathclyde (Argyllshire)
Map 10 NR39.
Kiloran Gardens
(2m N of Scalasaig)
Set close to Colonsay House, these peaceful gardens and woodlands are a maze of colour during the Spring, and are noted for their fine display of rhododendrons and shrubs, including embothriums and magnolias. The Gulf Stream encourages plants not normally found at this latitude.

Open: daily, dawn to dusk.

COMPTON
Surrey   *Map 4 SU94.*
Watts Picture Gallery
Down Lane
Memorial gallery with a collection of about 150 paintings by G F Watts who is buried by the nearby Watts Mortuary Chapel.

☏ Guildford (0483) 810235.
Gallery Open: Fri-Wed 2-6 Apr-Sep & 2-4 Oct-Mar; also 11-1 Wed & Sat. Chapel open daily.
& (ground floor only) Shop
✗

CORFE CASTLE
Dorset   *Map 3 SY98.*
Corfe Castle Museum
Tiny rectangular building, partly rebuilt in brick after fire in 1680. Small museum with old village relics and dinosaur footprints 130 million years old. Council chamber accessible by staircase at one end, the Ancient Order of Marblers meet here each Shrove Tuesday (open by appointment only).

☏ (0929) 480248.
Open: daily; Etr-Sep 8-7, Oct-Etr 8-5 (times are approximate).

CORRIESHALLOCH GORGE
Highland (Ross and Cromarty)
    Map 14 NH27.
(On A835 14m SE of Ullapool)
Spectacular canyon a mile long and 200 ft deep, varying in width from 50 ft to 150 ft. The Abhainn Droma plunges 150 ft over the Falls of Measach; a suspension bridge spans the gorge giving breathtaking views. The gorge is a special habitat for plant life, with high humidity and poor light.

Open: accessible at all reasonable times.
(NTS)

CORRIS
Gwynedd   *Map 6 SH70.*
Railway Museum
In village, 300 yards from A487
Museum in century-old railway building with photographs of operation of Corris narrow-gauge railway from 1890-1948. Items connected with railway are constantly added, and some old wagons are on show. Half mile of track between museum and old engine shed at Maespoeth has now been reinstated. Passengers not carried. Children's playground nearby.

☏ (065473) 343.
Open: 15 Jul-6 Sep Mon-Fri & BH periods 10.30-5.30 and as advertised locally during holiday season.
Shop.

COVENTRY
West Midlands   *Map 4 SP37.*
Coventry Cathedral
Priory Row
Outstanding cathedral designed by Sir Basil Spence, and consecrated in May 1962. It contains major works of art, including the Sutherland altar tapestry, the West Screen (a wall of glass engraved by John Hutton with saints and angels) and excellent stained glass.

☏ (0203) 27597.
Open: daily 8.30-7.30 (summer); 8.30-5.30 (winter) except during services.
⌷ ✗

Herbert Art Gallery and Museum
Jordan Well
Collections include social history, archaeology, folk life, industry, natural history, visual arts. Of special interest are the life collection of Graham Sutherland's studies for the 'Christ in Glory' tapes-

try in Coventry Cathedral, and the Frederick Poke collection of fine 18th-century English furniture and silver. Also a permanent exhibition of Coventry's history, and the Natural History live animal display.

☎ (0203) 25555 Ext 2315.
Open: Mon-Sat 10-6, Sun 2-5. (Closed: Good Fri & part Xmas.)
& Shop ✹

St Mary's Guildhall
Between Bayley Lane and Earl Street
Medieval guildhall, with minstrels' gallery, restored hall with portraits and Flemish tapestries and Caesar's watchtower.

☎ (0203) 25555 Ext 2874.
Open: Etr, then May-Oct, Mon-Sat 10-5, Sun 12-5 (subject to civic requirements — enquiry advised before visiting.)
& (ground floor only) ✹

COWES
Isle of Wight   Map 4 SZ49.
Maritime Museum and Public Library
Beckford Road
Ship models, photographs, paintings, books and other items showing the island's maritime past.

☎ (0983) 293341.
Open: Mon-Fri 9.30-6, Sat 9.30-4.30. (Closed: BHs.)
Shop ✹

COXWELL, GREAT
Oxfordshire   Map 4 SU29.
Great Coxwell Barn
Stone-built 13th-century barn. This is possibly the finest in England, with notably fine roof timbers.

Open: at all reasonable times.
(NT)

CRANBROOK
Kent   Map 5 TQ73.
Cranbrook Windmill
Seventy foot high Smock mill with eight sided three storey brick base and a four-storey, fixed wooden tower. The mill was built in 1814 by the millwright Humphrey for Henry Dobell. Wind powered, and now fully restored to working use for milling, it is maintained by the Cranbrook Windmill Association.

☎ (0580) 712256.
Open: Etr-Sep Sat & BH 2.30-5 (Donation box)

CRASTER
Northumberland   Map 12 NU22.
Kipper Curing (L Robson & Son Ltd.)
Haven Hill
Curing kippers has been carried out in this original smokehouse building since 1856, using traditional methods which visitors can see.

☎ Embleton (066 576) 223.
Open: Jun-mid Sep (ex BH), Mon-Fri 9.30-5, Sat 9.30-12
✹ Shop

CRATHIE
Grampian (Aberdeenshire)
*   Map 15 NO29.*
Crathie Church
Built in 1893 this small building is the parish church where the Royal Family worships when in residence at Balmoral.

☎ (03384) 208.
Open: Apr-Oct, 9.30-5.30. (Donations)
&

CRESWELL
Derbyshire   Map 8 SK57.
Creswell Crags Visitor Centre
(off Crags Road 1m E off B6042)
Limestone Gorge which was once the home of early man. Picnic site and a visitor centre, which explains the archaeological significance of the site with an exhibition and audio-visual programme which shows what life was like for our ancestors.

☎ Worksop (0909) 720378.
Open: Mar-Oct, Tue-Sun & BH Mons 10-5; Nov & Dec Suns only 10-5.
🚻 & Shop.

Glass from the Strathearn Collection, at Stuart Strathearn Glass, Crieff

·FREE·FACTORY·TOUR·
An Invitation to see the art of Glassmaking

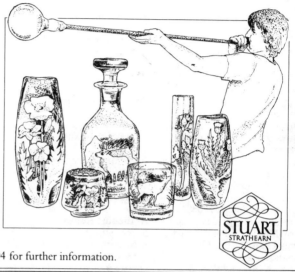

Factory open seven days a week.

Self-conducted tours showing the manufacture of crystal. Video on glassmaking and decoration.

Factory seconds shop open 9am–5pm Monday–Saturday, 11am–5pm Sundays. (extended hours during June – September)

Picnic Area.
Children's Playground.

Muthill Road, Crieff,
Perthshire,
Scotland PH7 4HQ.

Telephone Crieff (0764) 4004 for further information.

STUART STRATHEARN

CRICKLEY HILL COUNTRY PARK
Gloucestershire   Map 3 SO91.
(off A436)
On the extreme edge of the Cotswold scarp, 62 acres of countryside and scenery, the steep grassy slopes rich in flowers and butterflies. From the edge of the hill there are views to the Malverns, Forest of Dean, mountains of South Wales and the Severn Valley.

☎ Gloucester (0452) 863170.
Open: daily.
🍴

CRIEFF
Tayside (Perthshire)   Map 11 NN82.
Stuart Strathearn Glass
Muthill Road
Handmade lead crystal includes vases, rose bowls, honey pots, decanters and whisky glasses. The range is engraved with a wide variety of flowers and Scottish game. Self conducted tours enable the visitor to see at close hand all stages of manufacture. Video on glassmaking and decoration. Children's playground.

☎ (0764) 4004.
Open: Factory daily 9-5;
Shop Mon-Sat 9-5, Sun 11-5 (extended hours Jun-Sep).
🍴 🎡

CROMER
Norfolk   Map 9 TG24.
Lifeboat Museum
Situated in No 2 boathouse at the bottom of The Gangway. Covers both local lifeboat and general RNLI history. Also **Lifeboat Station** on pier.

☎ (0263) 512503.
Open: daily May-Sep 10-5.
Parties by arrangement.
♿ Shop.

CULROSS
Fife (Fife)   Map 11 NS98.
Culross Abbey
Cistercian monastery, founded by Malcolm, Earl of Fife in 1217. The choir is still used as the parish church and parts of the nave remain. Fine central tower, still complete.

Open: see page 4.
(AM)

CUSWORTH
South Yorkshire   Map 8 SE50.
Cusworth Hall Museum
18th-century house with fine chimney pieces and chapel in south-west wing. Museum of South Yorkshire life and sections of interest to children. Temporary exhibitions and many annual events. Also extensive grounds which are open all year, with fishing in ponds, cricket and football pitches. Children's study base, and research facilities.

☎ Doncaster (0302) 782342.
Open: all year Mon-Thu & Sat 11-5, Sun 1-5 (4pm Nov-

Feb). (Closed: Xmas.)
& (ground floor & gardens
only) Shop ✖

DANBY
North Yorkshire   Map 8 NZ70.
The Moors Centre
Lodge Lane
The former shooting lodge
offers full information and
countryside interpretation
service to visitors to the North
York Moors National Park.
The grounds include riverside meadow, woodland and
terraced gardens, children's
play area and brass rubbing
centre. Slides shown daily,
and also an exhibition about
the North York Moors. Bookshop information desk.

☎ Castleton (0287) 60654.
Open: daily Apr-Oct 10-5;
Nov-Mar Sun 12-4. Guided
walks Sun. Parties by
arrangement.
☞ ☴ & (ground floor &
garden) Shop ✖

DANEBURY RING
Hampshire   Map 4 SU33.
*(off unclass road 2½m NW
of Stockbridge)*
A fine Iron Age fort rising to
469 ft, much of it thickly
wooded with beech trees. Extensive excavations have
been carried out since 1969.
There is a nature trail and
leaflets are available at the
site.

Open: accessible at all
reasonable times.

DARLINGTON
Co Durham   Map 8 NZ21.
Art Gallery
Crown Street
Contains a permanent col-
lection of pictures but also has
temporary loan exhibitions
throughout the year.

☎ (0325) 462034.
Open: Mon-Fri 10-8, Sat
10-5.30. (Closed: Sun & all

weekend BH).
& ✖

Darlington Museum
Tubwell Row
Local social and natural history, archaeology and by-
gones. Observation beehive
and beekeeping exhibits, can
be seen approx May-Sep,
each year.

☎ (0325) 463795.
Open: all year Mon-Wed &
Fri 10-1 & 2-6; Thu 10-1; Sat
10-1 & 2-5.30. (Closed: Good
Fri, May Day, Xmas & New
Year's Day).
& (ground floor only) Shop
✖ (ex guide dogs)

DARTMOUTH
Devon   Map 3 SX85.
Agincourt House
Lower Street
A wealthy medieval mer-
chants' house, built 1380 and
restored in 1968 by the present owner. Two of the four
storeys are open to the public
and have an antique gallery,
with notable boudoir grand
piano in working order.

☎ (08043) 2472
Open: Mon-Fri 10-5.30, Sat
10-5, Sun 2.30-5. (Donations)
✖

Bayard's Cove Castle
Low, circular ruined stronghold, built by townspeople in
1537, with gunposts as at
Dartmouth Castle.

Open: accessible at all
reasonable times.
(AM)

DEDDINGTON
Oxfordshire   Map 4 SP43.
Deddington Castle
Mainly earthworks from outer
bailey and inner ward. Excavations have revealed
portions of a 13th-century
chapel.

Open: at all reasonable
times. (AM)

DEERHURST
Gloucestershire   Map 3 SO82.
Odda's Chapel
(off B4213 near River Severn)
Rare Saxon chapel, dating
back to 1056 and erected originally by the Lord of the
Manor. Attached to the old
house.

Open: at all reasonable
times.
& (AM)

DENMEAD
Hampshire   Map 4 SU61.
**Denmead Pottery &
Woodland Park**
In a woodland setting, a pottery manufacturers where the
latest ceramic plant and technology processes are used.
Visitors may walk around the
production area. For
children, the park has a lake,
pets enclosure and adven-
ture playground.

☎ Waterlooville (0705)
261942.
Open: Factory tours Mon-
Fri 9-4; shop daily 9-5.30.
☴
*See advertisement on page
119.*

DERBY
Derbyshire   Map 8 SK33.
**Derby Museum & Art
Gallery**
Antiquities, social and natural
history, militaria, Bonnie
Prince Charlie room (1745
rebellion), toy theatre collection and also temporary
exhibitions. There are
paintings by Joseph Wright of
Derby (1734-1797). Derby
porcelain and costumes.
Many temporary exhibitions
are held.

☎ (0332) 31111 Ext 405.
Open: Tue-Sat 10-5.
(Closed: Sun, Mon & BH.)

Shop ✖ (ex guide dogs)

Industrial Museum
Silk Mill, off Full St
Housed in an early 18th-century silk mill substantially rebuilt in 1910. The Rolls-Royce collection of aero-engines occupies the ground floor gallery, alongside the history of aviation from the Wright Brothers to the present day. 'An introduction to Derbyshire Industries' occupies the first floor gallery. Temporary exhibitions are held.

☎ (0332) 31111 Ext 740.
Open: Tue-Fri 10-5, Sat 10-4.45. (Closed: BH.)
& Shop ✖ (ex guide dogs)

DEVIZES
Wiltshire   Map 4 SU06.
Caen Hill Lock Flight
(½m W off A361)
An impressive flight of locks under restoration on the Kennet and Avon Canal, engineered by John Rennie and completed by 1810. In the space of only two miles there are 29 locks of which 17 are placed close together down Caen Hill. At the side of the locks large ponds were built to act as reservoirs. A good towpath runs along the southern bank of the canal; it is hoped to open the locks by 1990.

☎ (0380) 71279.
Open: accessible at all reasonable times.

DEWSBURY
West Yorkshire   Map 8 SE22.
Robinsons Canal Museum
Savile Town Wharf, Mill Street East
The museum housed in a former blacksmith's shop, features a display on the history of canals.

☎ (0924) 467976.

Open: Mon-Fri 9.30-4.30 (by request at weekends)

DINAS MAWDDWY
Gwynedd   Map 6 SH81.
Meirion Mill
In the Dyfi Valley, at the southern end of the Snowdonia National Park, is this working woollen weaving mill and retail shop in rural estate. Pack-horse bridge (AM). Field-walk on trackbed of Old Mawddwy Railway. Gardens and children's playground. Dog exercise area.

☎ (06504) 311.
Open: Apr-Oct daily including BH, Winter, Mon-Fri (ex Xmas Day) 10-5 & some weekends.
(Charge for educational visits.)
⌨ 🍴 & Shop.

DOLWYDDELAN
Gwynedd   Map 6 SH75.
Dolwyddelan Castle
Restored rectangular keep built in about 1200, with 13th-century curtain walls, and fine views.

Open: accessible at all reasonable times.
(AM)

DONCASTER
South Yorkshire   Map 8 SE50.
Museum & Art Gallery
Chequer Road
Prehistoric and Romano-British archaeology are on display, as well as British natural history, local history and costumes, British and European Art Collection, paintings, sculpture, ceramics, glass and silver. Temporary exhibitions are held.

☎ (0302) 734287.
Open: all year, Mon-Thu & Sat 10-5, Sun 2-5. (Closed: Xmas Day & New Years Day.)

⌨ (pre booked parties) &
(ground floor only)
Shop ✖

DONINGTON-LE-HEATH
Leicestershire   Map 8 SK41.
Donington-le-Heath Manor House
(near Coalville)
Medieval manor house of c.1280 with very few alterations.

☎ Coalville (0530) 31259.
Open: 26 Mar-28 Sep, Wed-Sun, also BH Mon & Tue, 2-6.
⌨ & (ground floor & gardens only) Shop ✖

DORCHESTER
Dorset   Map 3 SY69.
Maiden Castle
(1m SW)
Prehistoric earthworks the name being derived from Celtic 'Mai-Jun' (the stronghold by the plain). Huge, oval, triple-ramparted camp, with extensive plateau on summit. Complicated defensive system of ditches and ramparts.

Open: at all reasonable times.
(AM)

Old Crown Court
The court is contained in the Old Shire Hall, dating from 1796-97, and was the scene of the trial of the six Tolpuddle Martyrs in 1834 who were sentenced to transportation to Botany Bay in Australia for demanding a wage increase. The building is now a Tolpuddle Memorial.

☎ (0305) 65211 Ext 215.
Open: all year Mon-Fri 10-1 & 2-4. (Closed: PH.) Other times only by arrangement at adjacent West Dorset District Council.
✖

DORCHESTER-ON-THAMES
Oxfordshire   Map 4 SU59.

Dorchester Abbey and Museum
Archaeological finds from the Bronze Age through to Anglo-Saxon times with maps showing layout of village during Roman times and later, and a display of Roman material from Roman town of 'Dorocina'. The Abbey Church of SS Peter and Paul is the only remaining part of the Augustinian Abbey founded in 1140, enlarged in 13th and 14th centuries and 200 ft long. Of note are the fine Norman lead font and the Jesse Window in the north aisle which represents the Tree of Jesse.

☎ Museum, Oxford (0865) 340056; Abbey, Oxford (0865) 340007.
Open: Museum Etr-Apr Sat, Sun; May-Sep Tue-Sat & BH, 10.30-12.30 & 2-6, Sun 2-6; Abbey daily 9-7 or sunset if earlier.
Museum shop (⌨ Summer only Wed-Sun 3-5.30)
Abbey 🚻 ⴲ ✗

DORNOCH
Highland (Sutherland) Map 14 NH78.
Dornoch Cathedral
Founded in the 13th century by Gilbert, Archdeacon of Moray and Bishop of Caithness and largely destroyed by fire in 1570 but restored between the 18th and 20th centuries. Burial place for 16 Earls of Sutherland with at the western end a fine statue by Chantey of the first Duke of Sutherland.

Open: daily dawn-dusk.
🚻 ✗

Dornoch Craft Centre
Situated in the town jail, visitors can observe the weaving of tartans on Saurgr power looms. There is also kilt and soft toy making. The jail cells have a small exhibition.

☎ (0862) 810555.
Open: Mon-Sat 9.30-5; Sun Jul & Aug 12-5.
🚻 (ground floor only)

DOUGLAS
Isle of Man   Map 6 SC37.
Manx Museum
Items illustrate island's archaeology, history, natural history, folk life and art. Also National Reference Library.

☎ (0624) 75522.
Open: all year, Mon-Sat 10-5. (Closed: 25 & 26 Dec, 1 Jan, Good Fri & the morning of 5 Jul.)
Shop ✗ (ex guide dogs)

DOUNBY
Orkney   Map 16 HY22.
Click Mill
(NE of village, off B9057)
An example of one of the rare old Orcadian horizontal watermills, in working condition.

Open: at all reasonable times.
(AM)

DOVER
Kent   Map 5 TR34.
Dover Museum
Ladywell
The museum, founded in 1836, contains exhibits of local history, archaeology, ceramics, coins, natural history and geology. Monthly programme of exhibitions.

☎ (0304) 201066.
Open: Mon, Tue & Thu-Sat 10-4.45
🚻 Shop.

DOWLISH WAKE
Somerset   Map 3 ST31.
Perry's Cider Mills
A long established family run firm using traditional methods of cidermaking. The museum, which is housed in a modern thatched barn, includes wagons and carts and a fine collection of small farm tools. Also on display are photographs of cidermaking and nostalgic pictures of village life around 1900.

☎ Ilminster (04605) 2681.
Open: Mon-Fri 9-1, 2-5.30; Sat & Spring & Summer BH 9.30-1, 2-4.30 & Sun 9.30-1.
Shop.

DRE-FACH-FELINDRE
Dyfed   Map 2 SN33.
Museum of the Woollen Industry
A branch of the National Museum of Wales, it occupies part of a working mill, the Cambrian Mills. Its collection of textile machinery dates back to the 18th century and the exhibition traces the development of the industry from early days.

☎ Velindre (0559) 370929.
Open: Apr-Sep, Mon-Sat 10-5; Oct-Mar, Mon-Fri 10-5.(Closed: May Day.)
🚻 ⴲ (ground floor only)
Shop.

DRUMCOLTRAN TOWER
Dumfries and Galloway (Kirkcudbrightshire)   Map 11 NX86.
(5m NE of Dalbeattie)
A 16th-century tower house, three-storeys in height and built to an oblong plan, with a projecting tower or wing.

Open: see page 4. Key with keeper. (AM)

DRYSLWYN
Dyfed   Map 2 SN52.
Dryslwyn Castle
Ruined, 13th century, native Welsh stronghold on a lofty mound, important for its part in the struggles between the Welsh and English in the 13th century.

Open: accessible at any time. (AM)

DUDLEY
West Midlands   *Map 7 SO99.*
Museum & Art Gallery
St James's Road
Includes the Brooke Robinson collection of fine and decorative art. Geological Gallery and a wide variety of temporary exhibitions throughout the year.

☎ (0384) 55433 Ext 5530.
Open: Mon-Sat 10-5.
(Closed: BHs).
& (ground floor only) ✚

DUFFTOWN
Grampian (Banffshire)   *Map 15 NJ33.*
Dufftown Museum
The Tower, The Square
Small local history museum featuring Mortlach Kirk material. Temporary displays.

☎ Forres (0309) 73701.
Open: May-Sep, Mon-Sat 9.30-5.30 (6.30 in Jul & Aug) also Sun in Aug 2-6.30.
& Shop ✚

Glenfiddich Distillery
(N of town, off A941)
Situated by Balvenie Castle in the heart of Speyside country, the distillery was founded in 1887 by Major William Grant.

A visitor's reception centre houses a bar and a Scotch whisky museum. The theatre offers a programme in six languages covering the history of Scotland and Scotch whisky.

☎ (0340) 20373
Open: all year Mon-Fri 9.30-4.30 (Jun-Aug, Thu until 7.30 pm), also 11 May-13 Oct Sat 9.30-4.30, Sun 12-4.30.
(Closed: 23 Dec-5 Jan).
⊓ & (ground floor & gardens only) Shop.

DUFFUS
Grampian (Moray)   *Map 15 NJ16.*
Duffus Castle
(off B9012)
Motte and bailey castle, with 8-acre bailey surrounding rebuilt 15th-century hall and 14th-century tower, now broken into two halves.

Open: at all reasonable times.
(AM)

DUMFRIES
*Dumfries & Galloway
(Dumfriesshire)*   *Map 11 NX97.*
Old Bridge House
Mill Road
Built in 1662 the house over-

looks the River Nith and contains rooms furnished in period style to illustrate life in Dumfries over the centuries. Nearby is Devorgilla's Bridge, built in the 13th century by Devorgilla Balliol, who endowed Balliol College, Oxford.

☎ (0387) 53374.
Open: Apr-Sep, Mon-Sat 10-1, 2-5, Sun 2-5.
✚

Old Town Mill
Mill Road
Burns interpretation centre with exhibition of 'Robert Burns and Dumfries'.

☎ (0387) 64808.
Open: all year Tue-Sat 10-8, also Apr-Sep Mon 10-8, Sun 2-5.
Shop.

DUNBAR
Lothian (East Lothian)   *Map 12 NT67.*
John Muir Country Park
(W off A1087 & A198)
An attractive stretch of coastline forms this country park named after John Muir, a pioneer of conservation. The park, includes Belhaven Bay and Ravensheugh Sands, with waymarked paths and a clifftop nature trail giving good views to the Bass Rock and the Isle of May. A wide variety of wildlife reflects the diversity of habitats, which include cliff, dunes, saltmarsh, woodlands, scrub and grassland.

Open: accessible at all reasonable times.

DUNBLANE
Central (Stirlingshire)   *Map 11 NN70.*
Dunblane Cathedral
The Cathedral mostly dates from the 13th century but

*Perrys Cider Mills at
Dowlish Wake*

incorporates a 12th century tower. After the Reformation it became a ruin but was restored 1892-95.

☎ (0786) 823388.
Open: daily Apr-Sep, 9.30-12.30, 1.30-7; Oct-Mar, 9.30-12.30, 1.30-4.
&

DUNDEE
Tayside (Angus)   *Map 11 NO43.*
Barrack Street Museum
Barrack Street
Museum of Natural History; Scottish Wildlife of Lowlands and Highlands. Great Tay Whale. Some changes in displays may be caused by re-development.

☎ (0382) 23141.
Open: Mon-Sat 10-5.
Shop ✖

Broughty Castle Museum
Broughty Ferry (4m E)
15th-century castle rebuilt as estuary fort in 19th century. Displays of arms and armour, seashore wildlife, Dundee's former whaling industry and history of former Burgh of Broughty Ferry.

☎ (0382) 76121 or 23141
Open: Mon-Thu & Sat 10-1 & 2-5. Sun 2-5 (Jul-Sep only).
⊓ Shop ✖

Dundee Art Gallery and Museum (McManus Gallery)
Albert Square
Major Art Gallery with changing exhibitions of local and national interest. Important Scottish and Victorian collections. Local history displays cover Trade and Industry, Social and Civic History. Restricted displays of archaeology during redevelopment in 1986. McManus Galleries is one of Dundee's finest Victorian buildings by Gilbert Scott.

☎ (0382) 23141.
Open: Mon-Sat 10-5.
& Shop ✖

Mills Observatory
Balgay Park, Glamis Road
Observatory, built in 1935, with fine Victorian 10-inch Cooke refracting telescope and other instruments. Gallery displays on astronomy and space exploration, and small planetarium.

☎ (0382) 67138 or 23141.
Open: Apr-Sep Mon-Fri 10-5, Sat 2-5; Oct-Mar, Mon-Fri 3-10, Sat 2-5.
Parties booked in advance.
⊓ Shop ✖

DUNFERMLINE
Fife (Fife)   *Map 11 NT08.*
Andrew Carnegie Birthplace Museum
Junction of Moodie Street and Priory Lane.
The cottage in which the great philanthropist was born in 1835. New displays tell the exciting story of the weaver's son who gave away 350 million dollars and how the Carnegie Trust still spend his money on philanthropic causes.

☎ (0383) 724302.
Open: all year daily. Apr-Oct Mon-Sat 11-5 (Wed 8pm), Sun 2-5; Nov-Mar 2-4.
& (ground floor only) Shop
✖ (ex guide dogs)

Dunfermline Abbey
Pittencrieff Park
Benedictine house founded by Queen Margaret. The foundations of her church remain beneath the present Norman nave. The site of the choir is now occupied by a modern parish church, at the east end of which are remains of St Margaret's shrine dating from the 13th century. King Robert the Bruce is buried in the choir and his grave is marked by a modern brass. Guest house was a royal palace where Charles I was born.

Open: see page 4. (AM)

Dunfermline District Museum
Viewfield Terrace
Interesting and varied displays of local history, domestic bygones and damask linen. Periodically, special exhibitions are held at the museum.

☎ (0383) 721814.
Open: all year, Mon-Sat 11-5. (Closed: Sun & BHs).
✖

Pittencrieff House Museum
Pittencrief Park
Situated in a rugged glen, with lawns, hothouses and gardens, overlooked by the ruined 11th-century Malcolm Canmore's Tower. Fine 17th-century mansion house, with galleries displaying local history, costume and temporary exhibitions.

☎ (0383) 722935 or 721814.
Open: May-Aug Mon & Wed-Sun 11-5
⊓ & (ground floor & gardens only).

DUNGENESS
Kent   *Map 5 TR01.*
'A' Nuclear Power Station
Building open throughout the year for organised group tours by pre-arrangement any weekday and to the general public on Wed, tours at 2pm & 3pm, 11 Jun-24 Sep, 12 Jun-25 Sep. Tickets obtainable from the local South Eastern Electricity Board shops. Children under 14 not admitted.

☎ Lydd (0679) 20461 Ext 238.
& (by arrangement) ✖

DUNKELD
Tayside (Perthshire)   Map 11 NO04.
Dunkeld Cathedral
High Street
The present building dates from the 13th century. The nave is now a roofless ruin but the choir has been restored and is used as the parish church. The nave arcade is supported on heavy drum columns reminiscent of an earlier period.

☎ (03502) 601.
Open: Apr-Sep, Mon-Sat 9.30-7, Sun 2-7; Oct-Mar, Mon-Sat 9.30-4. Sun 2-4. (Donations)
& ✂

Hermitage
(2m W, off A9)
A tree garden was created here by the Second Duke of Atholl in the 18th century. Today, there is a wide variety of trees including a Douglas Fir over 180 ft tall. Among the wildlife is the red squirrel. Two follies, Ossian's Hall and Ossian's Cave, can be visited on the nature trail.

☎ Pitlochry (0796) 3233.
Open: accessible at all reasonable times.
& (NTS)

Little Houses
Dating from after the Battle of Dunkeld in 1689. Trust display of photographs of the restoration scheme and an audio-visual show are in the Tourist Information Centre.

☎ (03502) 460.
Open: 28 Mar-May & Sep-23 Dec, Mon-Sat 10-1 & 2-4.30, Jun-Aug, Mon-Sat 10-6.
Shop (NTS)

Loch of The Lowes Wildlife Reserve
Variety of wildlife. Great crested grebes and other waterfowl in natural surroundings can be watched through high powered binoculars from observation hide. There is an exhibition and slide programme in the visitor centre.

☎ (03502) 337.
Open: daily Apr-Sep 10-7 (Jun-Aug open until 8.30pm). (Times subject to change.) Hide open at all times. Special arrangements for parties booked in advance.
& (ground floor only) Shop ✂

DUNOON
Strathclyde (Argyllshire)
Map 10 NS17.
Scottish White Heather Farm
(5m SW of Dunoon)
Extensive gardens, including white heathers, sprays, coloured heather and conifers for sale.

☎ Toward (036987) 237.
Open: all year 9-6. Visitors advised to phone in advance during winter months.
&

DUNWICH
Suffolk   Map 5 TM47.
Dunwich Museum
St James Street
Contains the history and relics of the ancient city of Dunwich. Also flora and fauna of the area.

☎ Westleton (072873) 358.
Open: Apr-Oct, Sat & Sun 2-4.30. Also Tue & Thu, May-Sep & daily in Aug. (Subject to availability of volunteers.)
Shop ✂

DURHAM
Co. Durham   Map 12 NZ24.
Durham Cathedral
One of the most outstanding examples of Romanesque architecture in Europe, begun in 1093 by Bishop William of St Calais. Much of the original building remains. The nave shows the first use of ribbed vaulting on an extensive scale in a church. Also of note are the Chapel of Nine Alters, the Lady Chapel, the tomb of Venerable Bede, 8th-century illuminated manuscripts and the Sanctuary Door Knocker.

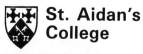

☎ (0385) 62367.
Open: daily, May-Sep
7.15-8; Oct-Apr, Mon-Sat
7.15-6.15, Sun 7.15-5
(Donations).
(Treasury: Admission
charge, Mon-Sat 10-4, Sun
2.30-4.)
(Tower: Admission charge,
Mon-Sat 10-3.30.)
⛨ (☞ Mon-Sat 9.30-5 Sun1-5)
Shop Museum

St Aidan's College Grounds
Windmill Hill
The College was designed
by Sir Basil Spence, and built
in the early sixties. The spa-
cious and well-stocked
grounds, landscaped by Pro-
fessor Brian Hackett, are at
their best during July, when
the shrub beds are in flower.
Features include a laburnum
walk and a reflecting pool,
well stocked with aquatic
plants and fish. From the garden there are fine views of
Durham Cathedral.

☎ (0385) 65011.
Open: all year, daily from
9-dusk.
Donations to NGS.
☞ (by prior arrangement)
⛨ (ground floor only) ✈
(garden only)
See advertisement on page 43

University Botanic Garden
A teaching and research
garden with specific
collections of tropical and
arid zone plants. Himalayan,
Scandinavian and other areas
of world fauna.

☎ (0385) 64971 Ext 657.
Open: daily. ✈

EASTBOURNE
East Sussex   Map 5 TV69.
Lifeboat Museum
Grand Parade
The museum displays details
of the work carried out by the
various lifeboats which have
been on station at East-
bourne. There are also displays illustrating the work of
the RNLI, a selection of lifeboat models, the original sails
and oars from the last sailing
lifeboat at the station, various
types of gear worn by lifeboat
men, together with descriptions and accompanying
photographs of notable
rescues.

☎ (0323) 30717.
Open: Jan-Mar weekends
only, Apr-Dec daily 9.30-6.
Shop.

Towner Art Gallery & Local History Museum
Manor Gardens, High Street
Georgian manor hose (1776)
with later alterations set in
pleasant gardens, containing
collection of 19th-and 20th-
century British works of art.
Frequent temporary exhi-
bitions. Museum has displays
of Eastbourne history.

☎ (0323) 21635 or 25112.
Open: all year Mon-Fri 10-5
& Sun 2-5. (Closed: Mon in
winter, Good Fri, Xmas day
and New Years day).
⛨ (ground floor & gardens
only) Shop ✈

EAST FORTUNE
Lothian (East Lothian)   Map 12 NT57.
Museum of Flight
East Fortune Airfield
The National Museums of
Scotland, former airship base
now displays the history of
aircraft and rockets and has
working exhibits which visitors may operate. Exhibits include a Supermarine Spitfire
Mk 16. De Havilland Sea
Venom, Hawker Sea Hawk
and Comet (4c).

☎ 031-225 7534.
Open: daily July & Aug
10-4, plus open days.
⛨ ✈

EASTHAM
Merseyside   Map 7 SJ38.
Eastham Country Park
Ferry Road
Seventy six-acre country
park with a fine nature trail,
unique views across the Mersey estuary and historical
features that include a bear
pit and the site of an ancient
river crossing, "Job's Ferry",
originally operated by a
brotherhood of monks.

☎ 051-327 1007.
Open: Park, at all
reasonable times; Visitor
Centre, Apr-Sep Sat, Sun &
BH 11-6; Oct-Mar, Sat, Sun &
BH (ex Xmas day) 12-4.
⛨ ☞ 🞕
See advertisement on page 143.

ECCLES
Gt Manchester   Map 7 SJ79.
Monks Hall Museum
Wellington Road
16th-century building with
later additions, housing a
small toy museum and ma-
terial of local interest
including a Nasmyth steam
hammer. There are frequent
temporary exhibitions.

☎ 061-789 4372.
Open: Mon-Fri 10-5, Sun 2-5.
(Closed: Good Fri, Xmas &
New Year's Day.) ⛨ ✈

EDINBURGH
Lothian (Midlothian)   Map 11 NT27.
Acheson House (Scottish Craft Centre).
140 Canongate.   Plan : F4.
This beautiful mansion, built
1633 and restored in 1937 by
R Hurd is now the head-
quarters of the Scottish Craft
Centre. There is a changing
display of crafts from ceramics to silverware.

☎ 031-556 8136/7370.
Open: Mon-Sat 10-5.30.

✈ ♿ (ground floor only)

Canongate Tolbooth
163 Canongate.   *Plan : F5.*
Dates from 1591 and shows a curious projecting clock. There is also a Brass-rubbing centre.

☎ 031-225 2424 Ext 6638.
Open: Jun-Sep Mon-Sat 10-6, Sun 2-5 during festival. Oct-May Mon-Sat 10-5.
Shop ✈

Calton Hill and Parthenon
Regent Road.   *Plan : F6.*
Rising to 335 ft it offers an impressive view of the city centre and Firth of Forth. On the top is a collection of monuments, including the National monument (1882), a partly completed copy of the Greek Parthenon, dedicated to the Scottish dead in the Napoleonic wars. Also the Nelson monument (1807), the Playfair (1826) and Dugald Stewart (1832) monuments.

Open: at all reasonable times.
(Nelson monument: Admission charge.)

City Art Centre
2 Market Street.   *Plan : E4.*
The Art Centre houses the City's permanent fine art collection comprising 3,000 paintings, drawings, prints and sculptures mostly by Scottish artists, dating from 17th century to the present. There is also a diverse programme of temporary exhibitions drawn from the UK and abroad.

☎ 031-225 2424 Ext 6650.
After 5pm & weekends 031-225 1131.
Open: Mon-Sat 10-5, (10-6 Jun-Sep) & Sun 2-5 during Edinburgh Festival.
⌂ (licensed) ♿ Shop ✈

Clan Tartan Centre
Pringle Woollen Mill, 70-74 Bangor Road, Leith (1m N), Not on plan
The Clan Tartan Centre offers the opportunity to find out (on the Pringle Archive Computer) if your name is linked to any of the Clans. A 15-minute film tells the history and development of the tartan. The shop sells a range of Pringle knitwear.

☎ 031-553 5161.
Open: daily Apr-Dec, 9-6; Jan-Mar, Mon-Sat 9-5.30.
♿ ⌂ ✈ Shop.

Fruit Market Gallery
29 Market Street.   *Plan : E4.*
A fine arts gallery with changing programme of exhibitions including contemporary art, paintings, sculpture, photographs and architecture.

☎ 031-225 2383.
Open: Tue-Sat, 10-5.30.
✈

George Heriot's School
Lauriston Place.   *Plan : D3.*
Dates from 1628 and was founded by George Heriot, the 'Jingling Geordie' of Scott's 'Fortunes of Nigel'.

☎ 031-229 7263.
Open: 7 Jul-22 Aug Mon-Fri 9.30-4.30.
♿ (ground floor only) ✈

Huntly House
142 Canongate.   *Plan : F4.*
Dating from 1570 and housing the City Museum of local history. Includes collections of silver, glass, and pottery.

☎ 031-225 2424 Ext 6689 (031-225 1131 after 5pm & weekends).
Open: Mon-Sat, Jun-Sep 10-6; Oct-May 10-5. (During

Edinburgh: an Acheson House craft design

Festival period only Sun 2-5).
Shop ✈

Lady Stair's House
Off Lawnmarket.   *Plan : D4.*
A restored town house dating from 1622, containing a museum of literary relics of Robert Burns, Sir Walter Scott and Robert Louis Stevenson.

☎ 031-225 2424 Ext 6593 (031-225 1131 after 5pm & weekends)
Open: Mon-Sat, Jun-Sep 10-6; Oct-May 10-5. (During Festival period only Sun 2-5).
Shop ✈

National Gallery of Scotland
The Mound.   *Plan : D4.*
One of the most distinguished of the smaller galleries in Europe, containing collections of Old Masters, Impressionists and Scottish paintings including: Raphael's Bridgewater Madonna, Constable's Dedham Vale, and master-

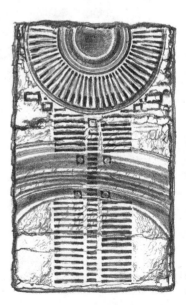

pieces by Titian, Velasquez, Raeburn, Van Gogh and Gauguin. Drawings, watercolours and original prints by Turner, Goya, Blake etc (these items can be shown on request Mon-Fri 10-12.30 & 2-4.30).

☎ 031-556 8921.
Open: Mon-Sat 10-5, Sun 2-5; winter lunchtime closure (Oct-Mar) 12-1 West Gallery, 1-2 East Gallery and New Wing. (Mon-Sat 10-6, Sun 11-6 during Festival).
ᕫ Shop ✈

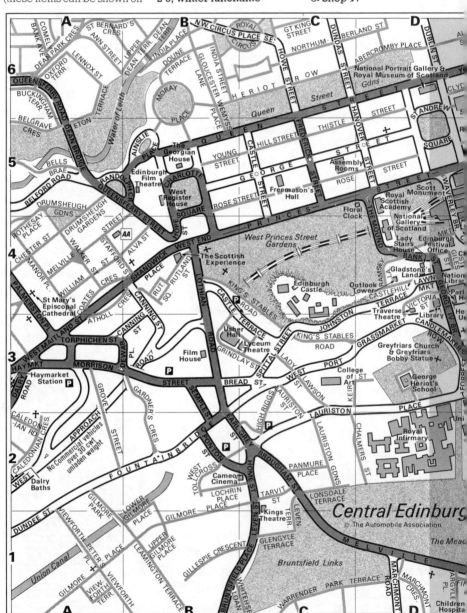

Central Edinburgh
© The Automobile Association

National Library of Scotland

George IV Bridge. Plan : **D4.**
Founded in 1682, this is one of the four largest libraries in Great Britain with nearly four and a half million books. There is an extensive collection of manuscripts, together with 19th-century music, Caxton bible and a map collection.

☎ 031-226 4531.
Open: Reading room Mon-Fri 9.30-8.30, Sat 9.30-1; Exhibition room Mon-Fri 9.30-5, Sat 9.30-1, Apr-Sep Sun 2-5. & ✈

Parliament House

East of George IV Bridge.
Plan : **D4.**
Dates from 1639, but façade was replaced in 1829. The Hall has a fine hammer-beam roof. The Scottish Parliament met here before the Union of 1707. Now the seat of Supreme Law Courts of Scotland.

☎ 031-225 2595.
Open: Mon-Fri 10-4.
☞ (closed Mon & when court in recess)
& (ground floor only)
✈ (ex guide dogs)

Register House

(East end of Princes Street).
Plan : **E5.**
Designed by Robert Adam, it was founded in 1774. Headquarters of the Scottish Record Office and the repository for National Archives of Scotland. Changing historical exhibitions. Historical and Legal Search Rooms available to visitors engaged in research.

☎ 031-556 6585.
Open: all year Mon-Fri 9-4.45. (Closed: Certain PH.)
& (ground floor only) ✈

Royal Botanic Garden

Inverleith Row (¾m N), Not on plan
Famous garden, noted especially for the rhododendron collection, rock garden, plant houses and exhibition hall.

☎ 031-552 7171 Ext 260.
Garden open all year (ex Xmas day and New Year's day). Mar-Oct Mon-Sat 9-1

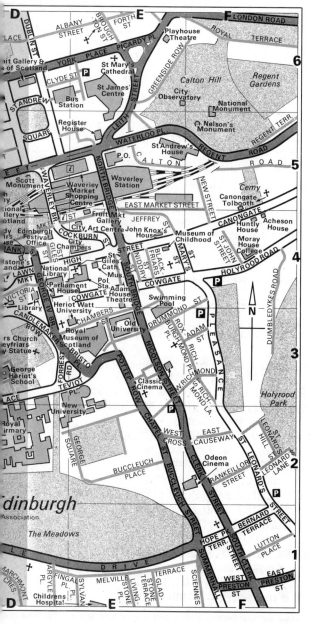

hr before sunset, Sun 11-1 hr before sunset; Oct-Mar Mon-Sat 9-sunset, Sun 11-sunset. Plant houses & exhibition hall open Mon-Sat 10-5, Sun 11-5 (from 10am during festival period).
☕ Apr-Sep ♿ Shop 🐕

Royal Museums of Scotland (formerly Museum of Antiquities)
1 Queen Street. Plan : **D6.**
Extensive collections and national treasures from earliest times to the present day, illustrating everyday life and history.

☎ **031-557 3550 Ext 279**
Open: Mon-Sat 10-5, (6pm during Festival) & Sun 2-5 (11-6 during Festival).
Shop 🐕

Royal Museum of Scotland (formerly Royal Scottish Museum)
Chambers Street. Plan : **E3.**
The most comprehensive display in Britain under one roof comprising the decorative arts of the world and ethnography, natural history, geology, technology and science. Lectures, gallery talks and films at advertised times.

☎ **031-225 7534.**
Open: Mon-Sat 10-5, Sun 2-5.
☕ ♿ Shop 🐕

Scottish National Gallery of Modern Art
Belford Road (½m W). Not on plan
New home of the national collection of 20th-century painting, sculpture and graphic art. Among many modern masters represented are Derain, Picasso, Giacometti, Magritte, Henry Moore, Barbara Hepworth, Lichtenstein and Scottish painting. Some sculpture is displayed. The gallery print room and library are also open to the public by appointment.

☎ **031-556 8921.**
Open: all year daily. Mon-Sat 10-5 & Sun 2-5. During Festival Mon-Sat 10-6, Sun 11-6.
☕ (licensed) ♿ Shop 🐕

Scottish National Portrait Gallery
Queen Street. Plan : **D6.**
Striking red Victorian building containing portraits of men and women who have contributed to Scottish history. The collection includes such popular figures as Mary Queen of Scots, James VI and I, Burns, Sir Walter Scott and Ramsay MacDonald. Many other artists, statesmen, soldiers

and scientists are portrayed in all media, including sculpture. Collections also illustrate the development of Highland dress. There is an extensive reference section of engravings, and photographs.

☎ 031-556 8921.
Open: all year daily, Mon-Sat 10-5 & Sun 2-5. (During Festival Mon-Sat 10-6, Sun 11-6)
& (telephone prior to visit) Shop ✶

Talbot Rice Art Centre
(Old University), South Bridge   Plan : *E3*.
Two main exhibition areas, one housing the university's permanently displayed Torrie Collection of 16th- and 17th-century European paintings and bronzes. The centre also promotes Scottish artists and has touring exhibitions.

☎ 031-667 1011 Ext 4308.
Open: Mon-Sat 10-5.
& ✶

West Register House
Charlotte Square.   Plan : *B5*.
The former St George's Church, designed by Robert Reid in the Greco-Roman style in 1811. Now an auxiliary repository for the Scottish Record Office and housing its museum. Search Room available to visitors.

☎ 031-556 6585.
Open: Mon-Fri 9-4.45.
(Closed: PH.)
& ✶

EDNASTON
Derbyshire   Map 8 SK24.
Ednaston Manor
A Lutyens house with garden of botanical interest. Large collection of shrubs, shrub roses, clematis and unusual plants, most varieties in containers for sale.

☎ Ashbourne (0335) 60325.
Open: Etr-Sep, Mon-Fri 1-4.30 & Sun 2-5.30. House not open.
☞ (Sun only) garden centre ✶

EDWINSTOWE
Nottinghamshire   Map 8 SK66.
Sherwood Forest & Visitor Centre
(½m N on B6034)
Probably the most famous forest in Britain but now consisting of scattered areas of woodland. The Visitor Centre has an exhibition on Robin Hood with information on forest wildlife found in the forest and walks, including one to the Mayor Oak, which lies about half a mile west.

☎ Mansfield (0623) 823202.
Open: Forest accessible at all reasonable times; Visitor Centre all year, daily 10.30-5.
& ☞ ⊓

ELCOT
Berkshire   Map 4 SU36.
Elcot Park Hotel
(5½m W of Newbury off A4)
16-acre garden overlooking the Kennet Valley with extensive views. Mainly lawns and woodland laid out by Sir William Paxton in 1848. Magnificent display of daffodils, rhododendrons and other shrubs in Spring.

☎ Kintbury (0488) 58100.
Open: all year, daily 10-6. (Charged on NGS Sun.)
☞ (Licensed Restaurant)
& (NGS)

ELGIN
Grampian (Moray)   Map 15 NJ26.
Pluscarden Abbey
(6m SW on unclass road)
The original monastery was founded by Alexander II in 1230. Restoration took place in the 14th and 19th centuries, and the Abbey has been re-

occupied by the Benedictines since 1948.

☎ Dallas (034389) 257.
Open: daily, 8am-8.30pm.
& (ground floor only) Shop

ELLISLAND FARM
Dumfries and Galloway (Dumfriesshire)   Map 11 NX98.
(6m NW of Dumfries off A76)
In this farm on the west bank of the Nith, Robert Burns lived from 1788 to 1791 and composed Tam O'Shanter and other poems and songs. Material associated with the poet is on display.

☎ Dumfries (0387) 74426.
No restriction on times of visiting, but visitors are advised to telephone in advance.
& (ground floor & gardens only) ✶

ELVASTON
Derbyshire   Map 8 SK43.
Elvaston Castle Country Park
Borrowash Road
Landscaped in the early 19th century, this attractive park has numerous walks, nature trails and fine formal gardens.

☎ Derby (0332) 71342.
Open: daily 9-dusk.
☞ (in season) ⊓ Shop

ELY
Cambridgeshire   Map 5 TL58.
Ely Cathedral
Rising like a beacon from the flat Fenland, Ely Cathedral is a superb architectural achievement of the Middle Ages. Most notable are the Octagon, the Lantern and the Lady Chapel, fine examples of 14th-century craftsmanship.

☎ (0353) 2062.
Open: daily, 7.30-7. (Admission charge for Stained Glass Museum).

⊡ ⅄ (entrance at south door)

ENFIELD

Gt London　　　see page 84.
Forty Hall
*Forty Hill.　London plan 2 : **39 E5**.*
Built in 1629 for Sir Nicholas Raynton, Lord Mayor of London, the Mansion was modified in the early 18th century. Contemporary plaster ceilings and screen, 17th- and 18th-century furnishings and paintings, ceramics and glass. Also exhibitions.

☎ 01-363 4046.
Open: all year Tue-Sun 10-6 (5pm Oct-Etr).
⊡ ⼓ Shop ⼘

EPPING FOREST AND CONSERVATION CENTRE

Essex　　　Map 5 TL40.
Six thousand acres of ancient woodland, grassland, heath, open water and marsh where the nightingale still sings in spring and early summer, given special protection by the 1878 Epping Forest Act for recreational and wildlife value. The Conservation Centre provides an interpretative and information service for the public and a base for ecological research.

☎ 01-508 7714
(Conservation Centre).
Open: Forest, at all times. Conservation Centre, Etr-Oct Wed-Sat 10-12.30 & 2-5, Sun & BH 11-12.30 & 2-5; Nov-Etr weekends only, Sat 10-12.30 & 2-5 (dusk if earlier), Sun 11-12.30 & 2-5 (dusk if earlier). Location between Chingford and Epping off A1069, A104 and B1393.

Ely Cathedral's 217 ft high West Tower is a landmark for miles around

EWELL

Surrey.　　　see page 84.
Bourne Hall Cultural Centre
Spring Street.
*London plan 2 : **40 C1***
18th-century house replaced by cultural centre, comprising museum, art centre, library, theatre hall and banqueting rooms. Collections embrace the human and natural history of the Epsom and Ewell area, and include costumes, dolls, toys and early photography. The Art Gallery has a continuous temporary exhibition programme. Other services include the identification of objects brought in by visitors.

☎ 01-393 9573.
Open: all year Mon-Sat; Mon, Wed & Thu 10-5 (8pm Tue & Fri) & 9.30-8 on Sat.
⊡ ⅄ ⼘

EWLOE

Clwyd　　　Map 7 SJ26.
Ewloe Castle
Remains of native Welsh castle, near where Henry II was defeated in 1157.

Open: accessible at all reasonable times.
(AM)

EXETER

Devon　　　Map 3 SX99.
The Devonshire Regimental Museum
Barrack Road, Wyvern Barracks
The exhibits cover the history of the Devonshire Regiment from its formation in 1685 to 1958 when the Regiment amalgamated with the Dorset Regiment. Exhibits include uniforms, weapons, medals, historical documents and military souvenirs collected by the Regiment over the years.

☎ (0392) 218178.
Open: all year Mon-Fri 9-4.30. (Closed: Sat, Sun & BHs.)
(Donations)
⅄ (ground floor only) Shop ⼘

Guildhall
High Street
Dates from 1330, partially rebuilt 1446, arches and façade, added 1592-5, fine displays of oil paintings, Guild Crests and civic silver and regalia.

☎ (0392) 56724.**
Open: all year Mon-Sat 10-5.15 (ex when used for Civic functions).
ⓗ (ground floor only) ✗

Royal Albert Memorial Museum
Queen Street.
Founded in 1865, and extended several times. Large permanent displays of fine and applied art, natural history and ethnography and local industry. Of particular interest are collections of Devon paintings, Exeter silver, glass, lace, costume, local and foreign natural history. Programme of temporary exhibitions.

☎ (0392) 56724.
Open: all year Tue-Sat 10-5.30.
ⓗ (by arrangement ground floor only) ✗

Spacex Gallery
42 Preston Street
The largest public fine art gallery in Devon. There is a continuous programme of the contemporary visual arts, plus regular film screenings, performances and poetry readings.

☎ (0392) 31786.
Open: all year, Tue-Sat 10-5.
ⓗ ☐ ✗

Tuckers Hall
Fore Street
Old Hall of the Weavers, Fullers and Shearmen, occupied since 1471 by their incorporation which was granted Royal Charter in 1479-81. Wagon-roof and panelling of 1638.

☎ (0392) 36244.
Open: Jun-Sep Tue, Thu & Fri 10.30-12.30; Oct-May Fri only 10.30-12.30.
✗

EXMOUTH
Devon.   Map 3 SY08.
Exmouth Museum
Sheppards Row
In the early stages of development with items from the town's past and present. Eventually to include a typical local kitchen of one hundred years ago and shipbuilding exhibits.

Open: Mon-Sat 10-12.30 and 2-4.30.

FAIRBURN INGS
West Yorkshire   Map 8 SE42.
(2 miles N of Ferrybridge, off unclass road W of A1)
Nature reserve and haven for small birds all year round. In spring and autumn, common, Arctic and more exotic black terns are regularly seen. Late summer and early autumn brings a large roost of swallows to the waterside vegetation. Colder months are noted for bringing an influx of wintering wildfowl.

Open: all year. Information centre and hide open weekends (one mile west of Fairburn village).

FAIRFORD
Gloucestershire   Map 4 SP10.
St Mary's Church
Glorious stained glass: 28 windows installed at the beginning of the 16th century have unusually been preserved intact.

☎ Cirencester (0285) 712467.
Open: daily 9.30-5.
ⓗ

FALKIRK
Central (Stirlingshire)   Map 11 NS87.
Falkirk Museum
District history exhibition with displays tracing the development of the area from earliest times up to the present day.

☎ (0324) 24911 Ext 2472.
Open: Mon-Sat 10.30-12.30 & 1.30-5.
ⓗ (ground floor only) Shop ✗

Rough Castle
One of the most remarkable forts on the Antonine Wall built by the Roman army in the 140's AD. The site covers one acre with double ditches and defensive pits.

Open: accessible at all reasonable times.
(AM)

FARNHAM
Surrey   Map 4 SU84.
Farnham Museum
Geology, archaeology, local history and art housed in Willmer House, a fine example of Georgian brickwork.

☎ (0252) 715094.
Open: Tue-Sat 11-5, BH Mons 2-5. Also open by prior arrangement only May-Aug Wed evenings. (Closed: 25 & 26 Dec).
ⓗ (ground floor only) Shop ✗

FENCE
Lancashire   Map 7 SD83.
Lake District Green Slate Co
Visitors can see slate from Coniston and Elterwater being cut with diamond saws and made up into fancy goods and gifts.

☎ Nelson (0282) 66952.
Open: Workshop and Shop Mon-Fri 8-5, Sat 8-4. (Closed: Xmas).

FILKINS
Oxfordshire   *Map 4 .SP20*
Cotswold Woollen Weavers
(¾m off A361)
In a splendid 18th-century barn, with traditional machinery to bring the Industrial Revolution to life. Exhibition gallery shows weaving processes and the history of wool in the Cotswolds.

☎ (036786) 491.
Open: Mon-Sat 10-6, Sun 2-6. (Parties by arrangement).
⌂ 🍴 🏛 Shop.

Swinford Museum
(4m NE of Lechlade on A361)
Old domestic articles, including cooking utensils, agricultural and rural craft tools.

☎ (036786) 365 (Apply to Mr Foster).
Open: Apr-Oct, Fri, Sat & Sun 9-6 by appointment. (Donations)
♿ 🏛

FINDON
West Sussex   *Map 4 TQ10.*
Cissbury Ring
(1 mile E)
Well preserved 60-acre Iron Age fort — the largest on the South Downs. It was occupied between the 5th and the 1st centuries BC and again in the 4th century AD. Extensive excavations have revealed flint mines, ploughing patterns and sites of huts. There are good views from the ramparts.

Open: accessible at all reasonable times.
(NT)

FINSTOWN
Orkney   *Map 16 HY31.*
Stenness Standing Stones
(3m SW on A965)
Remains of a stone circle,

second millennium BC. Nearby is the Ring of Brogar (c.2000 BC) consisting of a splendid circle of upright stones with a surrounding ditch.

Open: at all reasonable times.
(AM)

FLAMBOROUGH HEAD & BEMPTON CLIFFS
Humberside   *Map 8 TA17.*
(4m NE of Bridlington off B1259, B1255 & B1229)
Great chalk cliffs rising high above the North Sea between Flamborough Head and Bempton, where the largest breeding colony of seabirds in England includes gannets and kittiwakes. The cliffs are extremely dangerous and visitors should keep to footpaths and observation points. A good place for wildflowers.

Open: accessible at all times by public footpath.

FLINT
Clwyd   *Map 7 SJ27.*
Flint Castle
Ruined late 13th-century castle, erected by Edward I, with circular detached keep originally surrounded by moat.
Open: accessible at all reasonable times.
(AM)

FLIXTON
Suffolk   *Map 5 TM38.*
Norfolk & Suffolk Aviation Museum
A collection of aircraft and aviation spanning the years from the Wright Brothers to present day. There are sixteen aircraft on static display outside a large specially converted barn containing the smaller items relating to the history of flight.

☎ Broock (0508) 50614.
Open: Etr Sun-Oct, Sun & BH 10-5; Jun-Aug, Sun & Tue-Thu 7pm-9pm; also Jul & Aug Wed & Thu 12-5.
♿ (Assistance required)
Shop 🏛 (in museum).

FOCHABERS
Grampian (Moray)   *Map 15 NJ35.*
Baxters Visitors Centre
Family owned and internationally renowned for manufacturing high quality foods ranging from preserves and marmalades to Royal Game Soup. Audio-visual show and guided tours of the factory.

☎ (0343) 820393 Ext 241.
Open: Apr-Oct Mon-Fri; Shop 10-4; ½-hourly factory tours 10-11 & 2-3.
⌂ 🍴 🏛

FOLKESTONE
Kent   *Map 5 TR23.*
Museum & Art Gallery
Grace Hill
Displays of local history, archaeology and natural science. Temporary art exhibitions held.

☎ (0303) 57583.
Open: all year, Mon, Tue, Thu & Fri 9-5.30, Wed 9-1 & Sat 9-5. (Closed: BH).
🏛

FORRES
Grampian (Moray)   *Map 14 NJ05.*
Falconer Museum
Tolbooth Street
Displays of local history, wildlife, geology, ethnography and archaeological finds from Culbin.

☎ (0309) 73701.
Open: all year (ex BH); Oct-Apr Mon-Fri 10-4.30; May-Sep Mon-Sat 9.30-5.30 (6.30 in Jul & Aug), also Sun 2-6.30 Jul & Aug only.
♿ (ground floor only) Shop 🏛

Suenos' Stone
A notable 20ft-high Dark Age monument with a sculptured cross on one side and groups of warriors on the reverse.

Open: accessible at all reasonable times.
(AM)

FORT AUGUSTUS
Highland (Inverness-shire)
Map 14 NH30.
Great Glen Exhibition
Canal Side
History of the Great Glen from Pict to modern Scot. The Clans, battles and general history. Exhibits include rare antiques, weapons and mock smithy. Forestry exhibition and information on the canal and railway.

☎ (0320) 6341.
Open: Etr-Nov 9-5.
⊓ & Shop

FORTROSE
Highland (Ross & Cromarty)
Map 14 NH76.
Fortrose Cathedral
Partly dismantled by Cromwell for a fort at Inverness: the surviving portions of the 14th-century cathedral include the south aisle with vaulting and fine detail.

Open: accessible at all reasonable times. (AM)

FORT WILLIAM
Highland (Inverness-shire)
Map 14 NN17.
Inverlochy Castle
A well-preserved example of a 13th-century and later stronghold, noted for the famous battle fought nearby in 1645, when Montrose defeated the Campbells.

Under repair and interior not accessible. Can be viewed from outside.
(AM)

FOVANT
Wiltshire
Map 4 SU02.
Regimental Badges
(¾m SE on footpath)
The Regimental Badges line the scarp slope of Fovant Down and were cut into the chalk by regiments encamped in the area during the First World War. The badges can be viewed from the A30 east of Fovant or from the footpath which runs between Fovant and Chiselbury Hill Fort.

Open: accessible at all reasonable times.

FOWEY
Cornwall
Map 2 SX15.
St Catherine's Castle
Ruined stronghold erected in 16th century by Henry VIII to defend coast and restored in 1855.

Open: accessible at all reasonable times.
(AM)

FOXTON
Leicestershire
Map 4 SP68.
Foxton Locks
Constructed by Benjamin Bevan between 1810 and 1814 to raise the Grand Union Canal 75 feet. Arranged in two 'staircases', each with a series of five locks. At the halfway point is a passing pond. Nearby Foxton Barge Lift was completed in 1900 to raise boats up an inclined plane in 12 minutes, thus saving the passage through the locks. Dismantled in 1928, but partially restored and now an ancient monument.

Open: accessible at all reasonable times.
Shop.

GALASHIELS
Borders (Selkirkshre)
Map 12 NT43.
Peter Anderson Ltd
Woollen Mills

Nether Mill
Museum and exhibition of the past showing aspects of the towns development including health, education, labour and textiles. Conducted tours to see the manufacturing of tartan and textiles.

☎ (0896) 2091.
Open: Conducted tours Apr-Oct, Mon-Fri 10.30 & 2. Winter months by appointment; Museum Apr-Oct, Mon-Sat 9-5, Sun (Jun-Sep) 12-5.

GILLING EAST
North Yorkshire
Map 8 SE67.
Gilling Castle
14th-, 16th-, and 18th-century house, now preparatory school for Ampleforth College, with Elizabethan great chamber noted for panelling, painted glass and ceilings (rest of house not open to public). Fine gardens.

☎ Ampleforth (04393) 238.
Open: Great chamber & hall, Mon-Fri, 10-12 & 2-4. (Closed: Xmas & New Years day.)
Admission charge to gardens. ✗

GLASGOW
Strathclyde (Lanarkshire)
Map 11 NS56.
Bellahouston Park
Ibrox (2m W). Not on plan
171 acres of parkland only 3 miles from the city centre. Site of the Empire Exhibition of 1938. Sunken garden, walled garden and rock garden. Multi-purpose Sports Centre situated at west end of park, with adjacent all-weather Athletic Centre. Horse show.

☎ 041-427 4224 Park.
041-427 0558 Sports Centre.
Open: daily end Apr-Aug 8-10, Sep-Apr 8-5 (times approximate).
▱ (sports centre) &

Botanic Garden

(1m N). Not on plan
Established in 1817, it contains an outstanding. collection of plants. The Kibble Palace is a unique glasshouse with, among others, a famous collection of tree ferns. The main glasshouse contains numerous tropical and exotic plants. The 40 acres of gardens include systematic and herb gardens, and a chronological border.

☎ 041-334 2422.
The Kibble Palace. Open: daily 10-4.45 (4.15 in winter). The main glasshouse, Open: Mon-Sat 1-4.45 (4.15 in winter) Sun 12-4.45 (4.15 in winter). Gardens, Open: daily 7-dusk.
& (garden only)

The Burrell Collection

Pollok Country Park
(2½m SW). Not on plan.
The Burrell Collection was opened to the public by HM the Queen on 21 October 1983 in an award-winning gallery, which makes the most of its superb natural setting. The Collection was formed by Sir William and Lady Burrell and comprises more than 8,000 items. These include Chinese ceramics, bronzes and jades, Near Eastern rugs and carpets, Turkish pottery and artefacts from the ancient civilisations of Iraq, Egypt, Greece and Italy. European medieval art is represented by metalwork, sculpture, illuminated manuscripts, ivories and two of the most important museum collections in the world of stained glass and tapestries. The paintings range from the 15th to the early 20th centuries and include works by Memling, Bellini, Cranach, Rembrandt, Courbet, Millet, Boudin, Degas, Manet and Cezanne.

There are also important collections of British silver and needlework.

☎ 041-649 7151.
Open: Mon-Sat 10-5, Sun 2-5. (Closed: Xmas day & New Years day.)
🖵 ⏏ & Shop ✝ (ex guide dogs)

Cathedral

Castle Street.   Plan : **F3.**
The most complete medieval Cathedral surviving on the Scottish mainland, dating mainly from the 13th and 14th centuries.

Open: see page 4.
(AM)

City Chambers

George Square.   Plan : **E2.**
Opened by Queen Victoria in 1888, this impressive building, designed by William Young, occupies the eastern side of George Square and is the headquarters of Glasgow District Council. The building was built in Italian Renaissance style and is noted for its loggia, marble staircase and banqueting hall.

☎ 041-221 9600.
Open: Guided tours Mon-Wed, Fri 10.30 & 2.30. (Closed: BH.) (Telephone in advance.) ✝

Collins Gallery University of Strathclyde

Richmond Street.   Plan : **E2.**
A modern exhibition hall with a varied programme of temporary exhibitions of mainly visual arts and paintings and sometimes historical subjects.

☎ 041-552 4400
Ext 2682/2416.

Glasgow: Museum of Transport

Open: all year, Mon-Fri 10-5 & Sat 12-4.
(Closed: BH.)

Glasgow Art Gallery & Museum

Kelvingrove Park
(¼m NW). Not on plan
The finest civic art collection in Great Britain. All schools and periods of European painting with emphasis on Dutch 17th century, French 19th century and Scottish art from 17th century to the present day. Collections of pottery, porcelain, silver, sculpture, arms and armour, also archaeology, ethnography and natural history.

☎ 041-357 3929.
Open: Mon-Sat 10-5, Sun 2-5. (Closed: Xmas day & New Years day.)
🖵 & Shop ✝ (ex guide dogs)

Glasgow Museums & Art Galleries

Art Gallery & Museum	The Burrell Collection	The People's Palace	Pollok House
Kelvingrove	2060 Pollokshaws Road	Glasgow Green	2060 Pollokshaws Road
Glasgow G3 8AG	Glasgow G43 1AT	Glasgow G40 1AT	Glasgow G43 1AT
Tel: 041-357 3929	Tel: 041-649 7151	Tel: 041-554 0223	Tel: 041-632 0274
Museum of Transport	Haggs Castle	Provand's Lordship	Rutherglen Museum
25 Albert Drive	100 St Andrews Drive	Castle Street	Rutherglen
Glasgow G41-2PE	Glasgow G41 4RB	Glasgow G4 0RB	Glasgow G73 1DQ
Tel: 041-423 8000	Tel: 041-427 2725	Tel: 041-552 8819	Tel: 041-647 0837

Open all year except Christmas Day and New Year's Day   Mon-Sat: 10am-5pm Sun: 2-5pm Admission Free

Haggs Castle

100 St Andrews Drive,
(2m SW). Not on plan
Built in 1585, the castle houses a museum created for children. The theme is exploration of time — particularly the last 400 years since the castle was built. Activities in the adjacent workshop allow young visitors to become practically involved in the past. Easter, Summer and Autumn activity programmes, also Mary Queen of Scots Exhibition throughout 1986.

☎ 041-427 2725.
Open: Mon-Sat 10-5, Sun 2-5. (Closed: Xmas day & New Years day.)
Guided tours, only if booked in advance.
& (ground floor & garden only) Shop ✻ (ex guide dogs)

Hunterian Art Gallery The

University of Glasgow
(¼m NW). Not on plan
A major collection of works by James McNeill Whistler and Charles Rennie Mackintosh including reconstructed interiors from Mackintosh's Glasgow home. Also on display is a group of Dutch, Flemish, Italian and British 17th- and 18th-century paintings, bequeathed by the Gallery's founder, Dr William Hunter. There is a growing collection of 19th- and early 20th-century Scottish paint-

ings, contemporary British art and sculpture and a holding of old-master to modern prints. Winner of the 1983 Sotheby Award for the best UK Gallery. Sculpture Courtyard. Changing programme of print exhibitions.

☎ 041-339 8855 Ext 5431.
Main gallery open: Mon-Fri 10-12.30 & 1.30-5; Sat 9.30-1 (please telephone for details of public holiday closures).
Admission charge to Mackintosh House.
& Shop ✻

Hunterian Museum

The University of Glasgow
(¼m NW). Not on plan
The museum is named after the 18th-century physician, Dr William Hunter, who bequeathed his own collections to the University. The geological, archaeological ethnographical, numismatic and historical collections are exhibited in the main building of the University. Scottish Museum of the Year 1983 and 1984. Temporary exhibitions programme.

☎ 041-339 8855 Ext 4221.
Open: Mon-Fri 10-5, Sat 9.30-1.
(Please telephone for details of public holiday closures.)
& (ground floor. Lift by prior arrangement) Shop ✻

Hutcheson's Hall

158 Ingram Street.   Plan: **E2.**
Built in 1802-5 and designed by David Hamilton, the building is one of the most elegant in Glasgow's city centre, now Glasgow headquarters of the National Trust for Scotland. In 1876 it was reconstructed by John Baird who provided an impressive staircase and heightened the hall. There are statues of George and Thomas Hutcheson.

☎ 041-552 8391.
Open: all year, Mon-Sat 9-5.
(NTS)

Linn Park

Cathcart (4½m S).
Not on plan.
Comprises more than 200 acres of pine, deciduous woodland and riverside walks. Britain's first public park nature trail, (1965) features many varieties of flowers, trees, and insects. A children's zoo and a collection of British ponies and Highland cattle. There is also a ruined 14th-century castle.

☎ 041-637 1147.
Open: daily 7-dusk.
🖵 🍴 &

Mitchell Library

Kent Road.   Plan: **A4.**
The largest public reference library in Europe with more than a million volumes, founded in 1874, and named after

Stephen Mitchell, a Glasgow
tobacco manufacturer. There
is a special collection on
Robert Burns and Scottish
poetry.

☎ 041-221 7030.
**Open: all year, Mon-Fri
9.30-9 & Sat 9.30-5.**

Museum of Transport
*25 Albert Drive, near
Eglinton Toll (1m S on A77).
Not on plan*
A life-size presentation of
land transport, showing the
development of the bicycle,
horse-drawn vehicles, tram-
cars, Scottish motor cars from
vintage to present day and

railway locomotives, also the
Clyde Room and subway
Gallery with a reconstruction
of a Glasgow underground
railway station.

☎ 041-423 8000.
**Open: Mon-Sat 10-5, Sun
2-5. (Closed: Xmas day &
New Years day)**

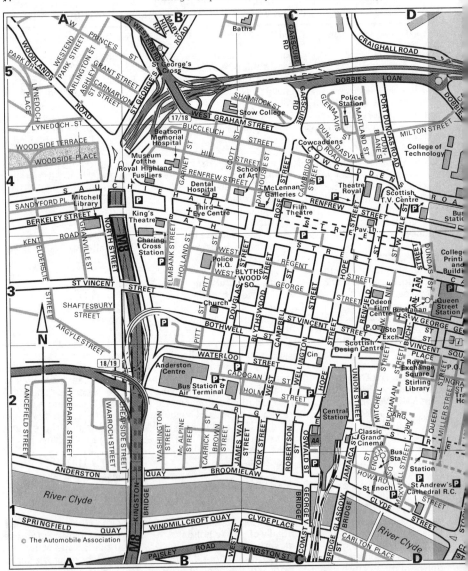

⌨ & Shop ✖ (ex guide dogs)

People's Palace Museum
Glasgow Green, off London Road (¼m SE). Not on plan
Contains a fascinating visual record of the history and life of the City. Exhibits include Medieval Glasgow, interest- ing relics of Mary, Queen of Scots, the Battle of Langside, the Tobacco Lords of the 18th century, and the history of the music hall. Fine examples of Glasgow craftsmanship, particularly pottery and special displays illustrating social and domestic life, including women's suffrage, tem- perance and the two world wars. A wide range of pictures of noteworthy people and places. Winter gardens are notable for tropical plants.

☎ 041-554 0223.
Open: Mon-Sat 10.30-5, Sun 2-5. (Closed: Xmas day & New Years day).
& (ground floor only) Shop ✖ (ex guide dogs)

Pollok Country Park
(2½m SW). Not on plan
Formerly a private estate, there are 361 acres of land containing an extensive collection of flowering shrubs and trees in a natural setting. There is a herd of 50 Highland cattle, a display rose garden, nature trails and jogging track. Demonstrations held fortnightly.
See also **Burrell Collection,** page 54.

☎ 041-632 9299.
Park always open.
Demonstration and display garden open: daily Mon-Thu 8-4, Fri 8-3; Sat, Sun (Etr-Sep) 8-4, (Oct-Etr) 8-6.30.
⌨ &

Also **Pollok House**
Situated within the grounds, a neo-Palladian building first constructed in 1752, but with later Edwardian additions, containing the famous Stirling Maxwell Collection of Spanish paintings, furniture etc.

☎ 041-632 0274.
Open: Mon-Sat 10-5, Sun 2-5. (Closed: Xmas day & New Years day.)
⌨ & Shop, Garden centre ✖ (ex guide dogs)

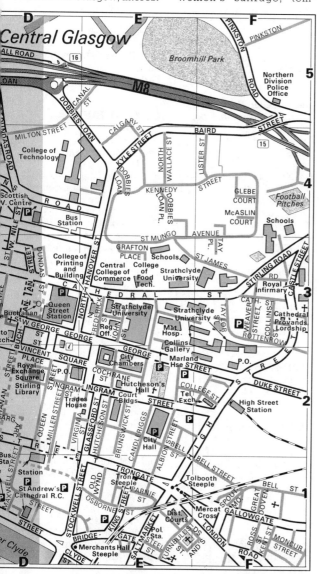
Central Glasgow

Provand's Lordship
3 Castle Street. *Plan :* ***F3.***
Built in 1471 as a manse serving the Cathedral and St Nicholas Hospital, this is the oldest house in Glasgow. Mary Queen of Scots is reputed to have stayed in the house, which now has period displays from 1500 onwards and a fine collection of 17th century Scottish furniture. Latterly a confectioner's shop, the machines which made the sweets can also be seen.

☏ 041-552 8819.
Open: Mon-Sat 10-5, Sun 2-5. (Closed: Xmas day & New Years day.)
Shop ✗ (ex guide dogs)

Provan Hall
Auchinlea Road (6½m E, off B806). Not on plan
Well restored 15th-century house considered most perfect example of a simple pre-Reformation house remaining in Scotland, set in Auchinlea Park. In the adjacent grounds are formal and informal gardens including garden for the blind.

☏ 041-771 6372.
For information on opening hours please telephone the above number.
♿

Regimental Museum of the Royal Highland Fusiliers.
518 Sauchiehall Street. *Plan :* ***B4***
The history of the Highland Light Infantry, The Royal Highland Fusiliers and the Royal Scots Fusiliers from 1678 to the present day. Exhibits include medals, pictures, uniforms, weapons, mementoes and records.

☏ 041-332 0961.
Open: all year, Mon-Thu 9-4.30 & Fri 9-4. (Closed: BH's.)
✗

Ross Hall Park
Crookston (5m W on A736). Not on plan
Beautifully kept gardens with artificial ponds, featuring a variety of aquatic plants and stocked with fish. Extensive heather and rock gardens and woodland nature trails.

☏ 041-882 3554.
Open: daily Apr-Sep 1-8, Oct-Mar 1-4.
♿

Rouken Glen Park
Thornliebank (4¾m S on A726). Not on plan
Fine park with lovely walks through the glen. Waterfall at head of the glen is a noted beauty spot. Large walled garden. Boating on picturesque loch.

☏ 041-638 1101.
Open: daily dawn-dusk.
☕ ⛱ ♿

Scottish Design Centre
72 St Vincent Street. *Plan :* ***D3.***
Scottish made goods and craft items are on sale here. There is also an exhibition centre with changing displays.

☏ 041-221 6121.
Open: all year, Mon-Fri 9.30-5 & Sat 9-5.
☕

The Stock Exchange
69 St George's Place. *Plan :* ***D3.***
Dating from 1877 this Venetian Gothic building is by John Burnet (Sen). Recently it has been rebuilt within the external walls. There is a visitors viewing gallery.

☏ 041-221 7060.
Open: all year, Mon-Fri 10-12.45, 2-3.30.

Victoria Park
Whiteinch (2½m W on A814). Not on plan
This park has the best known fossilized tree stumps of the prehistoric Coal Age period, discovered in 1887 and housed in the Fossil Grove building. The park has extensive carpet bedding depicting centennial events.

☏ 041-954 1746.
Fossil Grove building open: Mon-Fri 8-4, Sat, Sun pm only.
Park open: daily 7am-dusk.
⛱ ♿

GLASTONBURY

Somerset *Map 3 ST53.*

Glastonbury Tor
(¾m E of town centre off A361)
Rising to 521 ft, legend-rich Glastonbury Tor is also an excellent viewpoint, overlooking the Somerset levels. Crowning it is a 14th-century tower, the remains of a chapel destroyed in a landslip in 1271; near the foot is the Chalice Spring. Footpaths climb to the summit.

Open: accessible at all reasonable times.
(NT)

GLENDRONACH

Grampian (Aberdeenshire)
Map 15 NJ64.

Glendronach Distillery
(junc of B9001 & B9024)
Owned by William Teachers and Son Limited. Visitors can see the complete process of whisky making, including the malting barley rooms and distilling of spirits. Whisky has been made on the premises for over 160 years.

☏ **Forgue (046682) 202.**
Open: Guided tours Mon-Fri 10 & 2. (Other times by special arrangement.)
✗ Shop

GLENLIVET
Grampian (Banffshire)   Map 15 NJ12.
The Glenlivet Distillery Reception Centre
(off B9136, 12m SW of Dufftown, via B9009 and B9008)
The reception centre contains an exhibition of ancient artefacts used in malting, peat cutting and distilling. Distillery tour. Free whisky sample.

☎ Glenlivet (08073) 427.
Open: Etr-Oct, Mon-Fri 10-4.
🚻 (ground floor only) Shop
🍴

GLENMUICK AND LOCHNAGAR
*Grampian (Aberdeenshire)
Map 15 NO28.*
Glenmuick and Lochnagar Nature Reserve
(9m SW of Ballater on unclass road)
The nature reserve occupies a wild and remote area south of the River Dee. There are a variety of walks from the visitor centre at the Spittal of Glenmuick, including paths along Loch Muick and up to the summit of Lochnagar (3786 ft) where a variety of alpine plants can be seen. Visitors are requested to keep to footpaths. Weatherproof clothing and sturdy footwear are essential on all the walks.

☎ Ballater (0338) 55434.
Open: Visitor Centre daily, all year 10-5 (weather permitting).
🚻

GLOUCESTER
Gloucestershire   Map 3 SO81.
Gloucester Cathedral
Norman in origin with extensive rebuilding in the Perpendicular style. Two of its many treasures are the tomb of Edward II and the great east window.

☎ (0452) 28095.
Open: daily, 7.30-6 (ex during services).

City East Gate
Eastgate Street
Roman and medieval gatetowers and moat in an underground exhibition chamber. Adjacent to Bastion tower in Kings Walk.

☎ (0452) 24131.
Open: May-Sep, Wed & Fri 2-5, Sat 10-12 & 2-5. (Bastion tower, 26 Jul-Aug). 🍴

City Museum & Art Gallery
Brunswick Road
The Marling bequest of 18th-century walnut furniture, barometers and domestic silver. Paintings by Richard Wilson, Gainsborough, Turner, etc, supplemented by art exhibitions throughout the year. Local archaeology including Roman mosaics and sculptures, natural history including a freshwater aquarium.

☎ (0452) 24131.
Open: Mon-Sat 10-5. (Closed: BH's.)
🚻 (ground floor only) Shop 🍴
See advertisement on page 60

Folk Museum
99-103 Westgate Street
A group of half-timbered houses, (Tudor and Jacobean), furnished to illustrate

local history, domestic life and rural crafts. Civil War armour, Victorian toys, Severn fishing tackle, wooden ploughs, etc. Reconstructed Double Gloucester dairy and wheelwright's shop. Pin factory with 18th-century forge.

☎ (0452) 26467.
Open: Mon-Sat 10-5. (Closed: BH's.)
🚻 (ground floor only) Shop 🍴

Gloucester Docks
An inland Victorian port still preserved virtually intact in the heart of Gloucester, now being redeveloped as a major regional tourist, cultural and commercial centre. Famous as the location for filming the *Onedin Line*, the area has many listed buildings. Permission is needed to enter the docks, but most parts can be seen from outside vantage points.

☎ (0452) 502309 (Leisure Services Dept) or 25524 (Regional British Waterways Board).
Open: Vantage points at all times. For permission to

Gloucester Docks

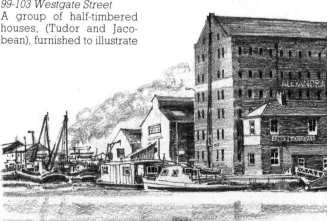

enter docks, contact British Waterways Board, Commercial Road, Gloucester GL1 2ES. Guided tours available.

House of the Tailor of Gloucester — Beatrix Potter Museum
9 College Court
A museum in miniature, housed in the building featured by Beatrix Potter in 'The Tailor of Gloucester'. The tailor's kitchen has been recreated and there is a working model of mice creating the waistcoat. On the ground floor, a bookshop sells Beatrix Potter books.

☎ (0452) 422856.
Open: Mon-Sat 9.30-5.30.

GODALMING
Surrey   Map 4 SU94.
Godalming Museum
Old Town Hall, High Street
Dates from 1814. On site of earlier building, and now museum of local history.

☎ (04868) 4104.
Open: Tue, Fri & Sat 3-5.
Extended hours during summer, please ring for details. Other times by appointment.
Shop

GOLSPIE
Highland (Sutherland) Map 14 NH89.
Golspie Burn Gorge and Waterfalls
(½m E of A9, ½m along unclass road signed Backies)
Waymarked paths, including one which follows the Golspie Burn towards Backies, running through the spectacular narrow gorge and climbing past waterfalls and deep dark pools. The gorge and surrounding area are heavily wooded with many interesting woodland plants. Display boards are sited at various

locations (summer only).

Open: accessible at all reasonable times. ⊟

GOMERSAL
West Yorkshire   Map 8 SE22.
Red House
Oxford Road
Off M62 (junc 26)
Built in 1660 of red brick, which because of its rarity at that time gave rise to its name. Associations with the Brontës, particularly Charlotte, who often spent weekends here with her schoolfriend Mary Taylor. She immortalised it in her novel 'Shirley' where it is described under the name of 'Briarmains'.

☎ Cleckheaton (0274) 872165.
Open: all year, Mon-Sat 10-5, Sun 1-5.
& (ground floor only) Shop ✖

GRASSINGTON
North Yorkshire   Map 7 SE06.
National Park Centre
Colvend, Hebden Road
Visitor centre featuring interpretative display on 'Walking in Wharfedale'. Audio-visual programme, maps, guides and local information.

☎ (0756) 752748.
Open: Apr-Oct daily from mid morning to late afternoon.
⊟ &

GRAYS
Essex   Map 5 TQ67.
Thurrock Museum
Orsett Road
Local history, agriculture, trade and industrial collections. Also Palaeolithic to Saxon archaeology of borough.

☎ Grays Thurrock (0375) 33325.

Open: all year, Mon-Fri 10-8 & Sat 10-5 (Closed: BH's.)
& ✖

GREENFIELD
Clwyd   Map 7 SJ17.
Greenfield Valley Heritage Park
Sixty acres of lakeside and wooded walks including 5 reservoirs, a farm and farm museum, monuments and Basingwerk Abbey remains. A nature and industrial heritage trail goes past the remains of cotton and wire mills.

☎ Holywell (0352) 714172.
Open: all year 10-5.
(Admission charge to farm)
& ⊟ (visitor centre)

GREENOCK
Strathclyde (Renfrewshire)
Map 10 NS27.
McLean Museum and Art Gallery
15 Kelly Street
James Watt memorabilia (he was born in Greenock), with exhibits from different cultures and displays of local history, natural history, shipping and an art collection.

☎ (0475) 23741.
Open: daily Mon-Sat 10-12, 1-5. (ex PH's.)
& (telephone beforehand)

GREENSTED-JUXTA-ONGAR
Essex   Map 5 TL50.
St Andrews Church
(1m W of Chipping Ongar on unclass road)
The only surviving wooden Saxon church in Britain with walls of solid oak, it is believed to date from the 7th century. In 1013 the body of King Edmund rested here on its way to Bury St Edmunds.

☎ Ongar (0277) 364694.
Open: daily, 9-dusk
(Donations)
✖

GRIMSBY
Humberside   Map 8 TA20.
Welholme Galleries
Welholme Road
Collection of Napoleonic and
later 19th-century ship
models, marine paintings and
fine china from Doughty
Bequest. Folk-life collections
and photographs of Lincolnshire life from collection of the
late W.E.R. Hallgarth.

☎ (0472) 59161 Ext 401.
Open: all year Tue-Sat 10-5.
(Closed: Xmas day & BHs.)
& Shop ✕ (ex guide dogs)

GROSMONT
Gwent   Map 3 SO42.
Grosmont Castle
Ruined Marcher stronghold,
rebuilt in 13th century by
Hubert de Burgh, on hill
above Monnow Valley. One
of three 'tri-lateral' castles of
Gwent.

Open: at all reasonable
times.
(AM)

GUILDFORD
Surrey   Map 4 SU94.
Guildford Castle
Castle Street
Early 12th-century rectangular, three-storeyed keep
affording fine views. The
castle ditch has been transformed into a flower garden,
seen at its best throughout the
summer. Brass rubbing display. Open air theatre during
summer.

☎ (0483) 505050.
Grounds open: daily dawn-
dusk. (Closed: Xmas day.)
Admission charge to keep.
& (gardens only) Shop ✕

Guildford House Gallery
155 High Street
Built in 1660, timber-framed
building containing richly
carved elm and oak staircase
and finely decorated plaster

ceilings. Monthly, temporary
art exhibitions, including
paintings and craftwork.

☎ (0483) 503406 Ext 3531.
Open: Mon-Sat 10.30-4.50.
(Closed: A few days prior
to each exhibition). For
details of exhibitions please
apply for leaflet.
& (ground floor only) Shop
✕

Guildford Museum
Castle Arch, Quarry Street
Local history, archaeology
and needlework.

☎ (0483) 503497.
Open: Mon-Sat 11-5.
(Closed: On certain PH.)
& (ground floor only) Shop
✕

HADDINGTON
Lothian (East Lothian) Map 12 NT57.
**St Mary's Pleasance and
Church**
Sidegate
Seventeenth-century re-
stored gardens belonging to
Haddington House including
rose, herb, meadow, cottage
and sunken gardens. Nearby
the Pleached Alley leads to St
Mary's Gate and the large
medieval church of St Mary's,
restored in 1973. Guided
tours are available.

☎ (062082) 3738.
Open: Apr-Sep Mon-Sat
10-4 & Sun 1-4.
(Donations)
& ⌐ Shop.

HADLEIGH
Essex   Map 5 TQ88.
Hadleigh Castle
Founded in 1231 by Hubert
de Burgh and rebuilt by
Edward III in the 14th
century. The walls are of
Kentish rag and the castle
retains two of its original
towers.

Open: accessible at any

reasonable time.
(AM)

HADLEIGH
Suffolk   Map 5 TM04.
Wolves Wood
(2m E on A1071)
An RSPB reserve located in
an ancient woodland, one of
the four surviving fragments
of the vast forests that once
covered this area. Interesting
plants and birds to be seen,
including five species of
orchid. Can be quite muddy.

☎ Norwich (0603) 615920.
Open: accessible at all
reasonable times.
✕

HADRIAN'S WALL
Cumbria/Northumberland
          Map 12 NY77.
Stretching 73 miles between
Bowness on Solway and
Newcastle upon Tyne,
Hadrian's Wall was built from
122AD to separate the
Romans from the Barbarians.
Originally about 15ft high and
10ft wide it had milecastles at
every Roman mile (1620
yards) and two equidistant
turrets between them.
Seventeen forts for up to 1000
soldiers each were built
along the wall, and running
parallel to the south of
Hadrian's Wall is the Vallum,
a ditch with mounds on either
side.
The best places to see the
wall are between Banks in
Cumbria and Chollerford in
Northumberland.

The following places are
accessible at all reasonable
times:
BIRDOSWALD, off B6318,
1¼m W of Gilsland. Roman
fort of Camboglanna visible
and section of wall.
GILSLAND, W of village.
Milecastle 48 and
Willowford Roman bridge.
CARVORAN, ¾m E of

Cloth was sold in the 315 rooms of Halifax Piece Hall

Greenhead. Fine section of wall running along crest of ridge.

CAWFIELDS, 2m N of Haltwistle on unclass road. Remains of Milecastle 42 and sections of wall.

BROCOLITIA, 4m W of Chollerford on B6318. Remains of Roman Fort and traces of the ditch Vallum. (Admission charges to Chester's Roman Fort and Housesteads Roman Fort).

HALIFAX

West Yorkshire   Map 7 SE02.

Bankfield Museum & Art Gallery

Boothtown Road, Akroyd Park

Built by Edward Akroyd in the 1860s, this Renaissance-style building, set in the centre of parkland on a hill overlooking the town, contains one of the finest and most representative collections of costume and textiles from all periods and all parts of the world. There are new galleries of costume and toys, with displays of local natural history and the museum of the Duke of Wellington's Regiment (including a display which re-opens mid summer '86). The Museum mounts regular temporary exhibitions, both from its collection, and also travelling art exhibitions.

☎ (0422) 54823 & 52334. Open: Mon-Sat 10-5, Sun 2.30-5. (Closed: Xmas & New Year's day). &丆 (ground floor & park only) Shop 🏴

Piece Hall

Unique and outstanding 18th-century cloth hall, restored and converted; museum, exhibition galleries; antique, craft and souvenir shops.

☎ (0422) 68725. Open: daily 10-5. (Closed: Xmas & New Year's day). Individual facilities vary. 🖳 & (ground floor only).

HALNAKER

West Sussex   Map 4 SU90.

Halnaker Mill

(1½m NE off A285)

Standing on Halnaker Hill (416ft) the windmill is a local landmark and has been partially restored. Built in 1740, it is the oldest tower mill in Sussex.

Open: accessible at any reasonable time.

HAMILTON

Strathclyde (Lanarks)   Map 11 NS75.

Hamilton District Museum

129 Muir Street

Local history museum in a 17th-century coaching inn with original stable and 18th-century Assembly Room with musicians gallery. Displays include prehistory, art, costume, natural history, agriculture and local industries of the past. Transport museum and Victorian kitchen.

☎ (0698) 283981. Open: Mon-Sat 10-5. & (ground floor only) Shop 🏴

See advertisement on page 64

The Cameronians (Scottish Rifles) Regimental Museum

Mole Hill, off Muir Street

Medals, banners, uniforms, documents and silver.

☎ (0698) 428688. Open: Mon, Tue, Thu-Sat 10-12 & 1-5, Wed 10-12. & 🏴

HAMPTON COURT

Gt London   see page 84.

Bushey Park

(off A308).   London plan 2 : 41 B2.

Less formal than its neighbour Hampton Court Park, with herds of deer roaming free. Mile-long Chestnut Avenue is ideal for horse riding close to the Hampton Court end, and

HAMILTON DISTRICT MUSEUM

Step into the past at Hamilton District Museum, a restored coaching inn, now the oldest building in the town. Re-live the coaching era in our restored stable and fascinating transport section. Stroll through the elegant 18th century Assembly Room with original plasterwork and musicians' gallery, and then savour the atmosphere of our reconstructed Victorian kitchen.

129 MUIR STREET, HAMILTON.
Telephone Hamilton 283981

the Diana Fountain marks the junction with an avenue of limes, a formal highway through an otherwise wild part of the park. North of the limes is the Longford River.

☎ 01-977 1328.
Open: all year 7-½ hour before dusk. ☐ ⑤

Hampton Court Palace
London plan 2 : 42 B2.
Built by Cardinal Wolsey in the early 16th century, the Palace has notable gatehouse, clock court and great hall. Large additions by Sir Christopher Wren, include Fountain Court, c.1689. Fine state apartments and banqueting rooms, kitchen and maze of special interest. Fine gardens (including knot gardens, Great Vine, King's Privy gardens and Wilderness) and park near River Thames.

☎ 01-977 8441.
Open: Gardens and grounds daily, summer 7-9 (or dusk) — winter 9-dusk. Kitchens, cellars and Tudor tennis courts Apr-Sep Mon-Sat 9.30-6, Sun 11-6. Admission charge: State apartments and maze. ⑤ ☐ Shop.

HARDKNOTT CASTLE ROMAN FORT
Cumbria   Map 7 NY20.
On Hardknott Pass above

Eskdale, 375ft square fort with three double gateways enclosing walled and ramparted area of almost three acres. Situated above western end of steep and narrow pass (maximum gradient 1 in 3), fort was occupied in mid-2nd century.

Open: accessible at all reasonable times.
(AM)

HARLOW
Essex   Map 5 TL41.
Harlow Museum
Passmores House, Third Avenue
The exhibits cover various aspects of local history from Roman to modern and also natural history and geology. Housed in an early Georgian building, set in gardens; part of the medieval moat from the earlier house can be seen.

☎ (0279) 446422.
Open: Tue & Thu 10-9, Fri-Mon & Wed 10-5. (Closed Xmas).
⑤ (ground floor & gardens only) Shop ✕

Mark Hall Cycle Museum & Gardens
Muskham Road, off First Avenue
History of the bicycle 1819-1980s, with fifty machines on display from an 1819 hobby horse to a 1982 plastic machine. Three

walled period gardens, Tudor herb garden and cottage garden.

☎ (0279) 39680.
Open: daily 10-5 (dusk in winter). (Closed: Xmas).
⑤ Shop ✕

HARRAY
Orkney   Map 16 HY31.
Corrigall Farm Museum
Restored Orkney farmstead dating from mid 19th century with grain-drying kiln, furnishings and implements of the period.

☎ (085677) 411.
Open: Apr-Sep Mon-Sat 10.30-1 & 2-5, Sun 2-7.
⑤ Shop ✕

HARTLEPOOL
Cleveland   Map 8 NZ53.
Gray Art Gallery & Museum
Clarence Road
Permanent collection of pictures. Museum collections feature local history, archaeology, engineering, Indian idols, porcelain, British birds, working blacksmith's shop in museum grounds. There are monthly temporary exhibitions.

☎ (0429) 66522 Ext 259.
Open: Mon-Sat 10-5.30, Sun 3-5. (Closed: Good Fri, Xmas & New Year's day).
⑤ (ground floor & gardens only) Shop ✕

Maritime Museum
Northgate
Collections feature the maritime history of the town and its shipbuilding industry. Also reconstructed fisherman's cottage, a ship's bridge and an early lighthouse lantern.

☎ (0429) 72814.
Open: Mon-Sat 10-5.
(Closed: Good Fri, Xmas & New Year's day).
Shop ✹

HASTINGS
East Sussex   Map 5 TQ80.
Fishermen's Museum
Rock a Nore Road
Former fishermen's church, now museum of local interest, including the last of Hastings luggers built for sail.

☎ (0424) 424787.
Open: Spring BH-Sep Mon-Thu, Sat & Sun 10.30-12 & 2.30-6.
Ġ ✹

Hastings Country Park
Main entrance off Coastguard Lane S of Fairlight Church
Opened in 1971 and covering 500 acres, the country park occupies four miles of the most attractive stretch of the Sussex coast, with several fine walks and five nature trails. Much of the area is well wooded. Interpretative Centre near Fairlight.

☎ (0424) 424242.
Open: Country Park accessible at all reasonable times. Interpretative Centre: Etr-Sep, Sat, Sun, BH 2-5
⊟ (✹ in Interpretative Centre).

Hastings Museums & Art Gallery
Cambridge Road
Collections of natural history of Hastings, archaeology and history of Hastings and neighbouring areas. Sussex ironwork and pottery. Fine and applied art. Durbar Hall (Indian Palace). Extensive collection of pictures, and a special Exhibition Gallery.

☎ (0424) 435952.
Open: Mon-Sat 10-1 & 2-5, Sun & BH 3-5. (Closed: Good Fri & Xmas).
Ġ (ground floor only) ✹

HAVANT
Hampshire   Map 4 SU70.
Havant Museum
East Street
The museum shares this late 19th-century building with a flourishing Arts Centre. Local history displays can be seen in two rooms off the main exhibition gallery. A display of firearms and their history, formed by C.G. Vokes, is on the first floor of the museum..

☎ (0705) 451155.
Open: Tue-Sat 10-5.
Ġ (ground floor only) Shop

HAWES
North Yorkshire   Map 7 SD89.
National Park Centre
Station Yard
Interpretative display relating to farming in the Yorkshire Dales. Audio-visual programme, maps, guides and local information available.

☎ (09697) 450.
Open: daily Apr-Oct, mid morning-late afternoon.
Ġ

HAWICK
Borders (Roxburghshire)
*   Map 12 NT51.*
Trowmill Woollen Mill
(2½m NE on A698)
There has been a mill here since the 1750s. Trowmill ground meal until about 1880 when it changed to woollen manufacture. The mill was powered by water until 1965

and by electricity until 1977. Visitors can see the various processes and stages of tweed being made at the new automated factory.

☎ (0450) 72555.
Open: daily 9-5.
⊟

HAWORTH
West Yorkshire   Map 7 SE03.
St Michael's Church
The tower is all that remains of the church in which Patrick Brontë (father of the celebrated writers Charlotte, Anne and Emily) preached, demolished by his successor the Reverend John Wade. In the crypt the Brontë family lie beneath an inscribed stone and commemorative plaque (except for Anne, who lies at Scarborough). The memorial chapel contains many documents associated with the family's life. In the churchyard are the graves of Martha Brown and Tabitha Aykroyd, servants of the Brontë household.

☎ (0535) 42329.
Open: daily 10-6
(Donation box).

HEBDEN BRIDGE
West Yorkshire   Map 7 SE02
F Walkley Clogs Ltd
(¾m SE on A646)
The firm was founded by Mr F Walkley at Huddersfield in 1946. This is the only surviving clog mill in Britain and visitors can see the complete process of clog-making, from the 100-year-old method to the modern methods used to make the latest leisure footwear.

☎ (0422) 842061.
Open: daily Mon-Fri 8-4.30, Sat & Sun 9-5 (ex 25, 26 Dec, 1 Jan).
⊟

HELSTON
Cornwall   Map 2 SW62.
Helston Folk Museum
Old Butter Market
Folk museum covering local
history and articles from The
Lizard Peninsula. Various
summer exhibitions are
regularly held.

☎ (03265) 61672.
Open: Mon, Tue, Thu-Sat
10.30-1 & 2-4.30, Wed
10.30-1. Touring schools
and visiting groups
welcome.
& Shop ✗

HENLEY-IN-ARDEN
Warwickshire   Map 4 SP16.
Guildhall
High Street
Gabled, timber framed building of 1448, restored in 1915,
with outside staircase leading
from Dutch-style garden to
hall with impressive roof
timbering.

☎ (05642) 2309.
Open: at any reasonable
time on application to
Caretaker, Guild Cottage.
(Donations)
✗

HEREFORD
Hereford and Worcester
                  Map 3 SO54.
**Hereford Museum & Art
Gallery**
Broad Street
Roman tessellated pave-
ments, natural history, bee
keeping display with observation hive, English watercolours, local geology and
county's archaeology, also
folk life and folklore material.
The exhibitions at City Art
Gallery are changed every
month.

☎ (0432) 268121 Ext 207.
Open: Tue, Wed & Fri 10-6,
Thu 10-5, Sat 10-5 (summer);
Sat 10-4 (winter).
& Shop ✗

HERTFORD
Hertfordshire   Map 4 TL31.
Hertford Castle
Castle was built by William
the Conqueror; the walls and
motte preserve the plan of his
structure. The Edward IV
gatehouse still remains, with
wings added in the 18th and
20th centuries. The grounds
are open to the public and
band concerts are held on the
open days.

☎ (0992) 552885.
Open: 1st Sun in each of the
months of May-Sep
2.30-4.30.
& (ground floor only).

HIGHDOWN
West Sussex   Map 4 TQ00.
Highdown
*(N off A259 halfway
between Worthing &
Littlehampton)*
Gardens laid out in chalk pit
on Highdown Hill, with rock
plants, flowering shrubs and
daffodils, as well as excellent
views. Gardeners Sunday,
1st Sun in May.

☎ Worthing (0903) 501054.
Open: all year Mon-Fri
10-4.30; weekends & BH's
Apr-Sep 10-8.
⌂ ⊟ &

HIGH WYCOMBE
Buckinghamshire   Map 4 SU89.
Wycombe Chair Museum
*Castle Hill House, Priory
Avenue*
Fine house set in gardens and
museum of chairs, old tools,
and chair-making apparatus.

☎ (0494) 23879.
Open: Tue-Sat 10-1 & 2-5.
(Closed: Sun, Mon & BHs).
& (ground floor only) Shop
✗

HIMLEY
Staffordshire   Map 7 SO89.
Himley Hall
(6m S of Wolverhampton off

A449)
Extensive parkland with 9
hole golf course, model
village, trout and coarse
fishing (extra charge). Hall
not open to the public.

☎ Dudley (0384) 55433 Ext
5425.
Grounds open: daily 8-8 or
½hr before dusk.
⌂ ⊟ &

HITCHIN
Hertfordshire   Map 4 TL12.
**Hitchin Museum & Art
Gallery**
Paynes Park
Contains local and natural
history collections, costume
and Victoriana. Regimental
Museum of the Hertfordshire
Yeomanry. Special tempor-
ary exhibitions changed
monthly. Good collection of
watercolours, especially
those by local Quaker artist
Samuel Lucas Snr 1805-1870.

☎ (0462) 34476.
Open: Mon-Sat 10-5.
(Closed: BH's.).
& (ground floor only) Shop
✗

HOLYHEAD
Gwynedd   Map 6 SH28.
**South Stack Cliffs (Nature
Reserve)**
(2m W on unclass road)
Covering 800 acres of an exposed headland with thou-
sands of sea birds including
guillemots, razorbills and
puffins. There are two areas
of maritime heathland; Holyhead Mountain and Penrhos
Feilw Common. A flight of 403
steps lead down to the South
Stack Lighthouse which is
reached by crossing a
suspension bridge. In clear
weather, Ireland can be seen
from the summit of Holyhead
Mountain (722ft).

☎ (0407) 2522.
Open: accessible at all

reasonable times; information centre Apr-Sep.

HOLY ISLAND (Lindisfarne)

Northumberland   Map 12 NU14.

Lindisfarne Liqueur Company

St Aidan's Winery

Visitors, although not allowed into the working area because of Customs and Excise restrictions, are welcomed into the winery showrooms where manufacturing of Lindisfarne Mead is explained (the recipe is a closely guarded secret). Products are on sale. Mead sampling sometimes possible.

☎ (0289) 89230.
Open: Etr-Sep daily; Oct-Mar Mon-Fri.
Opening hours depend on tide. Holy Island is accessible at low tide across a causeway with tide tables posted at each end. Shop.

HONITON

Devon   Map 3 ST10.

Honiton Pottery

30-34 High Street

Visitors can tour the pottery at leisure and see the several stages of the craft during normal working hours.

☎ (0404) 2106.
Pottery open: Mon-Thu 9-12 & 2-4.30, Fri 4. Shop Mon-Sat 9-5.30.
☞ (small coffee shop) Shop.

HORSHAM

West Sussex   Map 4 TQ13.

Horsham Museum

9 The Causeway

16th-century timbered house with walled garden planted with herbs and English cottage garden flowers. Displays include: costume and accessories, toys, early cycles, domestic life, Sussex rural crafts, local history, archaeology and geology. Regular temporary exhibitions throughout the year.

☎ (0403) 54959.
Open: Tue-Fri 1-5, Sat 10-5.
& (ground floor & garden) Shop ✶

HOVE

East Sussex   Map 4 TQ20.

Museum and Art Gallery

New Church Road

The museum contains local history, dolls, toys, coins and medals; a notable collection of British ceramics as well as an exhibition of 18th-century pictures, furniture and decorative arts. A large collection of 20th-century paintings and drawings are also on display.

☎ Brighton (0273) 779410.
Open: Tue-Fri 10-5, Sat 10-4.30 (ex BH's).
& (ground floor only) ✶

HOY

Orkney   Map 16 HY20.

Dwarfie Stane

(Off unclass road between Moness Pier and Rackwick)

Located in a remote glen south of Ward Hill, the Dwarfie Stane consists of a great block of sandstone, measuring 28ft long, 14ft wide and 8ft tall, into which a passage has been cut. No other such rock-cut tomb is known in Britain and it is believed to be about 5000 years old.

Open: accessible at all reasonable times.

HUDDERSFIELD

West Yorkshire   Map 7 SE11.

Art Gallery

Princess Alexandra Walk

Contains a permanent collection of British oil paintings, watercolours, drawings, sculpture from mid 19th century onwards. Temporary loan exhibition throughout the year. Scherer gallery of Bamforth photographs, lantern slides and postcards.

☎ (0484) 513808 Ext 216.
Open: Mon-Fri 10-6, Sat 10-4.
& ✶

Tolson Memorial Museum

Ravensknowle Park

Geology, natural history, archaeology, folk life, toys, development of cloth industry and collection of horse-drawn vehicles..

☎ (0484) 30591 & 41455.
Open: Mon-Sat 10-5, Sun 1-5. (Closed: Xmas).
& (ground floor & garden) Shop ✶

HULL

Humberside   Map 8 TA02.

Ferens Art Gallery

Queen Victoria Square

Contains a collection of works by European Old Masters; 19th-century marine paintings from Humberside; 20th-century English art and a regular programme of visiting exhibitions.

☎ (0482) 222737.
Open: Mon-Sat 10-5, Sun 1.30-4.30. (Closed: Good Fri, 25 & 26 Dec).
☞ (ex Sun) Shop ✶

Town Docks Museum

Queen Victoria Square

Displays include 'Whales and Whaling', 'Fishing and Trawling', 'Hull and the Humber', 'Ships and Shipping', plus Victorian Court Room.

☎ (0482) 222737.
Open: Mon-Sat 10-5, Sun 1.30-4.30. (Closed: Good Fri, 25 & 26 Dec).
☞ (ex Sun) & (ground floor only) Shop ✶

**Transport &
Archaeological Museum**
36 High Street
Development of road transport through the ages. Archaeology of Humberside and Roman mosaics, including the Horkstow Pavement.

☎ (0482) 222737.
Open: Mon-Sat 10-5, Sun 1.30-4.30. (Closed: Good Fri, 25 & 26 Dec). Shop ✖

Wilberforce House
23-25 High Street
Early 17th-century mansion, where William Wilberforce was born, with Jacobean and Georgian rooms and slavery displays. Secluded garden.

☎ (0482) 222737.
Open: Mon-Sat 10-5, Sun 1.30-4.30. (Closed: Good Fri, 25 & 26 Dec).
⊓ & (ground floor only)
Shop ✖

HUNTERSTON
Strathclyde (Ayrshire) Map 10 NS15.
**Hunterston 'B' Power
Station**
Nuclear Power Station of advanced gas-cooled reactor (AGR) type. Guided parties of about 12 are taken on tours of the premises and also see audio-visual presentation on nuclear power generation.

☎ West Kilbride (0294) 823668.
Open: May-Sep Mon-Sat at 10, 11.30, 2 & 3.30, Sun 2 & 3.30 (by telephone appointment only).
(Children 11+ accepted if

accompanied by an adult).
✖

HUNTINGDON
Cambridgeshire Map 4 TL27.
Cromwell Museum
Grammar School Walk
Restored Norman building, once a school where Oliver Cromwell and Samuel Pepys were taught, now Museum of Cromwellian relics.

☎ (0480) 52861.
Open: Apr-Oct, Tue-Fri 11-1 & 2-5, Sat & Sun 11-1 & 2-4; Nov-Mar, Tue-Fri 2-5, Sat 11-1 & 2-4, Sun 2-4. (Closed: BH, ex Good Fri).
Shop ✖

HUNTLY
Grampian (Aberdeenshire)
Map 15 NJ53.
Huntly Museum
The Square
Local history and changing special exhibitions every year. Governed by North East of Scotland Library Committee.

☎ Peterhead (0779) 77778.
Open: all year, Tue-Sat 10-12 & 2-4.
Shop ✖ (ex guide dogs).

ILKLEY
West Yorkshire Map 7 SE14.
Manor House Museum
Castle Yard, Church Street
Elizabethan manor house, built on site of Roman fort, showing exposed Roman wall and collections of Roman material. Exhibitions by regional contemporary artists and craftsmen.

☎ (0943) 600066.
Open: Apr-Sep, Tue-Sun 10-6; Oct-Mar 10-5. Also open BH Mon. (Closed: Good Fri & Xmas.)
& Shop ✖

White Wells
Wells Road
Built on the site of a natural spring when Ilkley was a fashionable spa town. The present building (1756, restored 1972) has two plunge baths, and a display on Ilkley Moor subjects.

☎ (0943) 600066.
Open: Apr-Sep, Sat, Sun & BH's, 11-12 & 2-5.

INGLISTON
Lothian (Midlothian) Map 11 NT17.
**Scottish Agricultural
Museum**
*Royal Highland
Showground*
Displays of original farming tools, equipment and models showing how the land was worked and life in rural Scotland.

☎ 031-333 2674.
Open: May-Sep, Mon-Fri 10-4, Sun 12-5.
Shop ✖ (ex guide dogs)

INVERFARIGAIG
Highland (Invernesshire)
Map 14 NH52.
Farigaig Forest Centre
(On B852, 2½m NE of Foyers)
Set on the wooded eastern shore of Loch Ness, and

Hunterston 'B'

housed in a converted stone stable, this Forestry Commission interpretation centre shows the development of the forest environment in the Great Glen. There are plenty of woodland walks nearby.

☎ Inverness (0463) 234353.
Open: daily Apr-Oct 9.30-6.
卂

INVERKEITHING
Fife (Fife)   Map 11 NT18.
Inverkeithing Museum
The Old Friary (founded in 1384) is home of the town museum. Exhibits show the history of the Old Royal Burgh with military, industrial, religious and domestic items.

☎ (0383) 413344.
Open: all year Wed-Sun, 10-12.30 & 2.30-5.
✻

INVERNESS
Highland (Inverness-shire)
               Map 14 NH64.
Museum and Art Gallery
Castle Wynd
Museum of the Highlands' social and natural history, archaeology and culture with a very good collection of Jacobite relics, bagpipes and Highland silver. Art gallery has interesting pictures of old Inverness and frequently changing exhibitions.

☎ (0463) 237114.
Open: all year, Mon-Sat 9-5.

& (ground floor only)
ᒣ (10-4) ✻

INVERURIE
Grampian (Aberdeenshire)
               Map 15 NJ72.
Inverurie Museum
Town House, The Square.
Thematic displays changing at four- or six-monthly intervals. There is a permanent local history and archaeology exhibition. Established in 1884, this museum is now governed by the North East Scotland Library Service Committee.

☎ Peterhead (0779) 77778.
Open: all year Mon-Fri 2-5, Sat 10-12.
Shop ✻ (ex guide dogs)

IONA
Strathclyde (Argyll)   Map 10 NM22.
Iona Abbey
This tiny island became an important Christian centre when St Columba brought Christianity from Ireland in 563AD, and it is still a place of pilgrimage. On the site of St Columba's monastery is a 13th-century abbey restored during the early part of the 20th century with more rebuilding and excavations since then.

☎ (06817) 314.
Open: accessible at all reasonable times.
(Donations)
ᒣ (Mar-Oct 10-4.30) 卂

✻ (in abbey and other buildings)

IPSWICH
Suffolk   Map 5 TM14.
Christchurch Mansion
Soane Street
16th-century town house with period furnished rooms, up to 19th century. Art gallery attached with Suffolk artists collection and exhibitions.

☎ (0473) 53246.
Open: Mon-Sat 10-5, Sun 2.30-4.30, (dusk in winter) (Closed: 24-26 Dec & Good Fri.)
Guided tours by written request to Director of Recreation & Amenities, Civic Centre, Civic Drive, Ipswich.
& (ground floor & gardens only) Shop ✻

The Museum
High Street
Local geology. Prehistoric to medieval archaeology in eastern counties, and natural history collection. Asia, Africa, America and Pacific gallery with commentary plus a Roman gallery.

☎ (0473) 213761.
Open: Mon-Sat 10-5.
(Closed: Sun, Xmas, Good Fri & some BH.)
& (ground floor only) Shop ✻

See advertisement for Noble Romans on page 70

IRVINE
Strathclyde (Ayrshire) *Map 10 NS34.*
Eglinton Castle & Gardens
Irvine Road, Kilwinning
Late 18th-century castle, built
for 13th Earl of Eglinton.
Castle ruin set in a 12-acre
garden. Site of the famous
Eglinton Tournament of 1839.

☎ (0294) 74166 Ext 373.
Open: all year during
daylight hours.
🅿 ♿

KEIGHLEY
West Yorkshire *Map 7 SE04.*
Cliffe Castle Museum
*Spring Gardens Lane (NW
of town on A629)*
Mansion of c.1878 given by
Sir Bracewell Smith. Contains
collections of natural and
local history, dolls, ceramics,
geological gallery, craft
workshops, and interesting
exhibitions programme. Play
area and aviary in adjacent
park. French furniture from
Victoria and Albert Museum.

☎ (0535) 64184.
Open: Apr-Sep, Tue-Sun
10-6; Oct-Mar, Tue-Sun 10-5.
Also open BH Mons.
(Closed: Good Fri & Xmas).
🛈 Shop ♿

KEITH
Grampian (Banffshire) *Map 15 NJ45.*
**Strathisla Distillery,
Chivas Bros Ltd**
Station Road
Claimed to be the oldest

established distillery in
Scotland, dating from 1786.
Visitors are given a tour
through various parts and
shown a film. Whisky sampling may be available to
visitors.

☎ (05422) 7471.
Open: Jun-early Sep, Mon-
Fri 9-4.30 (other times by
arrangement).
🛈 ♿

KELSO
Borders (Roxburghshire)
                         Map 12 NT73.
Kelso Abbey
Little but the abbey church
remains, and that only in
imposing fragments which
seem to consist almost wholly
of Norman and Transitional
work.

Open: see page 4
♿ (AM)

KESWICK
Cumbria *Map 11 NY22.*
Castlerigg Stone Circle
(1½m E on unclass road)
Dating from neolithic and post
neolithic periods these 38
standing stones are thought to
have been constructed for religious or otherwise cere-
monial meetings. A further 10
stones nearby form a
rectangle.

Open: accessible at all
reasonable times.
(AM)

KETTERING
Northamptonshire *Map 4 SP87.*
Alfred East Art Gallery
Sheep Street
Approximately 12 exhibitions
visit the gallery each year,
each lasting for about three
weeks.

☎ (0536) 85211.
Open: Mon-Wed, Fri & Sat
2-5. ♿ ♿
*See advert Pheasant Inn
Keyston, 13m E, page 71*

KEYHAVEN
Hampshire *Map 4 SZ39.*
**Keyhaven, Pennington
and Hurst (Nature
Reserve)**
Area of mudflats, marshes
and old salterns notable for its
breeding seabirds including
little, common and sandwich
terns and also the black-
headed gull. Golden sam-
phire, yellow horned poppy
and sea kale are among the
shingle plants. Visitors must
keep to the sea wall footpath
(Solent Way) during the
breeding season. Access at
Keyhaven and at Lymington.

Open: accessible at all
reasonable times.

KILMARNOCK
Strathclyde (Ayrshire) *Map 10 NS43.*
Dick Institute
Elmbank Avenue
Exhibits of geology (including
fossils), small arms, shells,
ethnography, numismatics,

and archaeological speci-
mens. Also art gallery,
(paintings and etchings) and
library containing Ayrshire
and Burns printed books.

☎ (0563) 26401.
Open: May-Sep; Mon, Tue,
Thu & Fri 10-8, Wed & Sat
10-5; Oct-Apr Mon-Sat 10-5.
& (ground floor only) ✸

**John Walker & Sons
Limited**
Hill Street
Home of the world's largest
selling Scotch whisky. Tour
begins with visit fo Barleith to
see the blending of whiskies
from all over Scotland, and
repair of oak casks by
coopers, followed by a tour
through the bottling halls at
Kilmarnock.

☎ (0563) 23401.
Open: Mon-Fri; tours 10 & 2
(ex company holidays).
Minimum age 14 years,
telephone in advance if
more than family.
✸

KILMARTIN
Strathclyde (Argyll)   Map 10 NR89.
Dunadd Fort
(3m S, off A816)
A prehistoric hillfort incorporating walled enclosures. It
was once the capital of the
ancient Scots kingdom of
Dalriada.

Open: at all reasonable
times.
(AM)

KILMUN
Strathclyde (Argyll)   Map 10 NS18.
**Kilmun Arboretum &
Forest Plots**
A large collection of conifer
and broadleaved tree
species planted in plots and
specimen groups.
Established by the Forestry
Commission in 1930 and now
extending to 100 acres on a
hillside overlooking the Holy
Loch. (Entrance and car park
at Forestry Commission
District Office, Kilmun, from
which an illustrated guide
book is available).

☎ (036984) 666.
Open: all year during
daylight hours.

KILSYTH
*Strathclyde (Stirlingshire)
                    Map 11 NS77.*
Colzium House & Estate
Partly a museum, with
attractive walled garden. Ice
house and old castle
associated with Montrose's
victory over the Covenanters
in 1645.

☎ (0236) 823281.
House open: Etr weekend-
Sep, Mon-Fri 9-5, Sun 10-6.
(Closed when booked for
private functions). Grounds
open at all times, Museum

open Wed 2-8.
⌨ 🏠 & (ground floor &
gardens only)

KINGS LYNN
Norfolk   Map 9 TF62.
St George's Guildhall
Kings Street
The largest surviving
medieval guildhall in
England, now used as a
theatre.

When not in use as a
theatre or cinema open:
Mon-Fri 10-1 & 2-5, Sat
10-12.30. (Closed: 1 Jan,
Good Fri, 25 & 26 Dec).
(NT)

KINGSTON ST MARY
Somerset   Map 3 ST 23.
Fyne Court
(3m N)
Nature reserve for asso-
ciated species of plants, with
nature trails, guided walks,
arboretum and countryside
interpretation centre. Events
through the summer, mostly
free.

☎ Kingston St Mary (082345)
587.
Open: daily 9-6.
✸

KINGUSSIE
*Highland (Inverness-shire)
                    Map 14 NH70.*
Ruthven Barracks
(½m SE of Kingussie)
The best preserved of the

four infantry barracks built by the Hanovarian Government in the Highlands following the Jacobite uprising of 1715.

Open: at any reasonable time.
(AM)

KIRKCALDY
Fife (Fife)   Map 11 NT29.
Art Gallery & Museum
War Memorial Grounds (next to Kirkcaldy Station)
A unique collection of fine Scottish paintings, historical displays and a full programme of changing art, craft and local history exhibitions.

☎ (0592) 260732.
Open: Mon-Sat 11-5, Sun 2-5. (Closed local Hols).
Shop ✗

John McDouall Stuart Museum
Rectory Lane, Dysart
Set in the National Trust restored 18th century house which was the birthplace of John McDouall Stuart (1815-1866) the first explorer to cross Australia. The award winning display describes his journeys and the Australian wilderness.

☎ (0592) 260732.
Open: Jun-Aug daily 2-5.
Shop ✗

KIRKHILL
Highland (Inverness-shire)   Map 14 NH54.
Moniack Castle (Highland Winery)
Seven miles from Inverness on the A862 Beauly road
Once a fortress of the Lovat chiefs and their kin, it is today the centre of an enterprise unique in Scotland — that of commercial wine making. The winery produces a wide range of wines including ''country wines'' such as Elder Flower and Silver

Birch, red and white wines and mead. An additional feature is the Wine Bar/Bistro.

☎ Drumchardine (046383) 283.
Open: Mon-Sat 10-5.
🍷 (licensed) ⚇ Shop.

KIRKWALL
Orkney   Map 16 HY41.
Grain and Rennibister Earth Houses
Grain Earth House (½m W off A965); Rennibister Earth House (At Rennibister Farm, 4m W off A965)
Both excellently preserved earth houses date from the Iron Age and can be reached by descending a short ladder to an underground chamber from which there is an underground passage with supporting pillars.

Open: Grain Earth House — Apply to keykeeper at Ortak shop in nearby Industrial Estate Mon-Sat 9-5. Rennibister Earth House — accessible at all reasonable times.
(AM)

Highland Park Distillery
(1m S on A961)
Traditional methods are used with peat fires to dry the barley, hand-beaten copper pot stills for distilling and old sherry casks to mature the finished product. The correct maturing period of at least twelve years is strictly observed. Visitors are shown the complete process of whisky making from the barley store to the warehouses.

☎ (0856) 3107.
Open: Mon-Fri, tours 10.30 & 3 (telephone beforehand).
✗

Cutting peat for Highland Park Distillery, Kirkwall

St Magnus Cathedral
Fine red and yellow sandstone Cathedral begun in 1137 by Earl Rognvald in memory of his uncle and predecessor Magnus, who was murdered by a rival about 1117. The polychrome stonework is considered to be the best of medieval age in Britain.

☎ (0856) 3535.
Open: daily Mon-Sat 9-1, 2-5.
✗

Tankerness House
Broad Street
Dating from the 16th century, this is one of the finest vernacular town houses in Scotland. It is now a museum of Orkney history with archaeological collections..

☎ (0856) 3191.
Open: Mon-Sat 10.30-12.30 & 1.30-5; May-Sep, Sun 2-5.
& (ground floor only) Shop
✗

KNOCKANDO
Grampian (Moray)   Map 15 NJ14.
Tamdhu Distillery
Visitors are able to see the complete process of whisky being made.

☎ Carron (03406) 221.
Open: Etr-Sep, Mon-Fri 10-4.
& (ground floor only) Shop

KNOWLTON
Dorset   Map 4 SU01.
Knowlton Circles
(3¼m SW of Cranborne on B3078)
Three large henge circles lying in a row, the eastern one is disected by the B3078 and measures 800ft across. The ruinous Norman Knowlton Church stands in the middle of the centre circle. There are several round barrows nearby.

Open: accessible at all reasonable times.
(AM)

LAKE VYRNWY
Powys   Map 6 SJ01.
(SE of Bala on B4393)
Large artificial lake with an interesting dam. Focal point for a Royal Society for the Protection of Birds reserve covering 16,000 acres, with two RSPB nature trails and hides. Wildlife display at Visitor Centre at the southern end of the lake, plus information on the area before and after the lake was formed.

☎ Llanwddyn (069173) 278.
Visitor Centre open: Etr-Spring BH weekends only; Spring BH-Sep Mon-Fri noon-6, Sat, Sun 11-6; Oct-Etr by prior arrangement.
᚛ & (Visitor Centre).

LAMB HOLM
Orkney Islands   Map 16 HY40.
Italian Chapel
(8m S of Kirkwall on A961)
Converted in World War II from a couple of Nissen huts to an ornate chapel, by Italian prisoners of war. These prisoners also built the nearby Churchill Barriers linking the islands of Orkney Mainland, Lamb Holm, Glimps Holm, Burray and South Ronaldsay.

☎ Holm (085678) 278.
Open: at all reasonable times.
(Donations).
& ✗

LANCASTER
Lancashire   Map 7 SD46.
City Museum
Market Square
Georgian building with archaeology, history collections and Museum of the King's Own Royal Lancaster Regiment.

☎ (0524) 64637.
Open: daily Apr-Oct 10-5; Nov-Mar 2-5. (Closed: Xmas & New Year).
& (ground floor only) Shop
✗

LAXFIELD
Suffolk   Map 5 TM27.
Laxfield & District Museum
The Guildhall
Housed in a 16th-century building, the museum contains mainly 19th-century items relating to village life. Displays change from year to year and include village shops, domestic interior, odd-job man's workshop, costume, the archaeology of Laxfield and photographs. Working beehive.

☎ Ubbeston (098683) 357.
Open: late May-Sep, Wed, Sat, Sun & BH 2-5. Midweek school parties by prior arrangement.

LEAMINGTON SPA
Warwickshire   Map 4 SP36.
Warwick District Council Art Gallery & Museum
Avenue Road
The art gallery specialises in British, Dutch and Flemish paintings and water colours of the 16th to 20th century. The museum contains ceramics, Delft, Saltglaze, Wedgwood, Whieldon, Worcester, Derby Ware etc, and an 18th-century glass collection. Temporary exhibitions.

☎ (0926) 26559.
Open: Mon-Sat 10-1 & 2-5; also Thu evenings 6-8. (Closed: Good Fri, 3 days Xmas & New Year's Day).
& ✗ (ex guide dogs).

LEEDS
West Yorkshire   Map 8 SE23.
Kirkstall Abbey
Abbey Road
Extensive and impressive

ruins of abbey founded in 12th century by Cistercian monks from Fountains Abbey. The chapter house, cloisters and abbot's lodgings are of interest.

☎ **Leeds (0532) 755821.**
Open: daily, dawn-dusk.
&

Leeds City Art Gallery
The Headrow

Permanent collection of Victorian and 20th-century paintings and sculpture, including work by Renoir, Courbet, Sisley, Bonnard, Vuillard and Derain, and

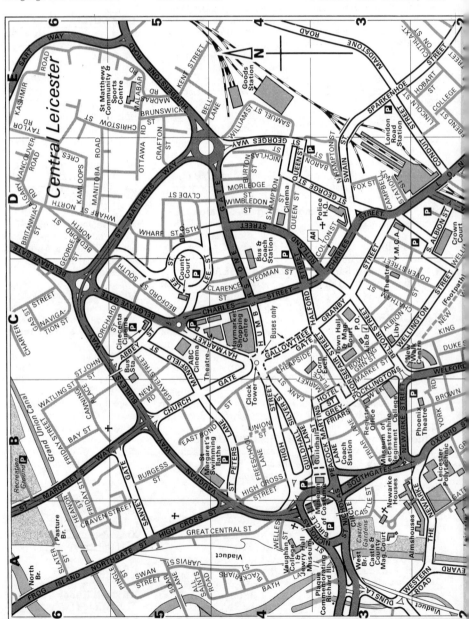

English watercolours. Also here, the Henry Moore Centre for the Study of Sculpture shows how sculptors have lived and worked in different times and countries.

☏ (0532) 462495.
Open: Mon, Tue, Thu, Fri 10-6, Wed 10-9, Sat 10-4, Sun 2-5. (Closed Xmas).

Roundhay Park (Canal Gardens)
Eighty-foot fountain, Coronation House and glasshouse, with Canal Gardens, rose gardens, a tropical plant house and an aquarium.

☏ (0532) 661850.
Open: daily, 9-dusk.
🖬 ₺

LEICESTER
Leicestershire   Map 4 SK50.
Belgrave Hall
Off Thurcaston Road (1m N) Not on plan
A fine early 18th-century house and gardens, now a museum with furnishings, stables with coaches and an agricultural collection.

☏ (0533) 666590.
Open: all year Mon-Thu & Sat 10-5.30, Sun 2-5.30. (Closed Xmas).
₺ (ground floor & gardens only) Shop ✹

Guildhall
Guildhall Lane.   Plan : **B3.**
Medieval Guildhall and later the Town Hall of Leicester, Great Hall, Mayor's Parlour, Library and police cells.

☏ (0533) 554100.
Open: all year Mon-Thu & Sat 10-5.30, Sun 2-5.30. (Closed: Fri and 25 & 26 Dec).
Shop ✹

Jewry Wall Museum & Site
St Nicholas Circle.   Plan : **A4.**
Museum of archaeology from prehistoric times to 1500. Remains of Roman baths and Jewry Wall.

☏ (0533) 554100.
Open: all year Mon-Thu &

Sat 10-5.30, Sun 2-5.30. (Closed: Fri and 25 & 26 Dec) Jewry Wall open: at any reasonable time.
₺ Shop ✹

John Doran Museum
East Midland Gas, Leicester Service Centre, Aylestone Road (½m S on A426) Not on plan.
Housed in an historic building (a part of the Aylestone Road Gasworks) the collection shows all aspects of the history of the manufacture, distribution and use of gas, with documentary material as well as old appliances and equipment.

☏ (0533) 549414 Ext 2192.
Open: Tue-Fri 12.30-4.30.

Leicestershire Museum & Art Gallery
New Walk.   Plan : **D2.**
Collections of 18th- to 20th-century English paintings and drawings, unique collection of 20th-century German Expressionist art, ceramics, silver, Egyptology. New geology and natural history environmental galleries in preparation. Extensive reference and study collections in Art and Natural Sciences with a very active educational programme.

☏ (0533) 554100.
Open: all year Mon-Thu & Sat 10-5.30, Sun 2-5.30. (Closed: Fri & Xmas).
₺ Shop ✹

Leicester Museum of Technology
Abbey Pumping Station, Corporation Road (1m N, off A5131) Not on plan.
Knitting gallery, power gallery, transport items, steam shovel. Original beam engines of 1891.

☏ (0533) 661330.

Open: all year Mon-Thu &
Sat 10-5.30, Sun 2-5.30.
(Closed: Fri & Xmas).
& (except beam engines)
Shop ✗

**Leicestershire Record
Office**
57 New Walk.   Plan : *E1.*
Extensive collection of official
and private archives, both
rural and urban, relating to
the County of Leicestershire.

☎ (0533) 554100.
Open: Mon-Thu 9.15-5, Fri
9.15-4.45, Sat 9.15-12.15.
(Closed: Sun & BH).
& Shop ✗

**Museum of Royal
Leicestershire Regiment**
Oxford Street.   Plan : *B3.*
Housed in Magazine Gate-
way the museum contains
mementos, battle trophies
and relics of the Leicestershire Regiment.

☎ (0533) 554100.
Open: Mon-Thu & Sat
10-5.30, Sun 2-5.30. (Closed:
Fri & Xmas).
Shop ✗

Newarke Houses
The Newarke.   Plan : *B3.*
Social history of the city from
1500 to present day. 19th-cen-
tury street scene. 17th-
century room, local clocks,
musical instruments.

☎ (0533) 554100.
Open: Mon-Thu & Sat
10-5.30, Sun 2-5.30. (Closed:
Fri & Xmas).
& Shop ✗

**University of Leicester
Botanic Gardens**
*Beaumont Hall, Stoughton
Drive South, Oadby (2½m
SE, off A6) Not on plan.*
The gardens occupy an area
of about 16 acres and include
botanical greenhouses, rose,
rock, water and sunken gar-

dens, trees, herbaceous borders and a heather garden.
They comprise the grounds of
four houses; Beaumont,
Southmeade, Hastings and
The Knoll, which are used as
student residences.

☎ (0533) 717725.
Open: Mon-Fri 10-4.30.
& garden centre ✗

**Wygston's House Museum
of Costume**
Applegate.   Plan : *B3.*
Displays of English costume
from 1769 to 1924. Recon-
struction of draper's, milli-
ner's and shoe shops of 1920s.

☎ (0533) 554100.
Open: Mon-Thu & Sat
10-5.30, Sun 2-5.30. (Closed:
Fri & Xmas).
& (ground floor only) Shop
✗

LEIGH
Gt Manchester   Map 7 SJ69.
**Pennington Flash Country
Park**
(1¼m SW on A572)
Once a derelict coalmining
wasteland, now a 1000-acre
country park including the
Flash, a 170-acre lake, numerous footpaths, thousands of
young trees and nature reserve, where a great variety
of birds can be observed.
The Information Centre has
an exhibition on park wildlife.

☎ (0942) 605253.
Open: Country Park
accessible at all reasonable
times. Information Centre:
All year, daily 9-5. (Closed
Xmas)
& ☐ ☐

LEISTON
Suffolk   Map 5 TM46.
Leiston Abbey
Remains of this 14th-century
abbey include choir and
transepts of church, and
ranges of cloisters. Georgian

house built into the fabric of
the abbey.

Open: accessible at any
reasonable time.
(AM)

LERWICK
Shetland   Map 16 HU44.
Clickheinen
(½m S of Lerwick)
A prehistoric settlement
which was occupied for over
1,000 years. Remains include
a partially demolished broch.

Open: see page 4.
(AM)

Fort Charlotte
(Overlooking harbour)
Artillery fort begun in 1665 to
protect Sound of Bressay in
Anglo-Dutch War; completed
in 1781 during American War
of Independence.

Open: see page 4.
(AM)

Shetland Museum
Lower Hillhead
A comprehensive local
museum of the Shetland
Islands from pre-history to the
present day. Displays of folk
life, shipping, archaeology,
art and textiles.

☎ (0595) 5057.
Open: all year Mon, Wed,
Fri 10-1, 2.30-5, 6-8. Tue, Sat
10-1, 2.30-5.
Shop

**Shetland Workshop
Gallery**
4-6 Burns Lane
The gallery is located in two
old dwelling houses in one of
Lerwick's oldest lanes.
Visitors can see local artists
and craftsmen at work.

☎ (0595) 3343.
Open: all year Mon, Tue,
Thu-Sat 9.30-1, 2-5.

LETCHWORTH
Hertfordshire   Map 4 TL23.
First Garden City Museum
296 Norton Way South
Thatched house with extension, containing the original offices of the architects of the Garden City, Barry Parker and Raymond Unwin. Displays explain the concept and development of Letchworth as the First Garden City.

☎ (0462) 683149.
Open: Mon-Fri 2-4.30, Sat 10-1 & 2-4. Other times by arrangement. (Closed Xmas).
&. (ground floor & gardens only) Shop ✻

Museum & Art Gallery
Broadway
Museum contains displays of archaeological material of North Hertfordshire including important Iron Age and Roman finds from Baldock. Natural history gallery. Monthly art exhibitions.

☎ (0462) 685647.
Open: Mon-Sat 10-5.
(Closed BHs).
&. (ground floor only) Shop
✻

LICHFIELD
Staffordshire   Map 7 SK10.
Lichfield Cathedral
Noted for its three graceful spires called the Ladies of the Vale. Begun in 1195, it was badly damaged during the Civil War, but three centuries of caring restoration have resulted in its present splendid condition. The Lady Chapel has lovely 16th-century stained glass windows.

☎ (05432) 22693.
Open: Mon-Sat 9-3.30, Sun 9-5.30.

Museum of the Staffordshire Regiment
(The Prince of Wales's) (3m SE)
Uniforms, badges and weapons, relics from the Sikh Wars, Crimea, Egypt, Sudan, South Africa and both World Wars. A medal display includes seven of the 13 Victorian Crosses awarded to men of the Regiment, which dates back to 1705.

☎ Whittington (0543) 433333 Ext 240.
Open: Mon-Fri 8.30-4.30.
&.

Solid Fuel Advisory Service Shire Horse Stables
Units 1 & 2, Birmingham Road
The shire horses of the Solid Fuel Advisory Service in their working environment, with the harness and vehicles they pull and a permanent display of solid fuel and appliances.

☎ (05432) 52809.
Open: daily 9-4. (Closed Xmas Day).

LINCOLN
Lincolnshire   Map 8 SK97.
Lincoln Cathedral
The west front is Norman, the transept, nave, St Hugh's Choir and Angel Choir date mostly from the 13th century. Its three towers dominate the

Lichfield's shire horses

skyline for many miles.

☎ (0522) 30320.
Open: daily Apr-Sep
7.15am-8pm; Oct-Mar
7.15-6.
⌨ ♿

LINDSEY
Suffolk   *Map 5 TL94.*
St James's Chapel
Rose Green
Small thatched flint and stone
chapel, built in the 13th
century.

Open: See page 4.
(AM)

LINLITHGOW
Lothian (West Lothian) Map 11 NT07.
Beecraigs Country Park
(2m S on unclass road)
700-acre pine woodland
country park, honeycombed
with waymarked paths. Trout
farm where visitors can feed
the thousands of trout in the
rearing ponds; red deer farm
with walkway and viewing
platform. Leisure-courses
include archery, fishing,
canoeing, sailing and
orienteering. An AA view-
point on Cockleroy Hill (913ft)
gives far reaching views to
the Bass Rock and to Great
Fell on Arran.

☎ (050684) 4516.
Open: Country Park
accessible at all reasonable
times; Park Centre Apr-Oct,
Mon-Thu 9-5, Fri 9-4, Sat 1-6,
Sun 10-6; Nov-Mar, Mon-
Thu 9-5, Sun 11-4.
⩋

LITTLEHAMPTON
West Sussex   Map 4 TQ00.
Littlehampton Museum
12A River Road
Six galleries of maritime
paintings, early photographs
of town and river, historic
maps, and local archaeology.
Special exhibitions are
sometimes held.

☎ (0903) 715149.
Open: Apr-Sep, Tue-Sat &
Oct-Mar, Thu-Sat 10.30-1 &
2-4.
♿ (ground floor only) Shop
🍴

LITTLE NESS
Shropshire   Map 7 SJ41.
Adcote School
(7m NW Shrewsbury off A5)
'Country Life' described this
as 'the most controlled,
coherent and masterly of the
big country houses designed
by Norman Shaw'. Includes
William Morris stained glass
windows and de Morgan tiled
fireplaces, also landscaped
gardens.

☎ Baschurch (0939) 260202.
Open: 24 Apr-11 Jul (ex
24-28 May) & 12-30 Sep,
daily 2-5. Other times by
appointment.
🍴

LIVERPOOL
Merseyside   Map 7 SJ39.
Anglican Cathedral
The largest Anglican
cathedral in the world: notable features include the
Gothic arches (the highest
ever built), the peals of bells
(the highest and heaviest in
the world), the cathedral
organ (which has nearly
10,000 pipes), and the stained
glass windows, one of which
contains some 18,000 sq ft of
glass. Architect Giles Gilbert
Scott supervised the con-
struction for more than half a
century, and has a memorial
in the cathedral. The foundation stone was laid in 1904 by
King Edward VII, and the
cathedral was consecrated in
October 1978, in the pres-
ence of HM Queen Elizabeth
II.

☎ 051-709 6271.
Open: daily 9-6.
(Donations).
⌨

Bluecoat Chambers
School Lane
A fine Queen Anne building
in Liverpool's city centre with
cobbled quadrangle and
garden courtyard. Built as a
charity school in 1717, it now
houses a gallery, concert hall,
artists' studio and craft shop.

☎ 051-709 5297.
Open: Mon-Sat 9-6.
Bluecoat gallery Tue-Sat
10.30-5. (Closed: Xmas, Etr
& BHs).
⌨ ♿ (ground floor &
gardens only) Shop.

Liverpool City Libraries
William Brown Street
One of the oldest and largest
public libraries in the
country, with over two million
books on the arts and
sciences.   Temporary
Exhibitions.

☎ 051-207 2147.
Open: Mon-Fri 9-9, Sat 9-5.
Guided tours by prior
arrangement.
⌨ ♿ 🍴

Metropolitan Cathedral
Plans to build a cathedral
here go back to the mid-19th
century, but the existing
structure was only conse-
crated in 1967 after five years
of building. The most striking
feature is the Lantern Tower,
containing over 25,000 pieces
of stained glass in a continuous progression of every
colour of the spectrum.

☎ 051-709 9222.
Open: daily 8-6.
(Donations).
⌨ ♿

Open Eye Gallery
90-92 Whitechapel
A constantly changing programme of photographic
exhibitions.

☎ 051-709 9460.

Liverpool: decoration in Anglican Cathedral

Open: Mon, Tue & Thu-Sat, 10-5.30. (Closed Xmas).

Sudley Art Gallery
Mossley Hill Road
Contains the Emma Holt Bequest of fine 19th-century British paintings and sculpture. A few French 19th-century paintings can also be seen.

☏ 051-724 3245.
Open: Mon-Sat 10-5, Sun 2-5. (Closed: Good Fri, Xmas Eve-Boxing Day & New Year's Day). (Donation). ✝

Walker Art Gallery
William Brown Street
Outstanding general collection of European paintings, sculpture and drawings dating from 1300 to the present day, especially notable for Italian and Netherlandish paintings.

☏ 051-227 5234 Ext 2064.
Open: Mon-Sat 10-5, Sun 2-5. (Closed: Good Fri,

Xmas Eve-Boxing Day & New Year's Day). (Donation). ♿ Shop ✝

LIVINGSTON
Lothian (West Lothian) Map 11 NT06.
Almondell & Calderwood Country Park
(1m E on B7015 & B8046)
Consisting of two adjoining estates formally owned by the Earl of Buchan and Lord Torphichen, with a variety of wildlife, wild flowers and birds. Over four miles of paths have been constructed, with a nature trail. Spring and early summer are the best times to visit for fine displays of daffodils and rhododendrons. There is a visitors' centre at Stables Cottage.

☏ Linlithgow (0506) 882254.
Open: Country Park accessible at all reasonable times; Visitor Centre all year Mon-Wed 9-12, 1-5, Thu 9-12, 1-4, Sun 10.30-12, 1-6 (Closed: 25, 26 Dec, 1 Jan).
♿ ㄓ (✝in visitor centre).

LLANALLGO
Gwynedd Map 6 SH48.
Din Lligwy Ancient Village
(1m NW off A5205)
Remains of 4th-century village, with two circular and seven rectangular buildings encircled by pentagonal stone wall.

Open: accessible at all reasonable times.
(AM)

LLANBERIS
Gwynedd Map 6 SH56.
Dolbadarn Castle
Native Welsh stronghold with 13th-century round tower.

Open: accessible at all reasonable times.
(AM)

LLANDRINDOD WELLS
Powys Map 3 SO06.
Llandrindod Wells Museum
Temple Street
Archaeological exhibits, and objects excavated from Roman Camp at Castell Collen to north of town. Paterson doll collection is on show. Victorian Spa gallery with period costume and 19th-century chemist's equipment. Temporary exhibitions.

☏ (0597) 4513.
Open: all year Mon-Fri 10-12.30 & 2-5, Sat 10-12.30 also 2-5 Apr-Sep.
♿ (ground floor only) Shop ✝

Rock Park Spa
Norton Terrace
Situated in an 18-acre wooded park, the Pump Room has been restored to its former glory and refurbished in Edwardian style, complete with pumps providing three spa waters for anyone to sample. In the Bath House there is an exhibition of the history of the spa and others in Wales.

☏ (0597) 4307.
Open: daily Apr-Oct 10-6 (other times by arrangement).
♿ ☕

LLANELLI
Dyfed Map 2 SN50.
Parc Howard Art Gallery & Museum
Situated in a pleasant park, and containing paintings. Llanelli pottery and museum exhibits. From Mar-Oct a programme of exhibitions of paintings, porcelain, sculpture etc is in operation.

☏ (05542) 3538.
Open: daily 10-6.
♿ (grounds only) Shop. ✝

LLANFIHANGEL-Y-PENNANT

Gwynedd *Map 6 SH60.*

Castell y Bere

(NW of Abergynolwyn on unclass road)

Built by Llywelyn the Great in 1221, Castell y Bere is a keep and bailey castle with two D-shape towers, a typical feature of Welsh castles. Although many of the walls are low there is some fine carved stonework still to be seen.

Open: accessible at all reasonable times. (AM)

LLANGYBI

Gwynedd *Map 6 SH44.*

St Cybi's Well

Rectangular structure, known also as Ffynnon Gybi, with dry-stone structure covering adjacent pool. Interior has wall niches and the corbelled beehive vaulting of a characteristically Irish type is unique in Wales.

Open: accessible at all reasonable times. (AM)

LLANIDLOES

Powys *Map 6 SN98.*

Old Market Hall

Half-timbered building, standing in open arches, with museum on upper floor.

**☎ Welshpool (0938) 4759.
Open: Etr, then Spring BH-Sep daily 11-1 & 2-5.
Shop ♿**

LLANSTEPHAN

Dyfed *Map 2 SN31.*

Llanstephan Castle

Remains of 11th- to 13th-century stronghold on west side of Towy estuary.

Open: accessible at all reasonable times. (AM)

LLANTHONY

Gwent *Map 3 SO22.*

Llanthony Priory

Augustinian foundation c.1108 most of the present structure being 12th- or 13th-century and including west towers, north nave arcade and south transept. Former Priest's House is now a hotel. The Honddhu valley scenery in the Black Mountains is very picturesque but roads are narrow especially northwards towards lofty Gospel Pass leading to Hay-on-Wye.

Open: at all reasonable times. (AM)

LLANTILIO CROSSENNY

Gwent *Map 3 SO31.*

Hen Gwrt

Rectangular enclosure of medieval house which is still surrounded by moat.

Open: at any reasonable time. (AM)

LLANTWIT MAJOR

South Glamorgan *Map 3 SS96.*

Town Hall

Originally 12th- and largely 17th-century medieval courthouse and market, known once as the 'Church Loft'. Retains original plan and comprises two storeys, curfew bell now in church.

**☎ (04465) 3707.
Open: all year Mon-Fri 9-4, by appointment.
♿**

LLANWRTYD WELLS

Powys *Map 3 SN84.*

Cambrian Factory

A sheltered workshop employing disabled persons operated by Powys County Council and the Royal British Legion. Visitors can see an outstanding example of a working mill and all the manufacturing process including wool sorting, dyeing, carding, spinning, warping, winding and weaving.

**☎ (05913) 211.
Open: Mill, all year Mon-Thu, 8.15-5, Fri 8.15-2.45. (Closed: weekends & BH.) Shop Mon-Fri, 8.15-5.30; Sat May-Sep 9-4.30, Oct-Apr 9-noon. (Closed: Sun & Xmas.)**

LOCHCARRON

Highland (Ross and Cromarty) *Map 14 NG83.*

Strome Castle

(3m SE)

A fragmentary ruin of a stronghold of the Macdonalds of Glengarry, blown up by Kenneth Mackenzie of Kintail in 1602. There are wide views across the Inner Sound to Scalpay, Raasay and the Coolins of Skye.

Open: accessible at all reasonable times. (NTS)

LOCH GARTEN

Highland (Inverness-shire) *Map 14 NH91.*

(2m E of Boat of Garten off B970)

The reserve became famous when ospreys returned here in the 1950's and they are still breeding on the north side of the loch. Access in that area is restricted to the signposted path and the observation hide where the birds can be viewed through telescopes. Other breeding birds include capercaillies, crested tits, red starts, siskins and Scottish crossbills. Red and roe deer are common, as are red squirrels.

**☎ Boat of Garten (047983) 694.
Open: Reserve, accessible at all reasonable times;**

Are you using the right oil?

INTRODUCING THE VISCO RANGE

The Visco range of multigrade oils has been developed by BP to suit different types of car and motorist.

All Visco oils contribute to the efficiency and condition of your car because they contain these vital additives:

● "Anti-wear" agents to prolong the life and reliability of your engine.

● A "detergent" to clean the inside of your engine, preventing the build-up of impurities which affect its performance.

● A "dispersant" to prevent the formation of "sludge".

● An "anti-oxidant" to guard against acid corrosion and the breakdown of the oil at very high temperatures.

PLUS

● Visco-Nova, our top of the range oil, contains two special performance ingredients unique to BP: LHC and Friction Shield. These combine to give the ultimate in engine protection and increased engine efficiency providing more miles to the gallon.

NOW CHOOSE THE BEST OIL FOR YOUR CAR

RECOMMENDED FOR NEW CARS

A new car is the biggest single investment, other than a house, that we ever make. Protect that investment with an oil tailormade for today's car – Visco-Nova.

Visco-Nova has been developed to meet the demands of the modern motor car. Visco-Nova has achieved greater fuel efficiency without loss of protection to the engine. It uses a special process called "Adsorption" which, by the use of a new additive called Friction Shield, electrochemically coats all metal surfaces with a protective film – ensuring protection for the engine where it's needed.

As well as containing the Friction Shield additive, Visco-Nova contains LHC (Lavera Hydrocracker Component) a base oil unique to BP which helps ensure that Visco-Nova stays stable under the most severe conditions.

Visco-Nova is the choice of the most discerning motorist who demands the latest in oil technology.

KEY BENEFITS

● PROTECTION – "FRICTION SHIELD" offers the ultimate in protecton.

● COLD STARTING – the lighter viscosity ensures that oil flows around the engine quicker.

● ENGINE COOLING – improved flow reduces high temperature build-up.

- FUEL SAVING – reduced friction leads to more miles to the gallon.
- APPROVED – motor manufacturers require 10W oils for new cars.

Visco 2000

THE UNIVERSAL MULTIGRADE

Visco 2000 is the most popular oil sold at BP garages. Used by motorists across the world, Visco 2000 has a long and proven record in reducing wear and tear on expensive engine components and giving longer life to batteries through easier starting. It is a premium quality 15W/40 multigrade engine oil, priced very competitively and can be used in all gasoline engine vehicles.

It meets the API/SF service qualification and satisfies the requirements of the world's car manufacturers.

KEY BENEFITS

- PROTECTION – offers a high level of protection against corrosion and engine wear.
- APPROVED – Visco 2000 is approved by, or meets the requirements of, major motor manufacturers.

Visco DIESEL

THE OIL FOR ALL DIESELS

BP have developed a new premium multigrade engine oil to provide better performance and protection for all diesel motorists. Diesel engines work differently to gasoline engines and therefore make different demands on their oil.

Visco Diesel is an advanced premium quality engine oil specifically formulated for use in diesel engines of all types and sizes, from road haulage and off-highway vehicles to turbo-charged sports saloon cars.

A VOTE OF CONFIDENCE

All the following manufacturers have approved Visco Diesel or have their standards/requirements met by its performance:

Ford	VAG	DAF	Perkins	Gardner
Leyland	Volvo	IVECO	Bedford	Caterpillar
Daimler Benz	Detroit	Cummins	Scania	MAN

KEY BENEFIT

- Visco Diesel can be confidently used to satisfy the engine lubrication requirements of any diesel powered vehicle engine.

THE KEY TO BETTER MOTORING

Do you keep your eye on the petrol gauge, anxious not to run out and fingers crossed that a full tank will last forever? You're not alone.

But, it might well be you're overlooking something just as important to your welfare and that of your car – OIL.

Without oil you are heading for trouble, breakdown and expensive repair bills.

One brief look under your bonnet can save you a great deal of time and money.

THINK OIL!

Start now and enjoy more miles to the gallon, increased life for the engine, easier starting and a host of other motoring benefits.

DO YOU NEED OIL?

After stopping the engine, allow a few moments for the oil level in the engine to settle. Pull out the dip-stick, wipe it clean and replace. Pull the dip-stick out again and now check the oil level. It should be on the upper of the two graduation marks – if it's not, you need oil.

TOPPING UP

The difference between the graduation marks on the dip-stick is usually 1 litre, so if the oil level is nearer the minimum than the maximum, you should top up with at least ½ litre of oil.

Remove the oil filler cap, pour in the oil.

Make sure that the level as shown on the dip-stick is never ABOVE the maximum mark.

CHECK REGULARLY

Contary to popular belief, every car, both new and old, consumes oil. In fact, if your car doesn't use oil, you have cause for concern, as the engine cannot be properly lubricated and this can lead to excessive wear and tear. The amount of oil your car needs depends on its age, the size of its engine, your personal style of driving and the type of motoring you do. For example, sustained high speed motorway cruising may consume more oil.

As a rule of thumb, you should check your oil at least once a fortnight or every 500 miles. Car manufacturers suggest an oil check EVERY TIME YOU FILL UP WITH PETROL.

REMEMBER,

It's not enough to keep an eye on the oil warning light. Don't wait for the light to flash to tell you oil is needed.

IT MIGHT BE
TOO LATE

Britain at its best.

WHERE TO BUY YOUR OIL

**Call in at the Oil Bar
at your local BP garage.**

shop and observation post end Apr & May daily 10-6.30, Jun-Aug 10-8.30.
🚻 🏃

LOCHORE MEADOWS COUNTRY PARK
Fife (Fife) Map 11 NT19.
(1½m N of Lochgelly on B920)
Developed on a mining wasteland, the country park covers nearly 1,000 acres and is dominated by Loch Ore. There are numerous trails, paths and other recreational facilities including sailing, canoeing, fishing and a nature reserve. The visitor centre has an interpretative display.

☎ Ballingry (0592) 860086.
Open: Park Centre daily Apr-Sep 9-8, Oct-Mar 9-4.30.
🚻 🏃 (🏃 in park centre)

LOCHWINNOCH
Strathclyde (Renfrewshire) Map 10 NS35.
Lochwinnoch Community Museum
Main Street
A series of changing exhibitions reflecting the historic background of local agriculture, industry and village life.

☎ (0505) 842615.
Open: Mon-Wed & Fri 10-1, 2-5 & 6-8, Sat 10-1 & 2-5.
🚻 🏃

LOGGERHEADS
Clwyd Map 7 SJ16.
Loggerheads Country Park
(on A494 between Ruthin and Mold)
A 67-acre country park in the valley of the River Alyn, which sometimes disappears down 'swallow holes' in the limestone country in dry weather. There is a 1½-mile nature trail and a restored corn mill near the information centre. A variety of woodland

birds may be seen.

☎ Llanferres (035 285) 586.
Open: Country Park, accessible at all reasonable times; information centre most summer weekends; corn mill by prior arrangement.

LONDON *Greater London.*

Plans 1 & 2 pages 82 to 85
Places within the London postal area are listed below in postal district order under East, North, South and West. Other places within Greater London or the surrounding area are listed under their respective place names.

Plan 1 covers Central London. A grid reference is given for each place, eg:
Guildhall Plan 1 : **F4.**
Plan 2 covers the surrounding area. Each place has a number — marked on the map — followed by a grid reference eg. **Keats House** Plan 2 : **12 D4.**

═══ EAST ═══

E1
St. Katherine Dock
Plan 2 : 1 E3.
Designed by Thomas Telford and forced to close after World War II, the dock basins and warehouses now offer a yacht marina, Historic Ship Collection and other attractions. A lovely place to wander round.

☎ 01-481 0043 (Historic Ship Collection).
Open: Docks at all times. Historic Ship Collection daily 10-5. (Closed: Xmas & New Year's day.) Historic Ship Collection admission charge.

🚻 🏕 🏃 (restricted in Historic Ship Collection)

E2
Bethnal Green Museum of Childhood
Cambridge Heath Road
Plan 2 : 2 E4.
A branch of the Victoria and Albert Museum. Its chief exhibits are toys, dolls and dolls' houses, model soldiers, puppets, games, model theatres, wedding dresses, children's costume and Spitalfield silks, all housed in a very attractive building.

☎ 01-980 2415.
Open: Mon-Thu & Sat 10-6, Sun 2.30-6. (Closed: Fri, Spring BH Mon, 24-26 Dec & New Year's day.)
🏃 Shop 🏃 (ex guide dogs)

Geffrye Museum
Kingsland Road Plan 2 : 3 E4.
A collection of furniture and woodwork from the Elizabethan period to 1939, including a reconstruction of John Evelyn's 'closet of curiosities', contained in the former almhouses built c.1713.

☎ 01-739 8368.
Open: Tue-Sat 10-5 Sun 2-5, BH Mons 10-5. (Closed: Good Fri, 24-26 Dec & New Year's day.)
🏕 🏃 (ground floor only)
Shop 🏃

E6
Interpretative Centre, St Mary Magdalene Churchyard Nature Reserve
Norman Road Plan 2 : 4 F4.
Displays relating to natural history and history of an interesting churchyard nature reserve.

☎ 01-519 4296.
Open: Tue-Thu & Sun 2-5.
Shop 🏃

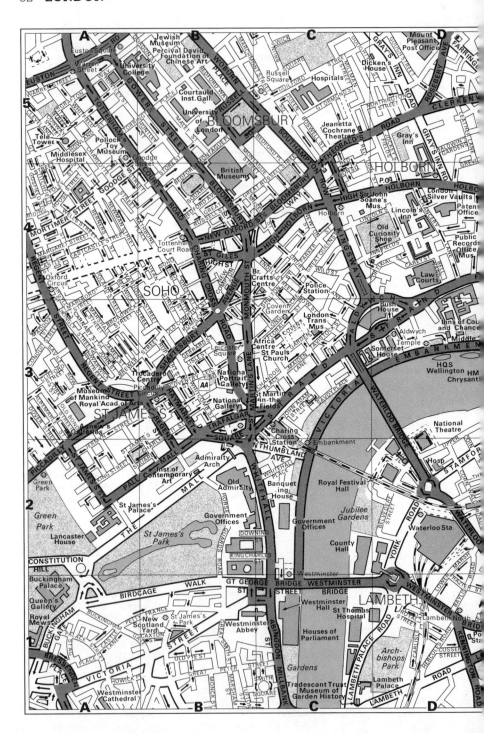

London Plan 1

E14

**National Museum of
Labour History**

*Limehouse Town Hall,
Commercial Road* Plan 2 : **5 E3**.
The visual history from late
18th century to 1945 is portrayed in two sections, from
autocracy to democracy, and
the turn to socialism 1881 to
1945. The prime concern of
this large and rare collection
is democracy over the last
200 years.

☏ 01-515 3229.
Open: Tue-Sat 9.30-5, Sun
2.30-5.30. Shop ✝

E15

**Passmore Edwards
Museum**

Romford Road Plan 2 : **6 F4**.
Greater London and Essex
archaeology, biology, geology and history.

☏ 01-519 4296.
Open: Mon-Wed & Fri 10-6,
Thu 10-6, Sat 10-1 & 2-5, Sun
& BH 2-5.
& (ground floor only) Shop
✝

E16

**North Woolwich Old
Station Museum**

Pier Road Plan 2 : **7 F3**.
Imposing restored station
building with three galleries
of photographs, models, an
original turntable pit. Each
Sunday a locomotive is in
steam.

☏ 01-474 7244.
Open: Mon-Sat, 10-5; Sun &
BH 2-5. (Closed: Xmas.)

E17

**Vestry House Museum of
Local History**

*Vestry Road, near
Hoe Street*
Plan 2 : **8 E5**.
A small museum located in a

London Plan 2

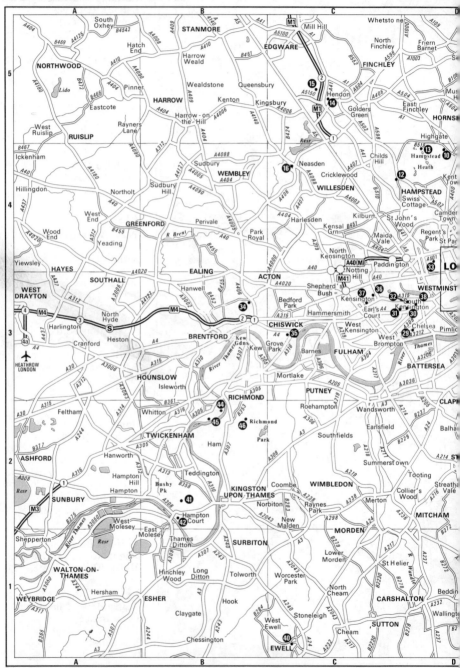

London Plan 2

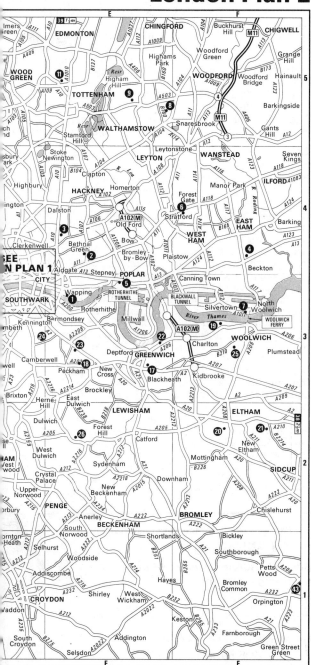

former 18th-century work-house standing in the con-servation area 'Walthamstow Village'. Historical items of local interest from the Stone Age onwards include a re-constructed Victorian par-lour. The Bremer Car, pro-bably the first British internal combustion engine car seen. Local archives are available for consultation by appoint-ment.

☎ 01-527 5544 Ext 4391.
Open: Mon-Fri 10-5.30, Sat 10-5. (Closed: BH.)
& (ground floor only) Shop
✻

William Morris Gallery
Water House, Lloyd Park, Forest Road
Plan 2 : **9 E5.**
William Morris lived in this house, known as 'Water House' from 1848-56. There are exhibits of his fabrics, wallpapers and furniture. Also ceramics by William de Morgan, furniture by Gimson and Barnsley and work by Mackmurdo and the Century Guild. Pre-Raphaelite pic-tures, sculpture by Rodin.

☎ 01-527 5544 Ext 4390.
Open: Tue-Sat 10-1 & 2-5, and 1st Sun in each month 10-12 & 2-5. (Closed: Mon & PH.)
Shop ✻

EC1
Museum of the Order of St John
St John's Gate, St John's Lane
Plan 1 : **E5.**
Sixteenth century Gatehouse, former entrance to the med-ieval Priory of the Order of St John of Jerusalem. Now head-quarters of the modern order whose charitable foundations include St Johns Ambulance and the Ophthalmic hospital in Jerusalem. Norman crypt and 15th-century Grand

Priory Church. A collection of paintings, silver, furniture and historical medical instruments, certificates, textbooks and memorabilia of notable early St John personalities and pioneers. Special features are St John's role in the development of medical transport and its service in the Boer and two World Wars.

☎ 01-253 6644 Ext 35.
Open: all year, Tue & Fri 10-6, Sat 10-4. Guided tours, Sat 11 & 2.30. (Closed: Etr, Xmas wk & BH.) (Donations)
&. (ground floor only) Shop ✖

National Postal Museum
King Edward Building,
King Edward Street
                    Plan 1 : F4.
Contains probably the finest and most comprehensive collection of postage stamps in the world. Included are: the RM Phillips collection of 19th-century Great Britain (with special emphasis on the One Penny Black and its creation); the Post Office Collection, a world-wide collection including practically every stamp issued since 1878; and the philatelic correspondence archives of Thomas de la Rue and Co who furnished stamps to over 150 countries between 1855 and 1965. Within these collections are thousands of

original drawings and unique proof sheets of every British stamp since 1840. Special exhibitions, and visits for up to 40 people may be arranged, with a guide and film show.

☎ 01-606 3769 & 01-432 3851.
Open: Mon-Thu (ex BH) 10-4.30, Fri 10-4.
&. (ground floor only) Shop ✖

EC2

Guildhall   *Plan 1 : F4.*
Rebuilt in 1411 but only the walls of the great hall, porch and crypt survive from the medieval building. It was severely damaged in the Great Fire and the Blitz. Restoration work, completed in 1954 was carried out to designs by Sir Giles Scott. Here the Court of Common Council, which administers the city, meets and entertains. The **Guildhall Library** contains an unrivalled collection of books, manuscripts, and illustrations on all aspects of London. The **Guildhall Clock Museum** with 700 exhibits illustrates 500 years of time keeping.

☎ 01-606 3030.
Open: Guildhall May-Sep, Mon-Sat 10-5, BH & Sun 2-5; Guildhall Library Mon-Fri 9.30-5. (Closed: BH); Guildhall Clock Museum

Mon-Fri 9.30-5. (Closed: BH.)
&. (ground floor only) ✖

Museum of London
London Wall   *Plan 1 : F4.*
The museum was formed by amalgamating the former London Museum and the Guildhall Museum. The present purpose-built premises were opened in 1976 and the museum is devoted entirely to London and its people. Everything on show contributes to the story of London during the past 2,000 years. Included are Royal treasures from the City, a barber's shop from Islington, sculptures from the Temple of Mithras, a 1930 Ford, Selfridge's lift, a medieval hen's egg, a Roman bikini and the Great Fire experience.

☎ 01-600 3699 Ext 240.
Open: Tue-Sat 10-6, Sun 2-6. (Closed: BH & Xmas.)
Parties by arrangement.
🖵 &. Shop ✖

Stock Exchange
Plan 1 : G4.
The centre of industrial finance, where stocks and shares in individual companies are bought and sold. The trading floor may be viewed from the gallery and guides are present to explain the scene. A colour film may be seen by prior arrangement.

The 'wedding cake' spire of St Bride's church, EC4

☎ 01-588 2355.
Open: Mon-Fri 9.45-3.15.
Last guided tour 2.30.
(Closed: PH's. Parties must book in advance.)
Shop ✸

EC3
Lloyd's of London
Plan 1 : G4.
The world's leading insurance market, moves into a new headquarters building of advanced design in Lime Street in May 1986. It incorporates a purpose-built exhibition encompassing Lloyd's 300 years in the City as well as a visitors viewing area.

☎ 01-623 7100.
Open: all year, Mon-Fri 10-4 (from early June 1986).
(Closed PH.)
✸

EC4
Central Criminal Courts
Old Bailey   *Plan 1 : E4.*
On the first two days of each session the judges carry posies of flowers and the courts are strewn with herbs, a custom dating from the time when it was necessary to disguise the stench of Newgate Prison. Most of the major trials of this century have been heard here including those of Crippen, Christie, Haig, the Kray brothers and more recently Peter Sutcliffe, the Yorkshire Ripper. When the courts are in session visitors may sit in the public galleries. It is often necessary to queue.

☎ 01-248 3277.
Open: Mon-Fri, 10.30-1 & 2-4.

Mansion House
Plan 1 : G4.
This Palladian building designed in 1739-53 by George Dance the Elder is the official residence of the Lord Mayor of London. The principal rooms are the Egyptian Hall, or dining room, and the Salon which contains 19th-century tapestries and an enormous Waterford glass chandelier.

☎ 01-626 2500 Ext 324.
Open: Tours Tue, Wed & Thu 11 & 2. For tickets apply to: Diary Secretary to the Lord Mayor. Tours last 1 hour.
✸

Middle Temple Hall
The Temple   *Plan 1 : D3.*
A fine example of Tudor architecture built during the reign of Queen Elizabeth I and completed about 1570. Hall features double hammer beam roof. Also stained glass showing shields of past readers. The most treasured possession is the 29 ft long high table, made from a sin-

gle oak tree of Windsor Forest. Another table was made from timbers of the Golden Hind in which Sir Francis Drake, a member of the Middle Temple, sailed around the world. Portraits of George I, Elizabeth I, Anne, Charles I, Charles II, James, Duke of York and William III line the walls behind the high table.

☎ 01-353 4355.
Open: Mon-Sat 10-12 & 3-4.30. (Closed: BH.)
✸

St Brides Crypt Museum
Fleet Street   *Plan 1 : E4.*
Internationally known as the 'parish church of the press'. It has been the site of seven previous churches, the existing structure having been meticulously restored to Wren's original design. A wealth of history and relics can be seen on permanent display in the crypt museum.

☎ 01-353 1301.
Open: Mon-Sat 9-5; Sun 9-8.

St Paul's Cathedral
Plan 1 : F4.
Wren's masterpiece, built in the late 17th and early 18th centuries is 515 ft long and 242 ft across at its widest point, crowned by a beautiful central dome rising to a height of 365 ft and 112 ft in diameter.

☎ 01-248 2705.
Open: daily Apr-Sep, 8-6; Oct-Mar, 8-5, subject to special services.
(Donations)

Telecom Technology Showcase
135 Queen Victoria St
Plan 1 : E3.
Two display floors featuring the past, present and future of Britain's telecommunications. There are many working exhibits charting 200 years of

progress from the earliest telegraphs, to satellites and optical fibres.

☎ 01-248 7444.
Open: Mon-Fri 10.00-5.00.
(Closed: BH.)
♿ Shop ✗ (ex guide dogs)

===== NORTH =====

N6
Highgate Cemetery
Swains Lane   Plan 2 : **10 D4.**
One of the private cemeteries which sprang up in the 1830's. The Eastern part is well known for the grave of Karl Marx. The Western part, decaying and overgrown through years of neglect, provides a marvellous backdrop for the magnificent tombs, vaults and buildings. Other famous Victorians buried here include George Eliot, Faraday and Charles Dickens's family.

☎ 01-340 1834.
Open: Eastern cemetery, daily, Apr-Sep 10-5, Oct-Mar 10-4 (Last admission ½ hour before closing); Western cemetery guided tours on the hour daily, Apr-Sep 10-4, Oct-Mar 10-3.
(Donations)

N17
Bruce Castle Museum
Lordship Lane   Plan 2 : **11 E5.**
An E-shaped part Elizabethan, part Jacobean and Georgian building, with an adjacent circular 16th-century tower, which stands in a small park. The museum contains sections on local history, postal history and the Middlesex Regiment, also known as the 'diehards'

☎ 01-808 8772.
Open: Prior to Etr 1986 Tue-Fri 10-5, Sat 10-12.30 & 1.30-5. (Closed: Sun, Mon &

BH.) From Etr 1986 daily 1-5. (Closed: Good Fri, Xmas & New Year's day)
(Donations)
Shop ✗

NW3
Keats House
Keats Grove   Plan 2 : **12 D4.**
Regency house, former home of the poet Keats. *Ode to the Nightingale* was written in the garden. Manuscripts and relics.

☎ 01-435 2062.
Open: all year, Mon-Sat 10-1 & 2-6, Sun & BH ½-5.
(Closed: Good Fri, Etr Sat, May Day, Xmas & New Year's day.)
Guided tours by appointment.
♿ (ground floor only) Shop ✗

Kenwood, Iveagh Bequest
Hampstead Lane Plan 2 : **13 D4.**
Mansion re-modelled c.1765 by Robert Adam, with fine grounds, bequeathed to the nation in 1927 by Lord Iveagh. Notable library, furniture, and works of art including paintings by Rembrandt, Hals, Vermeer, Reynolds and Gainsborough. Collections of 18th-century shoebuckles and jewellery. Summer exhibition. Concerts.

☎ 01-348 1286.
Open: daily; Apr-Sep 10-7; Feb, Mar & Oct 10-5; Nov-Jan 10-4.
(Charges for special exhibitions)
🅿 ♿ (ground floor & garden only) Shop ✗

NW4
Church Farm House Museum
Greyhound Hill   Plan 2 : **14 C5.**
Old gabled house, dating from 1660s, now museum of local interest. Period fur-

nished kitchen and dining room, with programme of changing exhibitions.

☎ 01-203 0130.
Open: all year. Mon-Sat 10-1 & 2-5.30 (Tue 10-1 only). Sun 2-5.30. (Closed: Good Fri, 25 & 26 Dec, 1 Jan.)
♿ (garden only) Shop ✗

NW9
Royal Air Force Museum
Entrance via M1, A41 (Aerodrome Road, off Watford Way) or A5 (Colindale Av, off Edgware Road)
Plan 2 : **15 C5.**
The museum, on the former Hendon airfield, covers all aspects of the history of the RAF and its predecessors. Over 40 aircraft are on display from the Bleriot X1 to the 'Lightning'. Twelve galleries depict over one hundred interesting years of military aviation history.

☎ 01-205 2266 Ext 38
Open: all year, Mon-Sat 10-6, Sun 2-6. (Closed: Good Fri, May Day, 24-26 Dec & 1 Jan)
RAF Museum free. Battle of Britain Museum admission charge.

NW10
Grange Museum
Neasden Lane (centre of roundabout)
Plan 2 : **16 C4.**
Dating from around 1700, the building originally formed part of the outbuildings of a large farm and was later converted into a gothic cottage. Permanent collections tell the story of the area that is now the London Borough of Brent. Changing temporary exhibitions, local history library, display on the British Empire Exhibition for which Wembley Stadium was built. Two

period rooms of late 19th century and early 20th century, and reconstructed draper's shop.

☎ 01-452 8311.
Open: all year, Mon-Fri 12-5 (8pm Wed), Sat 10-5. (Closed: BH.)
Parties by advanced booking only.
& (ground floor & gardens only) Shop ✖

═══ SOUTH ═══

SE1
Imperial War Museum
Lambeth Road   *Plan 1 : E1.*
Founded 1917 and established 1920 by Act of Parliament, this museum illustrates and records all aspects of the two World Wars and other military operations involving Britain and the Commonwealth since 1914. Extensive renovation and redevelopment will entail gallery closures from 1986 and a major interim exhibition on the two World Wars is being mounted while the work is in progress. Various reference departments, open by appointment only.

☎ 01-735 8922.
Open: all year, daily Mon-Sat 10-5.50, Sun 2-5.50. (Closed: Good Fri, May Day, 24-26 Dec, New Year's Day.)
& Shop ✖ (ex guide dogs)

Tradescant Trust Museum of Garden History
St Mary-at-Lambeth, Lambeth Palace Road.
Plan 1 : C1.

Historic building and newly made period knot garden containing 17th-century plants. Nearby stand the tombs of the John Tradescants (father & son) and Captain Bligh of the 'Bounty'. Temporary exhibitions. Enquiries to: The Tradescant Trust, 74 Coleherne Court, London SW5 0EF.

☎ 01-373 4030.
Open: Mon-Fri, 11-3; Sun 10.30-5. (Closed: From 2nd Sun in Dec to 1st Sun in Mar.)
⚲ & (ground floor & gardens only) Shop

SE3
Rangers House
Chesterfield Walk
Plan 2 : 17 E3.
Suffolk collection of Jacobean and Stuart portraits housed in 18th-century villa, former home of Philip Stanhope, 4th Earl of Chesterfield. Collection contains a set of portraits by William Larkin, among the finest to survive from the Jacobean period and a small collection of Old Masters. Three first floor rooms house the Dolmetsch collection of musical instruments, on loan from the Horniman Museum. Also chamber concerts and poetry readings. Educational programme, holiday projects and workshop.

☎ 01-853 0035.
Open: daily Mar-Oct 10-5; Nov-Feb 10-4. (Closed: Good Fri, Xmas.)
& (ground floor only) Shop ✖

SE5
South London Art Gallery
Peckham Road   *Plan 2 : 18 E3.*
Presents ten exhibitions a year. Exhibits include Victorian paintings and drawings; a small collection of contemporary British art; 20th-century original prints. A collection of topographical paintings and drawings of local subjects.

☎ 01-703 6120.
Open: only when exhibitions are in progress, Tue-Sat 10-6, Sun 3-6.
Shop ✖

SE7
Thames Barrier Centre
Unity Way   *Plan 2 : 19 F3.*
Described by some as the 'Eighth Wonder of the World', the ⅓-mile span barrier built to save London from disastrous flooding is the world's largest movable flood barrier representing an extraordinary feat of British engineering. The nearby exhibition building has displays and an audio-visual programme explaining the flood threat and the construction of the £480 million project. Barrier gates are raised for testing monthly.

☎ 01-854 1373
Open: daily 10.30-5, (Apr-Sep 10.30-6). (Closed: Xmas & New Year's day.)
⚲ (licensed) 🍴 & (ex riverside) Shop ✖ (ex guide dogs)

Thames Barrier, SE7

SE9

Eltham Palace

Plan 2 : 20 F2.

Noted for great hall with remarkable 15th-century hammer-beam roof. An old bridge spans the moat.

☎ 01-859 2112 Ext 255. Advisable to contact Admin Officer before visit. Open: Nov-Mar, Thu & Sun 10.30-4; Apr-Oct, Thu & Sun 10.30-6. Opening arrangements subject to possible alteration. (AM)

Winter Gardens

Avery Hill Park   *Plan 2 : 21 F2.*
Approximately 750 species of tropical and temperate plants can be seen here in cold, temperate and tropical houses, a collection second only to the Royal Botanical Gardens at Kew. Nursery production unit open spring BH weekend. Tennis and putting available.

☎ 01-850 3217. Open: all year Mon-Fri 1-4, Sat, Sun & BH 11-4 (6pm summer). (Closed: 1st Mon each month & 25 Dec.) ♿

SE10

Royal Naval College

Plan 2 : 22 E3.
Group of buildings designed by Webb (late 17th century) and Wren (early 18th century), with additions by Hawksmoor, Vanbrugh and Ripley. Formerly Naval Hospital, becoming College in 1873. Chapel rebuilt in 18th century, and Painted Hall ceiling by Sir James Thornhill.

☎ 01-858 2154. Open: all year (Painted Hall & Chapel only) daily (ex Thu) 2.30-5 (last admission 4.45). (Closed Xmas day.) Shop ✗

SE15

Livesey Museum

682 Old Kent Road

Plan 2 : 23 E3.
Museum displays one major exhibition every year, dealing mainly with Southwark's past and present, including permanent exhibition of Southwark Street furniture.

☎ 01-639 5604. Open: when exhibition is in progress, Mon-Sat 10-5. ✗ ♿ (ground floor only) Shop

SE17

Cuming Museum

155/157 Walworth Road

Plan 2 : 24 D3.
Contains Roman and medieval finds from the suburb of Southwark, south of London Bridge. Examples from the local 'Delft' pottery industry, items associated with Dickens and Michael Faraday (born locally in 1791), the equipment of a family dairy firm which served the neighbourhood for over 150 years. Also a collection relating to London superstitions.

☎ 01-703 3324 Ext 32. Open: all year Mon-Fri 10-5.30 (7pm Thu), Sat 10-5. Shop ✗

SE18

Museum of Artillery in the Rotunda

Repository Road   *Plan 2 : 25 F3.*
Circular structure designed by John Nash, which stood at one time in St James's Park. It contains a very interesting collection of artillery.

☎ 01-856 5533 Ext 385. Open: all year, Apr-Oct, Mon-Fri 12-5, Sat & Sun 1-5; Nov-Mar, Mon-Fri 12-4, Sat & Sun 1-4. (Closed: Good Fri, 24-26 Dec & 1 Jan.) ⌂♿ (ground floor only) Shop

SE23

Horniman Museum

London Road   *Plan 2 : 26 E2.*
Displays from different cultures and large natural history collections including living creatures. Exhibition of musical instruments from all parts of the world. Extensive library and lectures and concerts in spring and autumn. Special exhibitions. Education Centre programmes.

☎ 01-699 2339. Open: all year Mon-Sat 10.30-6, Sun 2-6. (Closed: 24-26 Dec.) ⌂ shop ✗ (ex guide dogs)

SW1

Buckingham Palace — Changing the Guard

Plan 1 : A1.
The forecourt of Buckingham Palace is patrolled by troops from the Brigade of Guards, the Queens personal bodyguard. The Changing of the Guard, a ceremony lasting about half an hour, takes place most mornings and is a very popular and colourful ceremony.

☎ 01-730 3488 (London Tourist Board). Takes place 11.30, subject to alteration (summer daily, winter alternate days).

Houses of Parliament

Plan 1 : C1.
A mid 19th-century building in Gothic style based on a design by Sir Charles Barry with additional detail by Augustus Pugin, the original building having been destroyed by fire in 1834. Two chambers are set either side of a central hall and corridor, the House of Lords to the south and the House of Commons to the north. The clock tower, 320 ft high, contains Big Ben, the hour bell weighing 13½ tons, and the Victoria tower stands

340 ft high. The House of Commons suffered bomb damage in 1941 and a new chamber was constructed to the design of Sir Giles Gilbert Scott and opened in 1950.

☏ 01-219 3090 & 3100.
To gain admission to the Strangers' Galleries join the queue at St Stephens entrance from approx 4.30 pm Mon-Thu, approx 9.30am Fri (House of Commons) or from approx 2.30pm Tue & Wed, from 3pm Thu & occasionally 11am Fri (House of Lords) or by arrangement with MP (House of Commons) or Peer (House of Lords). Free although guides require payment if employed.
♿ (by arrangement) bookstall 🐕 (ex guide dogs)

also **Westminster Hall**
Built 1097-99 by William Rufus, it is the oldest remaining part of Westminster. The glory of the hall is the cantilever or hammerbeam roof, the earliest and largest roof of its kind in existence, built between 1394 and 1401.

☏ 01-219 3090.
Open: Mon-Thu, am by arrangement with an MP only.
Free although guides require payment if employed.
♿ (by arrangement) 🐕 (ex guide dogs)

Tate Gallery
Millbank Plan 2 : **27 D3.**
Opened in 1897 the gallery houses the national collections of British painting of all periods, modern foreign painting and modern sculpture. There is also a large collection of contemporary prints. Hogarth, Blake, Turner, Constable and the Pre-Raphaelites are particularly well-represented in the British Collection and the Modern Collection traces the development of art from Impressionism through postwar European and American art including Abstract Impressionism and Pop, to the present day.

☏ 01-821 1313 & Recorded Information 01-821 7128.
Open: all year Mon-Sat 10-5.50, Sun 2-5.50. (Closed: Good Fri, May Day, 24-26 Dec & 1 Jan.) (Special exhibitions admission charge.) Free lectures, films and guided tours most days.
☕ (licensed) 12-3 (closed Sun) ☕ (coffee shop) ♿ Shop 🐕 (ex guide dogs)

Westminster Cathedral
Ashley Place Plan 1 : **A1.**
The largest and most important Roman Catholic church in England; a Byzantine structure completed in 1903 just seven years after the foundation stone was laid. Built entirely of red brick with contrasting bands of Portland stone, its interior is ornamented with marble and beautiful mosaics.

☏ 01-834 7452.
Open: daily, 7am-8pm. (Donations)

SW3

IBA Broadcasting Gallery
70 Brompton Road
Plan 2 : **28 D3.**
This permanent exhibition recreates nearly a century of television and radio. A multi-screen audio visual presentation shows how ITN covers an important and developing story in the course of a day's news programmes. Different stages of a typical production can be seen in a son et lumiére display. Working exhibition of Victorian parlour entertainment and replicas of experimental models used by pioneers.

☏ 01-584 7011.
Open: Tours, Mon-Fri at 10, 11, 2 & 3 (tours take approx one hour). Children under 16 only allowed access if part of an organised group.

National Army Museum
Royal Hospital Road
Plan 2 : **29 D3.**
Contains a permanent chronological display of the history of the British, Indian and Colonial forces from 1485. Among the exhibits are uniforms, weapons, prints, photographs, manuscripts, letters, glass, china, silver and relics of British commanders and mementoes of Britain's soldiers. There is a special display of the orders and decorations of the Duke of Windsor and also those of five great field marshals — Lords Roberts, Gough, Kitchener and Wolseley and Sir George White VC. The picture gallery includes portraits by Beechy, Romney and Lawrence, battle scenes and pictures of Indian regiments. The reading room is open Tue-Sat 10-4.30 to holders of readers' tickets, obtainable by written application to the Director.

☏ 01-730 0717.
Open: all year Mon-Sat 10-5.30, Sun 2-5.30. (Closed: Good Fri, May Day, 24-26 Dec & 1 Jan)
Lectures etc for school parties.
♿ Shop 🐕

SW7

Geological Museum
Exhibition Road Plan 2 : **30 D3.**
Established at present premises in 1935, the Geological Museum now forms part of the British Museum (Natural

History). Exhibits include a piece of the Moon and the largest exhibition on basic earth science in the world — The Story of the Earth. This is split into four main sections: the Earth in Space, which includes an exhibit showing that an observer 150 million light years away, looking through an immensely powerful telescope, would see dinosaurs roaming around in a Jurassic landscape. The Earth's Interior and Crust; Geological Processes; and Geological Time. There is also a collection of fine gemstones, showing them in their parent rock, in natural crystal form and in their final cut state. The regional geology of Great Britain and ore deposits of the world are also displayed. Other exhibitions are British Fossils, Britain Before Man and Treasures of the Earth (new).

☎ 01-589 3444.
Open: all year Mon-Sat 10-6, Sun 2.30-6. (Closed: Good Fri, May Day, 24-26 Dec & 1 Jan.)
Shop ✗ & (ex mezzanine floor)

Natural History Museum
Cromwell Road   Plan 2 : **31 D3**.
In the Hall of Human Biology visitors can learn more about the way their bodies work, while 'British Natural History' shows over 2,000 of our native plants and animals. A new exhibition 'Whales and their Relatives' explores the life of sea mammals. Other permanent exhibitions include 'Man's Place in Evolution', 'Origin of Species', 'Dinosaurs and their living Relatives' and 'Introducing Ecology'. In other parts of the Museum there are many traditional displays of living and fossil plants and animals, minerals, rocks and

meteorites from the national collections. Exhibits of special interest include a life-size model of a blue whale, the Cranbourne meteorite, a specimen of a coelacanth (a fish known as a living fossil) and the British bird pavilion where visitors can hear recordings of many different bird songs.
Please note: as the museum is currently reorganising its public displays, some of the galleries may be temporarily closed. There are public films and lectures on Tue, Thu and Sat. Leaflet available on request.

☎ 01-589 6323.
Open: daily, Mon-Sat 10-6, Sun 2.30-6. (Closed: Good Fri, May Day, Xmas, New Year's day.)
⌨ & (ex British Natural History Exhibition) Shop ✗

Science Museum
Exhibition Road   Plan 2 : **32 D3**.
Extensive collections, including aero-engines; agriculture; astronomy; atomic and nuclear physics; rail; road; sea and air transport; civil, electrical, marine and mechanical engineering, telecommunications, domestic appliances, 'Gas Industry' gallery, etc. Two galleries with items from the Wellcome Collection of the History of Medicine, galleries on Printing, Paper making and Lighting. Also children's gallery with many working demonstrations: this is always a favourite. A new exhibition on space technology opens mid July 1986. New gallery of Plastics.

☎ 01-589 3456 Ext 632.
Open: daily, Mon-Sat, 10-6, Sun 2.30-6. (Closed: Good Fri, May Day, 24-26 Dec & 1 Jan.)
⌨ & Shop ✗

═══ WEST ═══

W1

Agnew's Galleries
43 Old Bond Street   Plan 1 : **A3**.
London galleries established in 1860 as expansion of the Vittore Zanetti art business which originated in Manchester. Thomas Agnew, who entered the business in 1817, later became a partner. In 1932 a limited company, Thomas Agnew and Sons, was formed. Annual exhibitions include a water-colour exhibition devoted to English watercolours and drawings of the 18th and 19th centuries in Jan & Feb, and a selling exhibition of Old Master paintings from the 14th to 19th centuries. There are also exhibitions of French and English drawings from c.1800 to the present day, work by English painters of this century and loan exhibitions in aid of charity. Many works pass through Agnew's on their way to famous art galleries and museums.

☎ 01-629 6176.
Open: all year Mon-Fri, 9.30-5.30 (6.30pm Thu, during major exhibitions). (Closed BH.)
& Admission charge for some loan exhibitions.

Museum of Mankind
6 Burlington Gardens
Plan 1 : **A3**.
Houses the exhibitions, library and offices of the ethnography department of the British Museum. Its collections embrace the art and material culture of tribal, village and other pre-industrial societies, from most areas of the world excluding Western Europe. Also archaeological collections from the Americas and Africa. A few important pieces are on permanent exhibition, but the

museum's policy is to mount a number of temporary exhibitions usually lasting for at least a year. A separate store in Shoreditch contains the reserve collection which can be made available for serious study by arrangement. Film shows and educational services also available.

☎ 01-437 2224 Ext 43.
Open: all year Mon-Sat 10-5, Sun 2.30-6. (Closed: Good Fri, May Day, 24-27 Dec & 1 Jan.)
Shop ✸ (ex guide dogs)

Wallace Collection
Hertford House,
Manchester Sq   *Plan 2 : 33 D4.*
An outstanding collection of works of art bequeathed to the nation by Lady Wallace in 1897, displayed in the house of its founders. Includes pictures by Titian, Rubens, Gainsborough and Delacroix together with an unrivalled representation of 18th-century French art including paintings, especially of Watteau, Boucher and Fragonard, sculpture, furniture, goldsmiths' work and Sèvres porcelain. Also valuable collections of majolica, European and oriental arms and armour.

☎ 01-935 0687.
Open: all year Mon-Sat 10-5, Sun 2-5. (Closed: Good Fri, May Day, 24-26 Dec & 1 Jan.)
&. Shop ✸

W3

Gunnersbury Park Museum
Popes Lane   *Plan 2 : 34 B3.*
Early 19th-century former Rothschild mansion, in fine park, now museum of local interest for the London Borough of Ealing and Hounslow showing archaeological discoveries, transport items,

costume and topographical and social material. Rothschild coaches on display. Rothschild Victorian kitchens open to public on certain summer weekends. Changing exhibitions. Crafts shows.

☎ 01-992 1612.
Open: Mar-Oct (end of British Summer Time) Mon-Fri 1-5, Sat, Sun & BH 2-6; Nov-Feb, Mon-Fri 1-4, Sat, Sun & BH 2-4. (Closed: Good Fri & 24-26 Dec.)
&. (ground floor only) Shop Nursery ✸

W4

Hogarth's House
Hogarth Lane,
Great West Road
Plan 2 : 35 C3.
17th-century house where Hogarth lived for 15 years, with engravings, drawings and other relics.

☎ 01-994 6757.
Open: all year Mon, Wed-Sat 11-6, Sun 2-6 (4pm Oct-Mar). (Closed: Tue & Good Fri, 1st two weeks Sep, last 3 weeks Dec & New Year's Day.)

W8

Commonwealth Institute
Kensington High Street
Plan 2 : 36 C3.
Contains over 40 exhibitions depicting life in the countries of the Commonwealth. Library, art gallery, Arts Centre.

☎ 01-603 4535.
Open: Mon-Sat 10-5.30, Sun 2-5. (Closed: Good Fri, May Day, 24-26 Dec & 1 Jan.)
Special exhibitions admission charge.
🍴 (licensed) &. Shop ✸

W14

Leighton House
12 Holland Park Road
Plan 2 : 37 C3.
Leighton House is a uniquely

opulent and exotic example of High Victorian taste. Built for the President of the Royal Academy, Frederic, Lord Leighton, by George Aitchison, the main body of the house was completed in 1866. The fabulous Arab Hall, with its rare middle-eastern tiles, fountain and gilded decoration, is a 19th-century Arabian Nights' creation finished in 1879. Fine Victorian paintings by Lord Leighton and his contemporaries hang in the rooms, and there are three galleries for exhibitions of modern and historic art. The quiet garden is ornamented with Lord Leighton's sculpture.

☎ 01-602 3316.
Open: all year, Mon-Sat 10-5 (6pm during temporary exhibitions). (Closed BH.)
Garden open Apr-Sep 11-5.
🚻 &. (ground floor) ✸

WC1

British Museum
Great Russell Street
Plan 1 : B4.
Founded in 1753, one of the great museums, showing the works of man from all over the world from prehistoric to comparatively modern times. The galleries are the responsibility of the following departments: Egyptian; Greek and Roman; Western Asiatic; Prehistoric and Romano-British; Medieval and Later; Coins and Medals; Oriental; Prints and drawings. Each year, special exhibitions focus more detailed attention on certain aspects of the collections. Programmes on request. Gallery talks (Mon-Sat) Lectures (Tue-Sat) and Films (Tue-Fri). Children's trail at all times.

☎ 01-636 1555.
Open: all year, Mon-Sat 10-5, Sun 2.30-6. (Closed:

National Portrait Gallery

Good Fri, May Day, 24-26 Dec & 1 Jan.)
🍽 (licensed) & Shop
✠ (ex guide dogs)

Jewish Museum
Woburn House, Tavistock Square
Plan 1 : B5.
Opened in 1932, a museum of ritual and domestic arts and antiques. Many of the interesting variety of items relate to Anglo-Jewish history dating from the 13th century.

☎ 01-388 4525.
Open: Tue-Fri 10-4; Sun 10-12.45. (Closed: Jewish & PH.)

Percival David Foundation of Chinese Art
53 Gordon Square *Plan 1 : B5.*
A unique collection of Chinese ceramics, dating from between the 10th and 18th centuries, the Sung, Yuan, Ming and Ch'ing dynasties. Presented to London University by Percival David in 1951.

☎ 01-387 3909.
Open: Mon, 2-5, Tue-Fri 10.30-5, Sat 10.30-1.

WC2

Africa Centre
King Street *Plan 1 : C3.*
The centre is a charity and of particular interest to those who wish to learn more about African culture. For those who wish to browse there are displays of paintings, photographs and craftware by African artists.

☎ 01-836 1973.
Open: Mon-Fri 9.30-5.30, Sat 10-4.

British Crafts Centre
43 Earlham Street *Plan 1 : C4.*
Programme of special exhibitions and retail display including wallhangings, furniture, studio ceramics, pottery, wood, jewellery etc; books and magazines for craft and design.

☎ 01-836 6993.
Open: all year, Mon-Fri 10-5.30, Sat 11-5. (Closed: Sun & BH.)
& (ground floor only) ✠

London Silver Vaults
Chancery Lane *Plan 1 : D4.*
Fine collection of antiques and modern silverware in an underground location. Visitors can browse and traders are happy to talk about their wares, look up hallmarks and explain histories.

☎ 01-242 3844.
Open: Mon-Fri, 9-5.30, Sat 9-12.30.

National Gallery
Trafalgar Square *Plan 1 : B3.*
Founded by vote of Parliament in 1824, but was first opened in the present building in 1838. The gallery houses the national collection of masterpieces of European paintings from the 13th to 19th century. Collection includes van Eyck's Arnolfini Marri-

age, Velazquez's The Toilet of Venus, Leonardo da Vinci's cartoon 'The Virgin and the Child with SS Anne and John the Baptist', Rembrandt's Belshazzar's Feast, Titian's Bacchus and Ariadne, and many more. Lunchtime lectures and guided tours daily; quizzes and worksheets available for children. Constantly changing programme of exhibitions, usually highlighting certain aspects of the collection.

☎ 01-839 3321 & recorded information: 01-839 3526.
Open: daily Mon-Sat 10-6, Sun 2-6. (Closed: Good Fri, May Day, Xmas period & 1 Jan.)
🍽 (licensed) & Shop ✠

National Portrait Gallery
2 St Martin's Place
Plan 1 : B3.
Contains national collection of portraits of the famous and infamous in British history, including paintings, sculpture, miniatures, engravings, photographs, and cartoons. Special exhibitions several times a year.

☎ 01-930 1552.
Open: all year Mon-Fri 10-5, Sat 10-6, Sun 2-6. (Closed: Good Fri, May Day, 24-26 Dec & 1 Jan.)
(Charges for special exhibitions).
Shop ✠

Public Record Office Museum
Chancery Lane *Plan 1 : D4.*
The Public Record Office contains records of central government dating from the Norman Conquest to the present day. The museum contains a small selection of the several million separate documents kept in the Office including the Domesday Book, Shakespeare's will,

various royal letters and other documents.

☎ 01-405 3488 Ext 475
Open: Mon-Fri 1-4 (ex official holidays). Parties at other times by arrangement.
Shop ✺

St Paul's Church
Covent Garden   Plan 1 : C3.
The first new Anglican church to be built in London after the Reformation, St Pauls was designed by Inigo Jones for the 4th Earl of Bedford, between 1631 and 1633. It has long associations with the theatre since both the Theatre Royal, Drury Lane and the Royal Opera House are in the parish. Amongst the famous buried here are Claude Duval the highwayman, Grinling Gibbons, Thomas Arne, composer of *Rule Brittania*, and the actress Vivien Leigh. J. M. W. Turner was baptised here.

☎ 01-836 5221.
Open: Mon-Fri 9.30-4.30.

Sir John Soane's Museum
13 Lincoln's Inn Fields.
Plan 1 : C4.
The house of Sir John Soane (1753-1837), the architect, built in 1812 and containing his collections of antiquities, sculpture, paintings, drawings, and books, including the

Sarcophagus of Seti I (1292 BC). The Rake's Progress and the Election series of paintings by William Hogarth. Architectural Drawings Collection open by appointment.

☎ 01-405 2107.
Open: all year Tue-Sat 10-5. (Closed BH.)
& (ground floor only) ✺

LOWESTOFT
Suffolk   Map 5 TM59.
Royal Naval Patrol Service Association (Naval Museum)
Sparrows Nest Gardens
The museum includes collections of hundreds of photographs from World War II, models of minesweepers and naval ships, war relics, war medals, naval uniforms and the 'Victoria Cross' room.

☎ (0502) 86250.
Open: daily Etr BH & May-Oct, 10-12 & 2-4.30. Coach parties by appointment.
⌂ (licensed) & (ground floor only) Shop

LUDGERSHALL
Wiltshire   Map 4 SU25.
Ludgershall Castle
(7m NW of Andover on A342)
Norman motte and bailey castle with large earthworks and flint walling of later royal castle.

Open: at all reasonable times.
(AM) & (part of site only)

LUTON
Bedfordshire   Map 4 TL02.
Museum and Art Gallery
Wardown Park
Collections illustrate natural history, culture, and industries of Luton and Bedfordshire with particular reference to straw hat and pillow lace trade. 'Luton Life' gallery includes a reconstructed street display.

☎ (0582) 36941.
Open: daily, Mon-Sat 10.30-5, Sun 1.30-6 (1.30-5 in winter). (Closed: Sun Dec-Jan, Xmas & New Year's day.)
& (ground floor only) Shop ✺

LYDFORD
Devon   Map 2 SX58.
Lydford Castle
Midway between Okehampton & Tavistock off A386
Remains of mid 12th-century stone keep, altered a century later. The lower floor was once a prison and the upper floor became Stannary Court, established to administer local tin mines.

Open: at all reasonable times.
(AM)

LYDIARD PARK
Wiltshire   *Map 4 SU18.*
(1m N of M4 (junc 16) on unclass road)
Fine Georgian mansion set in pleasant park, together with the adjoining parish church of St Mary, which contains memorials to the St John family.

☎ Swindon (0793) 770401.
Open: daily, Mon-Fri 10-1 & 2-5.30, Sun 2-5.30. (Closed: Good Fri & Xmas.)
🚗 🚌 ♿ Shop ✕

LYTHAM ST ANNES
Lancashire   *Map 7 SD32.*
Premium Bonds Office, ERNIE
Moorland Road
Talk and film on ERNIE (Electronic Random Number Indicator Equipment).

☎ (0253) 721212.
Open: tours Mon-Thu 1.45.
🚗 ✕

MACCLESFIELD
Cheshire   *Map 7 SJ79.*
Macclesfield Museum and Art Gallery
West Park, Prestbury Road
Contains a notable collection of Egyptian antiquities, oil paintings and sketches including work by CF Tunnicliffe ARA and Landseer, and drawings and prints of a topographical nature. Also a small silk exhibition and a stuffed Giant Panda.

☎ (0625) 24067.
Open: Etr Sat-Sep, Tue-Sun 2-4.30; Oct-Sat before Etr, Sat & Sun & BH 2-4.30.
✕

MADRON
Cornwall   *Map 2 SW43.*
Lanyon Quiot
(2m NW on unclass Road)
One of the best examples of a megalithic tomb in Britain dating from between 2000-1600 BC: a large granite slab

18 inches thick, almost 9ft wide and 17ft long balanced on three upright stones.

Open: accessible at all reasonable times. (NT).

MAIDENHEAD
Berkshire   *Map 4 SU88.*
Henry Reitlinger Bequest
Oldfield, Guards Club Road
Collection of pottery, sculpture, paintings, drawings, ceramics and glass.

☎ (0628) 21818.
Open: Apr-Sep, Tue & Thu 10-12.30 & 2.15-4.30, first Sun in each month 2.30-4.30. Other times by prior arrangement in writing.
♿ (ground floor only) ✕.

MAIDSTONE
Kent   *Map 5 TQ75.*
Museum and Art Gallery
Chillington Manor, St Faith's Street
Rebuilt in 1562 with medieval wing brought from East Farleigh. Now museum and art gallery, containing Japanese room, Anglo-Saxon jewellery, glass and volume II of the Lambeth Byelaw circa 1170. Exhibitions by local and national artists. Includes Museum of Royal West Kent Regiment.

☎ (0622) 54497.
Open: all year, Mon-Sat 10-5.30. (Closed BH) During rebuilding some galleries may be closed.
✕

MALHAM
North Yorkshire   *Map 7 SD86.*
Yorkshire Dales National Park Centre
Visitor Centre with interpretative display and audiovisual theatre for group use. Maps, walks, guides and other information are all available.

☎ Airton (07293) 363.
Open: daily Apr-Oct. Mid morning to late afternoon.
♿

MANCHESTER
Gt Manchester   *Map 7 SJ89.*
City Art Gallery
Mosley Street   *Plan : D4.*
A sumptuous display of the city's treasures in an architectural masterpiece of the Greek Revival. Paintings by the Old Master, Stubbs, Gainsborough, Turner, and the Pre-Raphaelites. Outstanding collections of decorative arts, furniture, and sculpture.

☎ 061-236 9422.
Open: daily Mon-Sat 10-6, Sun 2-6.
✕ Shop

Fletcher Moss Art Gallery
Stenner Lane, off Wilmslow Road, Didsbury (5½m S of city off A5145) *Not on plan*
Small gallery, set in the botanical gardens, and devoted to the story of Manchester. Old maps, paintings and drawings illustrate the City's meteoric rise. Also an important collection of paintings by A Valette and L S Lowry.

☎ 061-236 9422.
Open: Apr-Sept, Mon, Wed-Sat 10-6, Sun 2-6.
✕ ♿ (ground floor only).

Fletcher Moss Botanical Gardens
Wilmslow Road, Didsbury, (5½m S of city on A5145) *Not on plan.*
The park was presented to the city early this century and has been transformed into beautiful botanical gardens. Because of its sheltered position the rock garden can grow Alpine, dwarf and other unusual plants. In addition there are conifers, rhododendrons, many rare shrubs and plants, an orchid house

and wild garden.

☎ 061-434 1877.
Open: daily, 7.45-dusk.
☞ (closed Tue & Sat) ♿

Gallery of English Costume
Platt Fields, Rusholme, (2m SE of city) Not on plan
Famous costume collection displaying the changing styles of everyday clothes and accessories of the last 400 years or more, including contemporary fashion. The costume library is available to students engaged in research on request.

☎ 061-224 5217.
Open: daily (ex Tue) 10-6, Sun 2-6, Nov-Feb closes 4pm.
♿ (ground floor only) Shop ✻

Gallery of Modern Art
Athenaeum, Princess Street Plan : **D4.**
Modern British and European painting, sculpture, prints, and decorative art, from Sickert to Hockney. Often replaced by temporary exhibitions.

☎ 061-236 9422.
Open: daily Mon-Sat 10-6, Sun 2-6.
Shop ✻

Greater Manchester Museum of Science & Industry
Liverpool Road Station, Castlefield Plan : **B4.**
Steam and internal-combustion machine tools, electrical exhibits, paper-making, printing and textile machinery and optical equipment among other exhibits. Stationary mill engines etc regularly demonstrated. Static display of railway locomotives and rolling stock. Bookshop.

☎ 061-832 2244 for museum.
Open: daily 10.30-5.
(Closed Xmas.) Children under 11 only admitted if accompanied by an adult.
☞ licensed ♿ Shop ✻

Greater Manchester Police Museum
Newton Street Plan : **F5.**
Occupying the old Newton Street police station, built in 1879. The ground floor displays a reconstructed 1920s charge room and cell corridor. The first floor has police uniforms and equipment, a forger's den and a photographic gallery.

☎ 061-855 3290.
Open: daily Mon-Fri 9.30-3 (by appointment only).
✻

John Rylands University Library of Manchester
Deansgate Plan : **C4.**
Famous library, dating from 1851, containing over 3 million books, 17,000 manuscripts, extensive archival collections and c 600,000 title in microform. Rare books division in the architecturally distinguished Rylands memorial building in Deansgate, holds regular exhibitions and lectures.

☎ 061-834 5343.
Open: daily Mon-Fri 10-5.30, Sat 10-1. (Closed BH & Xmas-New Year.)
✻

Manchester Museum
The University, Oxford Road. (1m SE of city) Not on plan
Contains exhibits of archaeology and natural history including an extensive collection from Ancient Egypt, rocks, minerals, fossils, coins and native craftsmanship and huge study collections of over 8

million specimens. Frequent temporary exhibitions, and lectures.

☎ 061-273 3333.
Open: daily Mon-Sat 10-5. (Closed Good Fri, May Day & Xmas-New Year.)
♿ Shop ✻

Whitworth Art Gallery
University of Manchester, Whitworth Park (1½m SE of city) Not on plan
Founded in 1889 by Royal Charter. The principal collections are British watercolours including work by Blake, Turner, the Pre-Raphaelites and 1939-45 War Artists; Continental water-colours including works by Cézanne, Van Gogh and Picasso; Old Master drawings and prints, including examples by leading Renaissance masters such as Pollaiuolo, Mantegna and Dürer, and fine collection of Japanese prints; textiles, including the Whitworth Tapestry, designed by Paolozzi in 1968; historic wall-papers; and contemporary works of art. Frequent special exhibitions.

☎ 061-273 4865.
Open: daily Mon-Sat 10-5 (Thu until 9pm).
(Closed: Good Fri & Xmas to New Year.)
☞ (licensed) ♿ Shop ✻ (ex guide dogs).

Wythenshawe Horticultural Centre
Wythenshawe Park, Northendon (5½m S of city, off A5103) Not on plan
The 5½ acre centre provides a splendid all year round display of plants, much of which is used for the parks and gardens throughout the city. The extensive glasshouses contain the Tropical House with pineapples, oranges and bananas while

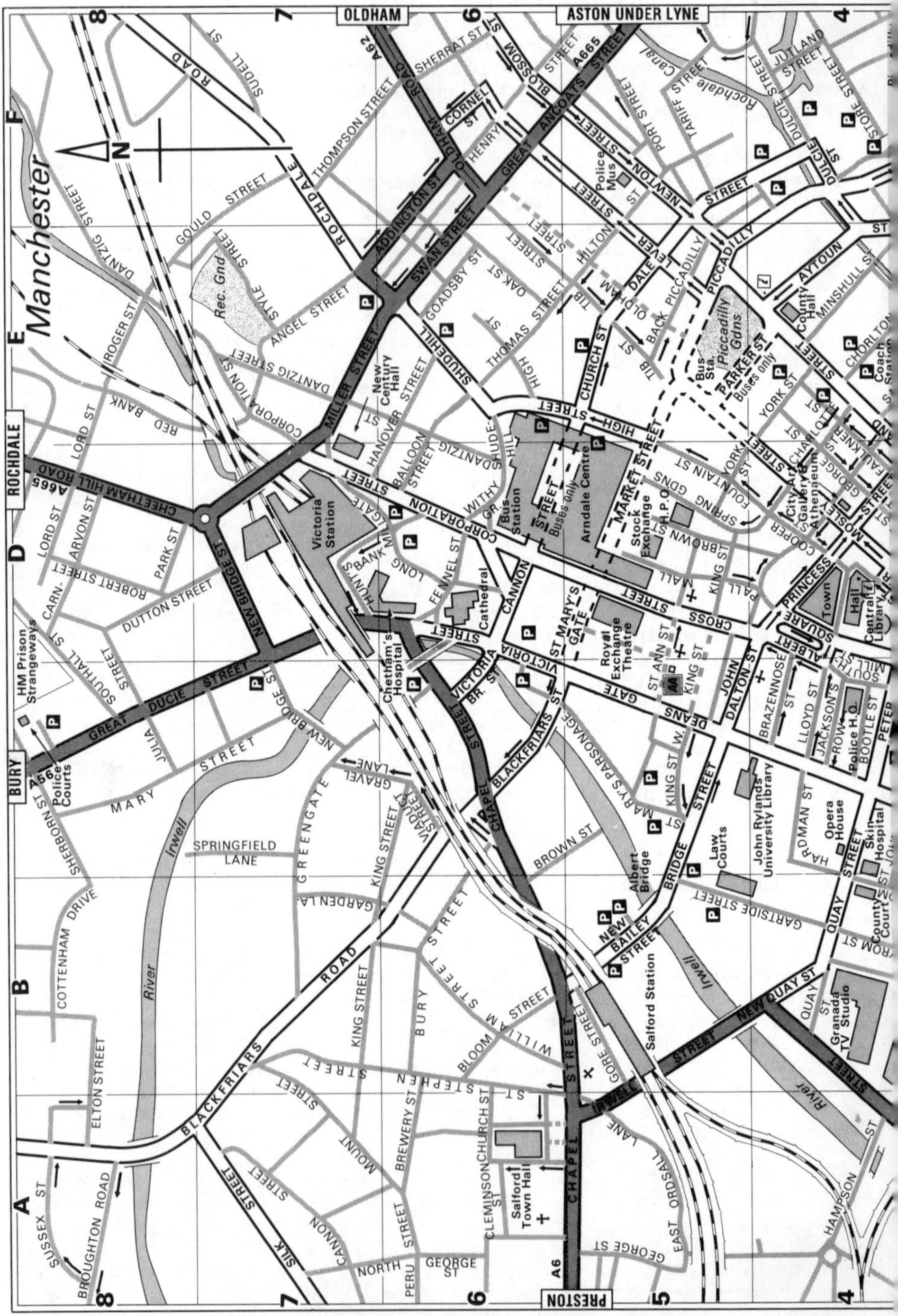

Manchester

N

OLDHAM
ASTON UNDER LYNE
A62
A665
ROCHDALE
BURY
ROCHDALE HILL ROAD
A665
A6
PRESTON

SHERRAT ST
CORNEL
BLOSSOM ST
NEWTON STREET
GREAT ANCOATS STREET
Rochdale Canal
PORTUGAL STREET
TARIFF STREET
DULCIE STREET
PORTLAND STREET

Police
Mus
PICCADILLY
Piccadilly
Gdns
Bus
Sta
Buses only

THOMPSON STREET
ROCHDALE ROAD
SUDELL STREET
GOULD STREET
STYLE STREET
DANZIG STREET
Rec. Gnd
ANGEL STREET
DANZIG STREET
ADDINGTON STREET
SWAN ST
OLDHAM STREET
HENRY STREET
GREAT ANCOATS STREET
BOLTON STREET
LEVER STREET

New
Century
Hall
MILLER STREET
HANOVER STREET
BALLOON STREET
CORPORATION STREET
SHUDEHILL
GOADSBY ST
OAK ST
THOMAS STREET
HIGH STREET
CHURCH ST
HIGH STREET
OLDHAM ST
DALE ST
BACK PICCADILLY
PICCADILLY
County
Hall
Coach
Station
Chorlton
AYTOUN ST
MINSHULL ST
YORK ST
PARKER ST

Victoria
Station
RED BANK
CHEETHAM HILL ROAD
DANZIG STREET
HANGING DITCH
WITHY GROVE
MARKET STREET
Arndale
Centre
Bus
Station
Stock
Exchange
H.P.O.
SPRING GDNS
BROWN STREET
FOUNTAIN ST
MARKET STREET
City
Art Gallery
Athenaeum
COOPER ST
PRINCESS STREET
FAULKNER ST
GEORGE ST

ROGER ST
LORD ST
ARVON ST
LORD ST
CARN.
PARK ST
ROBERT STREET
DUTTON STREET
NEW BRIDGE STREET
Cathedral
LONG MILLGATE
FENNEL ST
HUNTS BANK
VICTORIA STREET
CANNON STREET
CROSS STREET
ST MARY'S GATE
KING ST
PALL MALL
Town
Hall
Central
Library
Hall
St
Peter

HM Prison
Strangeways
SOUTHALL STREET
JULIA STREET
GREAT DUCIE STREET
NEW BRIDGE STREET
Chetham's
Hospital
VICTORIA BR
DEANSGATE
ST ANN ST
KING ST
Royal
Exchange
Theatre
JOHN DALTON ST
BRAZENNOSE ST
LLOYD ST
JACKSONS
ROW
Police H.Q.
BOOTLE ST

Police
Courts
SHERBORN ST
MARY STREET
GRAVEL LANE
GREENGATE
CHAPEL STREET
ST MARY'S PARSONAGE
KING ST W
BLACKFRIARS ST
Opera
House
Skin
Hospital
ROMAN ST
DEANSGATE
John Rylands
University Library
SPRINGFIELD
LANE
KING STREET
WATER STREET
BROWN ST
Albert
Bridge
Law
Courts
BRIDGE STREET
NEW BAILEY STREET
GARTSIDE STREET
QUAY ST

COTTENHAM DRIVE
River Irwell
GARDEN LA
KING STREET
BURY STREET
WILLIAM STREET
BLOOM ST
Salford Station
Irwell
QUAY ST
NEW QUAY ST
QUAY ST
Granada
TV Studio
River

ELTON STREET
BLACKFRIARS ROAD
MOUNT STREET
BREWERY ST
STEPHEN STREET
CHURCH ST
Salford
Town Hall
CLEMINSON ST
CHAPEL STREET
GORE STREET
EAST ORDSALL LANE
HAMISON

SUSSEX ST
BROUGHTON ROAD
CANNON STREET
NORTH ST
PERU STREET
GEORGE ST
GEORGE ST

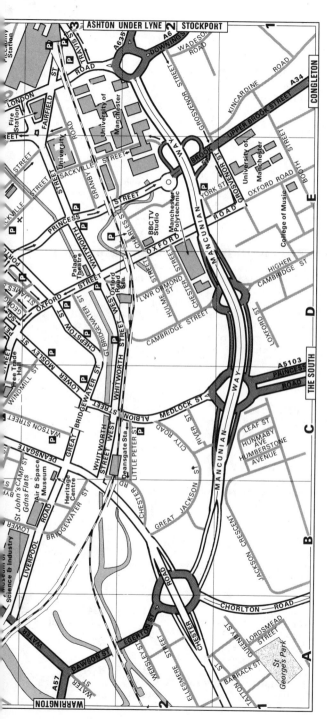

the Cactus House contains the
Charles Darrah collection.

☎ 061-945 1768.
Open: daily 10-4 (no plants
for sale).
✉

MANSFIELD
Nottinghamshire   Map 8 SK55.
Museum & Art Gallery
Leeming Street
New display of William Bil-
lingsley porcelain, lustreware
and Wedgwood. Water-
colours of old Mansfield.
Many temporary exhibitions.
There is also a natural history
gallery.

☎ (0623) 22561 & 646604.
Open: daily Mon-Fri 10-5 &
Sat 10-1 & 2-5.
♿ Shop ✉

MARKET
HARBOROUGH
Leicestershire   Map 4 SP79.
Harborough Museum
*Council Offices, Adam &
Eve Street*
Museum illustrating the long
history of the Harborough
area, particularly the town's
role as a marketing and social
focus, hunting centre and
mediaeval planned town.

☎ (0858) 32468.
Open: daily Mon-Sat
10-4.30, Sun 2-5.
(Closed: Good Fri & Xmas.)
♿ (Sat, Sun & BH by
arrangement)
Shop ✉

MARSDEN
West Yorkshire   Map 7 SE01.
**Tunnel End Canal Museum
& Countryside Centre**
Reddisher Road
Displays on the history of
canals, housed in the former
tunnel keeper's cottage at the
entrance to the Standedge
Tunnel on the Huddersfield
Narrow Canal. Also an inter-
pretative centre devoted to

this part of the Pennines.

☎ Huddersfield
(0484) 846062.
Open: Tue-Sun 11-4; Etr-Oct
11-5.
⊼ ⌷ (Sun) ✗ (in museum).

MARYPARK
Grampian (Banffshire)   Map 15 NJ13.
Glenfarcias Distillery
(1m W)
One of the finest Highland
Malt whiskies is produced
here. There is an exhibition,
museum, craft shop and
visitor centre. Museum and
exhibition now in French,
German and Swedish.

☎ Ballindalloch (08072) 257.
Open: all year Mon-Fri
9-4.30; Jul-Sep also Sat 10-4.
(Closed: 25 Dec & 1 & 2
Jan.)
& (ground floor only) Shop

MARYPORT
Cumbria   Map 11 NY03.
Maritime Museum
*Shipping Brow, 1 Senhouse
Street.*
Material of local and general
maritime interest. Photo-
graphic display illustrating
Maryport's history.

☎ (090081) 3738.
Open: Etr-Sep; Mon, Tue,
Thu-Sat 10-12 & 2-4. Also
Sun 2-4.30.
Shop ✗

MELROSE
Borders (Roxburghshire)
Map 12 NT53.
Priorwood Garden
Special garden with flowers
for drying. Visitor centre
adjacent to Melrose Abbey
and 'Apples through the
Ages' orchard walk.

☎ (089682) 2555.
Open: Apr & 1 Nov-24 Dec,
Mon-Sat 10-1 & 2-5.30; May-
Jun & Oct, Mon-Sat 10-5.30,
Sun 1.30-5.30; July-Sep,

Mon-Sat 10-6, Sun 1.30-5.30.
Donations.
(NTS)

MELTON MOWBRAY
Leicestershire   Map 8 SK71.
Melton Carnegie Museum
Thorpe End
Museum illustrating past and
present life of the area.

☎ (0664) 69946.
Open: Etr-Sep, Mon-Sat
10-5, Sun 2-5; Oct-Etr, Mon-
Fri 10-4.30, Sat 10.30-4.
(Closed: 1 Jan, Good Fri &
25-26 Dec.)
Shop ✗

MENAI BRIDGE
Gwynedd   Map 6 SH57.
Tegfryn Art Gallery
Cadnant Road
A private gallery, standing in
its own pleasant grounds near
to shores of the Menai Straits.
Exhibition of paintings by
contemporary and prominent
artists including many from
North Wales. Pictures may
be purchased.

☎ (0248) 712437.
Open: daily 10-1 & 2-5
(Closed: Mon Oct-Etr).
& (ground floor only)

MERTHYR TYDFIL
Mid Glamorgan   Map 3 SO00.
Garwnant Forest Centre
*(5m N of Merthyr Tydfil off
A470)*
A focal point for the many
forest facilities in the Brecon
Beacons, with displays on the
farming, water supply and
forestry of the valleys. Trails
and adventure play area.

☎ (0685) 3060.
Open: Etr-Sep, Mon-Fri,
10.30-4.45, BH 12-6.
Weekends Apr, Sat & Sun
2-4, May & Sep 2-5, Jun 2-6 &
Jul & Aug 1-6.
Other time, telephone for
details.
Party ⊼ Shop.

Joseph Parry's Cottage
4 Chapel Row
Birthplace of musician and
composer Joseph Parry. Exhibition of his life and works and
display of momentoes of
Welsh male voice choirs.
Open air museum with ex-
cavated section of Glamor-
ganshire Canal and exhibits
illustrating local industrial
and social history.

☎ (0685) 73117.
Open: Jun-Aug Mon-Fri;
Sep-May Mon, Wed & Fri
1.30-4.30. (Closed BH.)
Shop.

MIDDLESBROUGH
Cleveland   Map 8 NZ42.
Dorman Museum
Linthorpe Road
Displays of local, social, industrial and natural history. A
permanent display of re-
gional and Linthorpe pottery
together with a regular varied
programme of temporary
exhibitions.

☎ (0642) 813781.
Open: Mon-Fri 10-6, Sat
10-5. (Closed: Xmas Day.)
& (ground floor only) Shop
✗

MILLPORT
*Great Cumbrae Island, Strathclyde
(Bute)   Map 10 NS15.*
Museum of the Cumbraes
Garrison House
The museum tells the story of
life on and around the Cumbraes and features many old
photographs, including some
of steamers which achieved
fame on the Millport run.

☎ (0475) 530741.
Open: Jun-Sep Tue-Sat
10-4.30
&

MILNATHORT
Tayside (Kinross-shire) Map 11 NO10.
Burleigh Castle
A 16th-century tower house,

with a courtyard enclosure and roofed angle tower, dating from 1582.

Open: see page 4 Application to key keeper. (AM).

MILNGAVIE
Strathclyde, (Dunbartonshire)
Map 11 NS57.
Lillie Art Gallery
Station Road
A permanent collection of 20th-century Scottish paintings are included in this modern purpose built art gallery. There are also displays of sculpture and ceramics, and temporary exhibitions of contemporary art.

☎ Glasgow 041-956 2351. Open: all year, Tue-Fri 11-5 & 7-9, Sat, Sun 2-5. ⅃ ✘

MINSTER-IN-THANET
Kent
Map 5 TR36.
Minster Abbey
One of the oldest inhabited houses in Kent with some 11th-century work. Now home of a religious order.

☎ Thanet (0843) 821254. Open: all year, May-Oct, Mon-Fri, 11-12 & 2-4.30, Sat 11-12 & 3.30-5; Oct-Apr, Mon-Sat 11-12. Donations (alms box) ⅃ Shop

MINTLAW
Grampian (Aberdeenshire)
Map 15 NK04.
Aden Country Park
(1m W Mintlaw off A950)
230 acres of beautiful woodland set in open farmland. The grounds of a former estate, the Park is the home of many varieties of plants and animals which can be explored by a network of footpaths including a specially developed nature trail. The semi-circular farm steading is

now home to the North East of Scotland Hertitage Centre, providing an experience of estate life in the 1920s. Craft Workshops.

☎ (07712) 2857. Park open: all year. Buildings open: mid May-Sep, 12-6. ⅃ (Table licence) (May-Sep) ⅃ ⅃ (ground floor gardens only) Shop ✘

MISTLEY
Essex
Map 5 TM13.
Mistley Towers
Twin, square porticoed towers, remaining features of church erected originally by Robert Adam c 1776. A hall was built at about the same time of which only the Adam Lodges constructed in 1782 still stand.

Open: towers accessible at all reasonalble times. ⅃ (exterior only) (AM)

MOEL FAMAU
Clwyd
Map 7 SJ16.
Moel Famau Country Park
(3½m NE of Ruthin. N of unclassified road between Loggerheads and Llanbedr-Dyffryn-Clwyd
The country park is situated on the Clwydian Range and includes the highest summit, Moel Famau 1817ft. From here there are excellent views stretching from Snowdonia to Liverpool and beyond. A tower was planned for the summit to mark George III's golden jubilee but never reached its full intended height and collapsed during a storm in 1862. The easter slope of Moel Famau has a forest rich in wood-loving birds. There is a forest trail.

Open: accessible at all reasonalble times. ⅃

MOFFAT
Dumfries and Galloway (Dumfrieshire)
Map 11 NT00.
Ladyknowe Mill
Small mill where visitors can see garments being made. Showroom for the sale of woollens, tweeds and tartans.

☎ (0683) 20134. Open: daily May-Oct 8.30-5.30; Nov-Apr 10-4. ⅃ (licensed) Shop ✘

MONMOUTH
Gwent
Map 3 SO51.
The Kymin
(1¾m E off A4136)
This 800ft vantage point has views of nine counties. The hilltop is crowned by a Naval temple built in 1800 in commemoration of Britain's victories at sea and decorated with plaques commemorating fifteen admirals and their most famous battles.

Open: accessible at all reasonable times. (NT)

MONTGOMERY
Powys
Map 7 SO29.
Montgomery Castle
Overlooking the small town of Montgomery, the castle was built by Henry III about 1223 on the site of an earlier Norman motte and bailey. For a time it was the home of the powerful Marcher family of Mortimer and the Herberts and it was here that the poet George Herbert was born in 1593. Assaults by Parliamentaries during the Civil War in 1644 left the castle in ruins.

Open: accessible at all reasonable times. (AM)

MONTROSE
Tayside (Angus)
Map 15 NO75.
Montrose Museum and Art Gallery
Extensive collections cover-

ing local history from prehistoric times including the maritime history of the port, the Natural History of Angus and local arts.

☎ (0674) 73232.
Open: Apr-Oct, Mon-Sat 10.30-1 & 2-5, Sun (Jul & Aug only) 2-5; Nov-Mar, Mon-Fri 2-5, Sat 10.30-1 & 2-5.
& (ground floor only) Shop ✷ (ex guide dogs).

MORECAMBE
Lancashire   *Map 7 SD46.*
Morecambe Bay Nature Reserve
Hest Bank (2½m NE on A5105)
Morecambe Bay contains the largest area of tidal sand in the British Isles, a feeding ground for thousands of birds which can be seen at high tide on the 6000 acre RSPB reserve at West Bank. Waders, dunlins, oyster-catchers, curlews, ringed plovers, redshanks and bar tailed godwits are amongst the birds easily observed. Further north, there is a vast area of salt marsh backed by limestone cliffs. **Warning:** the advancing tide races across the sands and water channels are filled with deep water within minutes. There is an infomation centre at Hest Bank (west side of level crossing).

☎ (0524) 701601.
Open: Nature Reserve: accessible at all reasonable times. Information Centre & Shop: Apr-Sep Sat, Sun, Wed, Thu 10-5; Oct Sat, Sun, Wed 10-5.

MORCOMBELAKE
Dorset   *Map 3 SY49.*
S. Moores, Biscuit Factory
Biscuits have been made in Morcombelake since 1880 and daily output here now runs at about 60,000 biscuits.

Baking takes place during the morning and this is the best viewing time.

☎ Chideock (029 789) 253.
Open: all year Mon-Fri 9-5. Shop.

MORETON CORBET
Shropshire   *Map 7 SJ52.*
Castle
Triangular group comprising keep of c 1200, gatehouse altered in 1579, and notable Elizabethan range of the same date, all damaged by Parliamentary forces in 1644.

Open: at all reasonable times.
(AM) &

MOSTYN
Clwyd   *Map 6 SJ18.*
Art Gallery
12 Vaughn Street
This Art Gallery re-opened in 1979 and is housed in a building originally built as an art gallery by Lady Augusta Mostyn. Each year there is a series of temporary exhibitions together with talks, art films and workshop activities.

☎ Colwyn Bay (0492) 79201.
Open: all year Tue-Thu, Sat 11-5, Fri 11-8.
& ✷ (on a lead only).

MOTHERWELL
Strathclyde
(Lanarkshire)   *Map 11 NS75.*
Strathclyde Country Park
(1m NW)
Covering an area which lay derelict and neglected for years, now vast country park. The artificial loch (nearly two

miles long) has two beaches and various watersports, and a wide scope of other leisure activities are available, including nature trails and river-side walks. Overlooking the loch and the motorway which runs across the park is 120ft high, Hamilton Mausoleum, also open to the public.

☎ (0698) 66155.
Open: Country park at all reasonable time; Visitor Centre Etr-Sep, daily 10-4; Oct-Etr, Sat-Sun 10-4 (Admission charge Hamilton Mausoleum tours) &

MOUSA ISLAND
Shetland   *Map 16 HU42.*
Mousa Broch
The best preserved late pre-historic drystone tower in Scotland. It rises to a height of 40ft and, uniquely, is almost fully intact. Reached by boat from Leebottom on Mousa Sound.

Open: see page 4. Apply keeper.
(AM)

MOW COP
Cheshire/
Staffordshire   *Map 7 SJ85.*
Mow Cop Folly
Perched on a gritstone ridge

Mow Cop Folly, purpose-built as a ruin

rising to 1100ft, this Gothic folly was built in 1754 by Randle Wilbraham, to create a focal point on the skyline.

Open: accessible at all reasonable times.
(NT)

MUIRSHIEL
Strathclyde
(Renfrewshre)   *Map 10 NS36.*
Muirshiel Country Park
(4m NW of Lochwinnoch on unclass road)
Set in wild upland country, with trails and walks. Windy Hill (1036ft) gives fine views. Many woodland and moorland birds can be seen as well as small mammals and in June there are fine displays of rhododendrons. The visitor centre has a display of natural history. Guided walks can be arranged.

☎ Lochwinnoch (0505) 842803.
Open: park daily, dawn-dusk; visitor centre daily Apr-Sep 9-8; Oct-Mar 9-4.30.

MUSSELBURGH
Lothian (Midlothian)   *Map 11 NT37.*
Pinkie House
A fine Jacobean building of 1613 and later, incorporating a tower of 1390. Fine painted ceiling in the long gallery. The house now forms part of the Loretto School.

☎ 031-665 2059.
Open: mid Apr-mid Jul & mid Sep-mid Dec, Tue 2-5.

NEW ABBEY
Dumfries and Galloway
(Kirkcudbrightshire)   *Map 11 NX96.*
Shambellie House Museum of Costume
(¼m N on A710)
A costume collection, made by Charles Stewart of Shambellie, of European fashionable dress from the late 18th century to early 20th century.

Mainly women's clothes and accessories although some children's and men's clothes; also fancy dress costume.

☎ (038785) 375 or 031-225 7534.
(National Museums of Scotland)
Open: May-Sep, Thu-Mon 10-5.30, Sun 12-5.30.
Shop

NEWARK-ON-TRENT
Nottinghamshire   *Map 8 SK85.*
Millgate Museum of Social & Folk Life
Collection reflecting the domestic, commercial and industrial life of the district from Victorian times onwards, including printing, with craft workshops, still being developed.

☎ (0636) 79403.
Open: all year Mon-Fri 9-12 & 1-5; Apr-Sep also Sat & Sun 2-6.
Shop ✖

Newark District Council Museum
Local history, archaeology, natural history and art.

☎ (0636) 702358.
Open: all year Mon-Wed, Fri & Sat 10-1 & 2-5; Thu 10-1; Apr-Sep also Sun 2-5.
Shop ✖

Newark Town Hall
Market Place
Designed by the architect John Carr in 1773, the town hall is perhaps one of the finest of all Georgian town halls. On display is the town's collection of silver gilt and silver plate, generally of the 17th and 18th centuries. Other items of interest are early historical records and various paintings including a collection by Joseph Paul.

☎ (0636) 700200 & 700233.

Open: daily Mon-Fri, 10-12 & 2-4. (Closed BH Mon.) Other times by appointment.
&. (ground floor only) ✖

NEWBURN
Tyne and Wear   *Map 12 NZ16.*
Tyne Riverside Country Park
(between Newburn and Ovingham)
A long narrow country park based on footpaths along the banks of the River Tyne between Newburn and Ovingham. Sand martins and kingfishers may be seen on the river banks.

Open: accessible at all reasonable times.

NEWBURY
Berkshire   *Map 4 SU46.*
Newbury District Museum
The Wharf
In picturesque 17th- and 18th-century buildings. Displays include ballooning; Kennet and Avon Canal; traditional crafts; costume; Civil War battles of Newbury (with audio-visual); and local collections of archaeology, history, geology and birds. Also cameras, pewter and pottery. Temporary exhibitions throughout the year.

☎ (0635) 30511.
Open: Apr-Sep, Mon, Tue, Thu-Sat 10-6, Sun & BH 2-6; Oct-Mar, Mon, Tue, Thu-Sat 10-4.
&. (ground floor only) Shop
✖ (ex guide dogs)

NEWCASTLE-UNDER-LYME
Staffordshire   *Map 7 SJ84.*
Borough Museum
The Brampton
Local history, including Royal Charters, ceramics, dolls, display of firearms, and Victorian street scene.

☎ (0782) 619705.

Open: all year, Mon-Sat 9.30-1 & 2-6; May-Sep also Sun 2-5.30.
♿ (ground floor only) 🚫

Hobbergate Art Gallery
The Brampton
Permanent collection of 18th- and 19th-century English water-colours. Temporary exhibitions and picture loan scheme.

☎ (0782) 611962.
Open: Tue-Fri 2-6, Sat 9.30-1 & 2-6. (Closed BH.)
♿ (ground floor only) 🚫

NEWCASTLE-UPON-TYNE

Tyne and Wear *Map 12 NZ26.*

Laing Art Gallery
Higham Place
British paintings and water-colours from the 18th century to the present day with works by Reynolds, Turner, Burne-Jones and others including the Northumberland artist, John Martin. Also a collection of silver, ceramics and glass including a fine display of 18th-century enamelled glass by William Bailby of Newcastle. Temporary exhibition programme.

☎ (0632) 327734/326989.
Open: daily, Mon-Fri 10-5.30, Sat 10-4.30, Sun 2.30-5.30.
♿ Shop 🚫

Museum of Antiquities
University Quadrangle
The collection has been in the course of assembly since 1813, and was opened in its present form in 1960. Valuable collection of Roman and other antiquities, with models, reconstructions etc.

☎ (0632) 328511 Ext 3844/3849.
Open: Mon-Fri 10-5. (Closed Good Fri, 24-26 Dec & New Year's day & certain other BH's: telephone in advance)
♿ (prior arrangement) Shop 🚫

Museum of Science & Engineering
Blandford House, West Blandford Street
Motive power (engine) gallery; maritime gallery; special exhibitions, educational activities, plus supporting displays.

☎ (0632) 326789.
Open: Mon-Fri 10-5.30, Sat 10-4.30. (Closed Xmas & 1 Jan.)
♿ Shop 🚫 (ex guide dogs)

NEWCHAPEL

Surrey *Map 5 TQ34.*

London Temple Visitors Centre & Gardens
Pictures, films and beautiful gardens.

☎ Lingfield (0342) 833842.
Open: daily (ex Mon) 10-7 or dusk.
♿

NEW GALLOWAY

Dumfries & Galloway (Kirkcudbrightshire) *Map 11 NX67.*

Galloway Deer Museum
(5m SW off A712)
In a converted farm this museum not only features the deer but also shows aspects of the history and wildlife of the area, including a display of live trout.

Open: daily Apr-Oct 10-5.

NEWPORT

Dyfed *Map 2 SN04.*

Pentre Ifan Burial Chamber
(3m SE)
Remains of this chamber comprise capstone and three uprights with semi-circular forecourt at one end. Excavated 1936-37 when found to be part of vanished long barrow.

Open: at all reasonable times.
(AM)

NEWPORT

Gwent *Map 3 ST38.*

Fourteen Locks Picnic Area
(NW, off B4591)
The picnic area takes its name from the flight of fourteen locks designed by Thomas Dadford on the Crumlin arm of the Monmouthshire and Brecon Canal. The 'staircase' enabled barges to climb 168 ft in less than 1,000 yards, and has a series of 'top', 'header' and 'side' ponds. The canal ceased in 1930. Waymarked walks start from the interpretative centre.

☎ (0633) 894802 or Cwmbran (06333) 67711 Ext 676.
Open: Interpretative Centre Apr-Sep, Thu-Mon 10-5.30; Waymarked walks accessible at all reasonable times.
♿ 🧺

Museum & Art Gallery
John Frost Square
Archaeology and history of Gwent including Roman finds from Caerwent and Pontypool; Japanned ware; section on Chartist movement of 1838-40. Natural history and geology. Also collection of early English watercolours.

☎ (0633) 840064.
Open: Mon-Thu 9.30-5, Fri 9.30-4.30, Sat 9.30-4.
♿ Shop 🚫 (ex guide dogs)

NEWTONMORE

Highland (Inverness-shire) *Map 14 NN79.*

Clan Macpherson House & Museum
Relics and memorials of the Clan Chiefs and other Macpherson families. Prince

Be there...

at a 2000 B.C. burial[1]; see a Roman fort being built[2]; step aboard a railway guard's van[3]; discover a glass arcade[4]; meet a hero of Gallipoli[5]; experience the Great Fire of Newcastle[6]; navigate the Tyne[7]; visit a pit-head[8]; stroll through an Edwardian house[9]; take a glass with Mr. Beilby[10]...

...and be back in time for tea.

In our Museums the emphasis is on action, participation and fun. Out are the endless, old fashioned glass cases you pored over in hushed silence. In are... professionally designed displays, working models to play with, complete period room settings to browse through and sound effects to complete the picture...

So take part in history and learn as you travel through the centuries.

TYNE AND WEAR COUNTY COUNCIL MUSEUMS

for time travellers

1 Sunderland Museum & Art Gallery, Borough Road, Sunderland. 2 Arbeia Roman Fort & Museum, Baring Street, South Shields. 3 Monkwearmouth Station Museum, North Bridge Street, Sunderland. 4 Shipley Art Gallery, Prince Consort Road, Gateshead. 5 South Shields Museum & Art Gallery, Ocean Road, South Shields. 6 John George Joicey Museum, City Road, Newcastle upon Tyne. 7 Museum of Science & Engineering, Blandford House, West Blandford Street, Newcastle upon Tyne. 8 Washington 'F' Pit Museum, Albany Way, Washington. 9 Grindon Museum, Grindon Lane, Sunderland. 10 Laing Art Gallery, Higham Place, Newcastle upon Tyne.

TYNE AND WEAR COUNTY COUNCIL-WORKING FOR YOU

Charles Edward Stuart relics, including letters to the Clan Chief (1745) and a letter to the Prince from his father (the Old Pretender). Royal Warrants, Green Banner of the Clan, swords, pictures, decorations and medals. Also James Macpherson's fiddle, and other interesting historical exhibits. Highland Games 1st Sat in August.

☎ (05403) 332.
Open: May-Sep, Mon-Sat 10-5.30, Sun 2.30-5.30. Other times by appointment. (Donations)
⅋ ✻

NEWTON STEWART

Dumfries and Galloway (Wigtownshire)   *Map 10 NX46.*
Cree Weaving Mills
(½m N, on A714)
Producing high quality mohair products (from the fleece of the Angora goat). Visitors are shown weaving, brushing with natural teasles, and finishing processes for the outstandingly soft, light and warm wool.

☎ (0671) 2990.
Open: guided tours all year Mon-Fri 10-2.30; Shop Etr-Oct, Mon-Sat 9-5; Nov-Etr, Mon-Fri 9-5.
⅋ (ground floor only)

NEWTOWN

Powys   *Map 6 SO19.*
Robert Owen Memorial Museum
The Cross
Museum on the life and work of Robert Owen, born here in 1771. The pioneer of modern British socialism and father of the co-operative movement, Owen set up a very success-ful mill at New Lanark in the Industrial Revolution.

☎ (0686) 25580.
Open: all year, Mon-Fri 9-5.
⅋

Textile Museum
Commercial Street
Housed in the upper floor workshops of a woollen mill where handloom weavers once worked, the museum exhibits interesting relics from the days when Newtown had a thriving woollen industry. Exhibits include mill machinery, 19th century handlooms, cottage and mill shop fronts, and examples of wool and flannel.

Open: Apr-Oct, Tue-Sat 2-4.30.

W H Smith & Sons Ltd
High Street
The shop has been designed in the style of the 1920's. A small museum illustrates the history of the firm.

☎ (0686) 26280.
Open: during shop hours.

NORTHAMPTON

Northamptonshire   *Map 4 SP76.*
Abington Park
Large landscaped town park with lakes, well planted with trees and noted for its colour in the autumn. Garden for the blind. Aviary with wide variety of birds.

☎ (0604) 31454.
Open: at all reasonable times.
⅋

Carlsberg Brewery Limited
140 Bridge Street
Producing over 50 million gallons of lager annually, with the latest computer con-trolled equipment. Visitors can see the various brewing processes and at the end of the tour are invited to sample 'probably the best lager in the world'.

☎ (0604) 21621.
Open: tours Mon-Fri 9.15 &

2.15 (always telephone Visitors Department in advance).
⅋ ✻

Delapre Abbey
(½m S off A508)
16th- to 19th-century house with fine porch, built on site of Cluniac nunnery. Contains Northamptonshire Record Office and HQ of Northamp-tonshire Record Society.

☎ (0604) 62129.
Abbey grounds and Wall garden, open: all year dawn-dusk.
Certain parts of the interior shown Thu only, May-Sep 2.30-5; Oct-Apr 2.30-4.30.
✻

Hunsbury Hill Country Park
(1¾m S off A45)
The Iron Age hill fort on the summit of Hunsbury Hill (370 ft) is the centrepiece of the 98-acre park, with a topo-scope at the viewpoint over-looking Northampton. Sur-rounding attractions include an adventure playground, standard gauge railway and museum exploring the local ironstone industry.

☎ (0604) 67216 (evenings only).
Open: accessible at all reasonable times.
Admission charge railway and museum.
Ŧ

NORTH BERWICK

Lothian (East Lothian)   *Map 12 NT58.*
North Berwick Law
(S off B1347)
A conical volcanic peak rising to 613 ft to the south of the town and an excellent viewpoint. The summit is crowned by a watch tower

dating from Napoleonic times and an archway made from the jawbones of a whale.

Open: accessible at all reasonable times.

North Berwick Museum
Small museum in former Burgh school with sections on local and natural history, archaeology and domestic life. Exhibitions held throughout the summer.

☎ (0620) 3470.
Open: Jun-Sep, Mon-Sat 10-1 & 2-5, Sun 2-5.
✠

NORTH CREAKE
Norfolk   Map 9 TF83.
Creake Abbey
(1m N off B1355)
Church ruin with crossing and eastern arm belonging to a house of Augustinian canons founded in 1206.

Open: accessible at all reasonable times.
(AM)

NORTHINGTON
Hampshire   Map 4 SU53.
The Grange
(off B3046)
Built in the style of a Greek temple, this 17th-century mansion by William Samwell is one of the most important neo-classical country houses in Europe. Only viewable from the outside it features a massive Doric portico overlooking a lake. Display boards show the history of The Grange.

Open: Mon-Sat 9.30-6.30, Sun 2-6.30. (Closes 4.30 in winter.)

NORTH WOOTTON
Somerset   Map 3 ST54.
Wootton Vineyard
North Town House
A vineyard set in the foothills

of the Mendips, 3m from Wells, 9,000 vines specially imported from the Rhine and Alsace. The old farm buildings house a winery where fresh dry white wine is made. Visitors can walk in the vineyards and wines may be purchased direct from the cellar.

☎ Pilton (074989) 359.
Open: Mon-Sat 10-1 & 2-5.
Shop ✠

NORWICH
Norfolk   Map 5 TG20.
Cathedral
Herbert de Losinga, the first Bishop of Norwich, founded the cathedral in 1096. It is a superb building, and among its most notable features are the nave, with its huge round pillars, the bishop's throne (a Saxon survival unique in Europe), and the cloisters with their matchless collection of roof bosses.

☎ (0603) 626290.
Open: daily summer 7.30-7, winter 7.30-6.
(Donations)
& ☞ ✠

City Hall
St Peter Street
Civic Plate and Insignia dating from 1549 on show; also to be seen is the Council Chamber.

☎ (0603) 622233 Ext 743.
Open: Mon-Fri 10-4, visits by arrangement with the Director of Administration.
& (ground floor only) Shop

Royal Norfolk Regimental Museum
Brittania Barracks, Brittania Road.
Contains a fine collection of medals, uniforms and weapons, paintings, silver and trophies amassed by the Regiment.

☎ (0603) 628455.
Open: Mon-Fri 9-12.30, 2-4. (Closed BH.)
(Donations)
✠

St Peter Hungate Church Museum
Princes Street, near Elm Hill.
Fine church (1460), with hammer-beam roof and good Norwich painted glass, now museum of church art. Brass rubbing centre.

☎ (0603) 611277 Ext 296.
Open: Mon-Sat 10-5.
(Closed: Good Fri, Xmas & New Year's day).
& Shop ✠

NOTTINGHAM
Nottinghamshire   Map 8 SK53.
Brewhouse Yard Museum
Castle Boulevard
Housed in 17th-century buildings on a two-acre site. The museum depicts daily life in the city in post-medieval times with period rooms and thematic displays. Unusual rock-cut cellars open showing their uses in the past. The museum contains material which can be handled or operated by the public. The cottage gardens contain unusual local plants.

☎ (0602) 411881 Ext 67 or 48.
Open: all year daily 10-12 & 1-5, last admission 4.45pm. (Closed Xmas.) Parties must book.
& (ground floor only) ✠ (ex guide dogs)

Canal Museum
Canal Street
On ground floor and wharfage of 19th-century warehouse, the museum tells the history of the River Trent from the Ice Age to the present day. Includes local canal and river navigation, boats,

bridges, archaeology, etc.

☎ (0602) 598835.
Open: Apr-Sep, Wed-Sat
10-12 & 1-5.45, Sun 1-5.45;
Oct-Mar, Wed, Thu & Sat
10-12 & 1-5, Sun 1-5.
& Shop ✘

Green's Mill and Science Centre
Belvoir Hill, Sneinton
A partially reconstructed
tower mill restored to working order with flour milling.
The adjacent Science
Museum contains working
models and exhibits illustrating the importance to
science of George Green,
one time miller and dis-
tinguished mathematician.

☎ (0602) 503635.
Mill restoration due to be
completed by Jan 1986.
Open: Wed-Sun 10-12 & 1-5
also BH's. (Closed: Xmas
day.)
& (ex mill) Shop ✘

Costumes at Nottingham

Industrial Museum
*Courtyard Buildings,
Wollaton Park*
Housed in 18th-century stable
block are displays illustrating
Nottingham's industrial history and in particular the lace
and hosiery industries, together with exhibits on the
pharmaceutical industry, engineering, tobacco industry
and printing. New extensions
house a mid-19th-century
beam pumping engine, and
heavy agricultural machinery. Outside yards display a
horse gin from a local coal-
mine, Victorian street furniture etc.

☎ (0602) 284602.
Open: Apr-Sep, Mon-Sat
10-6, Sun 2-6; Oct-Mar, Thu
& Sat 10-4.30; Sun 1.30-4.30,
19th-century beam

pumping engine in steam
last Sun in each month &
BH.
Admission charge Sun &
BH.
(Ticket valid for both this
and Natural History
Museum, Wollaton Hall.)
& Shop ✘

Museum of Costume and Textiles
43-51 Castlegate
Displays include costume
from 1730 to 1960 in furnished
room settings of c.1790, 1830,
1860, 1885, 1910 and 1935.
Other rooms contain 17th-
century costume and em-
broidery, the Lord Middleton
collection, map tapestries of
Nottinghamshire, dress accessories from 18th century to
circa 1960. English, European
and Asian embroidery, knit-
ted woven and printed textiles. Also hand-and machine-
made lace.

☎ (0602) 411881.
Open: daily 10-5. (Closed
Xmas day.)
Shop ✘

Natural History Museum
Wollaton Hall
Housed in imposing
Elizabethan mansion by
Robert Smythson, dating from
1580-1588, and situated in
large park with deer.

☎ (0602) 281333 & 281130.
Open: Apr-Sep, Mon-Sat
10-7, Sun 2-5; Oct, Mon-Sat
10-5.30, Sun 1.30-4.30;
Nov-Mar, Mon-Sat 10-4.30,
Sun 1.30-4.30.
Admission charge Sun &
BH.
⬚ Etr-Sep ⊨ Shop ✘

NUNEATON
Warwickshire   Map 4 SP39.
Nuneaton Museum and Art Gallery
Riversley Park
A purpose-built structure,

situated in a pleasant public park, it houses a permanent collection of ethnography, archaeology, the George Eliot Collection and a display of fine miniatures painted by May B Lee (Lady Stott). From March to May the Nuneaton Festival of Art is held here.

☎ (0203) 326211 Ext 473.
Open: summer, Mon-Fri 12-7, Sat & Sun 10-7; winter 12-5 & 10-5.
& (ground floor only) Shop ✗

NUNEHAM COURTENAY
Oxfordshire   Map 4 SU59.
John Mattock Rose Nurseries
An internationally known rose growers with display gardens of hundreds of thousands of roses grown annually from leading rose hybridists.

☎ (086738) 265.
Open: Mon-Sat 9-6, Sun 10.30-6.
&

Oxford University Arboretum
(on A423 just S of the village)
50 acres of conifers and broad leaf trees.

☎ (0865) 242737.
Open: May-Oct Mon-Sat 8.30-5 & Sun 2-6.
& ✗

NUNNEY
Somerset   Map 3 ST74.
Nunney Castle
Moated structure modelled on French 'Bastille', built by Sir John de la Mere in 1373. Surrounded by one of the deepest moats in England.

Open: at all reasonable times.
(AM) & (exterior only)

OAKHAM
Leicestershire   Map 4 SK80.
Oakham Castle
off Market Place
Preserves a splendid Norman hall, with unique collection of presentation horseshoes.

☎ (0572) 3654.
Open: all year; Grounds, daily 10-5.30; Great Hall, Tue-Sat & BH 10-1 & 2-5.30; Sun 2-5.30; Nov-Mar closes 4pm. (Closed: Good Fri, Xmas day & Boxing day). Magistrates Court in session on Mon.
& Shop ✗ (in hall)

Rutland County Museum
Catmos Street
Local archaeology, especially Roman and Anglo-Saxon, craft tools and local history. Courtyard containing various farm wagons and agricultural implements. Temporary exhibitions. This is generally agreed to be one of the best collections of its kind.

☎ (0572) 3654.
Open: Apr-Oct, Tue-Sat & BH 10-1 & 2-5, Sun 2-5; Nov-Mar, Tue-Sat 10-1 & 2-5. (Closed: Good Fri, Xmas day & Boxing day).
& (ground floor only) Shop ✗ (unless carried).

OAKWELL HALL
West Yorkshire   Map 8 SE22.
In Nova Lane, near Birstall Smithies (6m SE of Bradford)
Elizabethan moated manor house (1583), with Civil War and Brontë connections. It was 'Fieldhead', in Charlotte Brontë's novel *Shirley*. There is a recently opened Country Park complex.

☎ Batley (0924) 474926.
Open: all year Mon-Sat 10-5, Sun 1-5.
⊓ Shop ✗

OBAN
Strathclyde (Agyll)   Map 10 NM83.
Caithness Glass
Oban Glassworks, Lochavullin Estate.
Visitors can see the art of paperweight making. Large seconds shop.

☎ (0631) 63386.
Open: all year Mon-Fri 9-5. May-Sept also Sat 9-12 noon.
& Shop ✗ (ex Shop).

Macdonald's Mill
(½m S of centre of Oban on A816)
Exhibition of the Story of Spinning and Weaving, with demonstrations of this ancient Scottish industry. Also showroom containing modern products.

☎ (0631) 63081.
Open: Mar-Oct Mon-Fri 9-7.30, Sat & Sun 9-5; demonstrations Mon-Fri only.
⌗ Shop ✗

OGMORE
Mid Glamorgan   Map 3 SS87.
Ogmore Castle
On River Ogmore with inner and outer wards and early 12th-century three-storeyed keep preserving hooded fireplace. West wall 40ft high, and dry moat around inner ward.

Open: see page 4.
(AM).

OLD CLEEVE
Somerset   Map 3 ST04.
John Wood Sheepskins
Visitors can see sheepskins being processed from their natural state, including tanning, dyeing and the crafting of various sheepskin products.

☎ Washford (0984) 40291.
Open: factory tours, Apr-Oct Mon-Fri 10.45 & 11.30,

2.15 & 3.00 (parties by appointment); showroom & shop all year Mon-Fri 9-4.30; Mar-Dec also Sat & BH 10-4.
& ✗

OLD DAILLY
Strathclyde (Aryshire) Map 10 NX29.
Bargany Gardens
(4m NE of Girvan on B734)
Woodland walks; with fine displays of snowdrops, blue-bells and daffodils in spring. Fine display of azaleas and rhododendrons round lily pond in May and June. Autumn colours. Many ornamental trees. Plants for sale.

☎ (046587) 227 or 274.
Gardens open: Mar-Oct daily until 7pm (or dusk).
(Donations)
ᕎᕎ

OLD KILPATRICK
Strathclyde (Dunbartonshire)
Map 11 NS47.
Auchentoshan Distillery
(on A82)
Guided tours showing brew-ing, distilling and warehou-sing of whisky, with sampling at the end.

☎ Duntocher (0389) 79476.
Open: tours between 9-3 Mon-Fri (telephone in advance)
✗

OLDMELDRUM
Grampian (Aberdeenshire)
Map 15 NJ82.
Glengarioch Distillery
Distillery Road
Formerly a tannery, the buildings were taken over as a distillery in 1794, and form part of the Oldmeldrum Con-servation Area. Display on the production of single malt Scotch Whisky.

☎ (06512) 2706.
Open: Mon-Fri, tours start 2.30 & 7.30 by appointment.

OLD WHITTINGTON
Derbyshire Map 8 SK37.
Revolution House
Old house, once known as Cock and Pynot (or Magpie) Inn, with 17th-century furnish-ings. Associated with the 1688 revolution.

☎ Chesterfield (0246) 32088.
Open: May day-second Sun in Sep, Wed-Sun & BH Mon, 11-12.30 & 1.30-5.30.
✗

ORPINGTON
Gtr London see page 84.
Priory Museum
The Priory, Church Hill,
London Plan 2 : 43F1.
13th- 14th-century clergy house with addition of 15th-century manor house. Now small museum of local interest where special exhibi-tions are held during the year.

☎ (0689) 31551.
Open: all year Mon-Wed, Fri, Sat 9-6 (5pm Sat) (Closed PH).
& (ground floor only) ✗

OSWESTRY
Shropshire Map 7 SJ23.
Old Oswestry
(½m N)
Iron Age hill fort covering 68 acres, with five ramparts and elaborate western portal. Abutted by part of prehistoric Wat's Dyke.

Open: accessible at all reasonable times.
(AM) &

OXFORD
Oxfordshire Map 7 SP50.
Ancient and picturesque University city on rivers Cherwell and Thames, dating back to 8th century. The University, the oldest in Britain, probably dates from c.1167 and consists of a large

number of colleges built over a period of several centuries, many of which are among the finest buildings of their ages. Access to some colleges is restricted to certain times and details may be obtained from the Official Information Bureau, Carfax Tower.

Ashmolean Museum of Art and Archaeology
Beaumont Street Plan : C3.
The oldest (1683) museum in the country, housed in C R Cockerell's building of 1845 (with later extensions). Its exhibits include archaeo-logical items of British, European, Mediterranean, Egyptian and Near Eastern origins. Also exhibited are coins and medals of all countries and periods, in the Heberden Coin Room; Italian, Dutch, Flemish, French, and English oil paintings, Old Master and modern drawings, water-colours, prints and minia-tures; European ceramics; English silver; Chinese and Japanese porcelain; painting and lacquer; Tibetan art; Indian sculpture and paintings; Islamic pottery and metalwork; Chinese bronzes; casts from the antique and objects of applied art. Temporary exhibits through-out the year.

☎ (0865) 512651.
Open: all year, Tue-Sat 10-4, Sun 2-4. (Closed: Etr & during St. Giles Fair in early Sep, Xmas period & 1 Jan.) (Donations)
Guided tours by arrangement.
& Shop ✗

Museum of the History of Science
Old Ashmolean Building,
Broad Street Plan : D3.
Contains the finest collection of early astronomical, mathe-

matical and optical instruments in the world. Housed in the Old Ashmolean Building, a fine example of 17th-century architecture which was originally built to hold the collection of Elias Ashmole. One of the most distinquished parts of the present display is the series of Islamic and European astrolabes, once used for astronomical calculations. Also early microscopes and other optical instruments, photographic apparatus, clocks and watches, air pumps etc. Of special interest are the penicillin material, H G J Moseley's X-ray spectrometer, and a prototype of Dr C R Burch's ultra violet reflecting microscope made in 1946.

☏ (0865) 243997.
Open: Mon-Fri 10.30-1 & 2.30-4. (Closed: BH, Xmas and Etr week).
Bookstall ✶

Museum of Oxford
St Aldates   Plan : **C2.**
Permanent displays of the archaeology and history of the university city from the earliest times to the present day. Temporary exhibitions. Facilities for parties.

☏ (0865) 815559.
Open: all year, Tue-Sat, 10-5. (Closed: Good Fri & Xmas).
Bookshop ✶

St Edmund Hall
College of Oxford University
                     Plan : **E3.**
This is the only surviving medieval hall and has a Norman crypt, 17th-century dining hall, chapel and quadrangle. Other buildings 18th- and 20th-century.

☏ (0865) 248180.
Open: all year, daily

7.30-dusk. (Closed: 23 Dec-1 Jan, Etr, Aug BH weekend-Tue).
&. (ground floor only) ✶

University Private Botanic Garden
High Street (by Magdalen Bridge)   Plan : **E2.**
Gardens of great botanical interest, founded in 1621, and the oldest in the country.

☏ (0865) 242737.
Open: all year Mon-Fri 8.30-5, (9-4.30 Oct-Mar), Sun 10-12 & 2-6 (2-4.30 Oct-Mar). Greenhouses open daily 2-4. (Closed: Good Fri & Xmas day.)
&. ✶

PAIGNTON
Devon   Map 3 SX86.
Oldway
19th-century house containing replicas of rooms at the Palace of Versailles. Picturesque gardens.

☏ Torquay (0803) 26244 Ext 286 for bookings, Paignton (0803) 550711 enquiries. House open: May-Sep, Mon-Sat, 10-1 & 2.15-5.15, Sun 2.30-5.30; winter Mon-Fri 10-1 & 2.15-5.15 (Closed: Sat & Sun.) Closed occasionally for Council purposes.
⌷ &. ✶ (ex guide dogs)

PAISLEY
Strathclyde (Renfrewshire)
                     Map 11 NS46.
Coats Observatory
49 Oakshaw Street
Dating from 1883 but recently renovated with modern technology, the Observatory has resumed a role of importance in the realms of astronomy and meteorology. There are displays relating to the history of the building, astronomy, meteorology and space flight, together with a small planetarium.

☏ 041-889 3151.
Open: all year Mon-Fri 2-5, Sat 10-1 & 2-5, BH 2-5; Jan-Mar also Thu 7-9pm weather permitting. (Closed Xmas & New Year).
Shop ✶

Paisley Museum and Art Galleries
High Street
Collection illustrates local, industrial and natural history of the town and district. Also a world-famous collection of Paisley shawls.

☏ 041-889 3151.
Open: Mon-Sat, 10-5. (Closed BH).
&. (ground floor only) Shop ✶

PALNACKIE
Dumfries and Galloway (Kircudbrightshire)   Map 11 NX85.
Orchardton Tower
A rare example of a circular tower built originally in the late 15th century.

Open: see page 4, on application to the Key Keeper.
(AM)

PAPA WESTRAY
Orkney   Map 16 HY45.
Knap of Howar
(W side of island near Holland House)
Recently confirmed as northwest Europe's oldest standing house. It was built over 5000 years ago and visitors can see how large flagstones have been used for cupboards, hearths and seating. Other finds in the house have included whalebone mallets and unique stone borers and grinders. There are many other prehistoric monuments on the island.

Open: accessible at all reasoable times.
(AM)

PENARTH

South Glamorgan   Map 3 ST17.

Turner House

A small gallery holding temporary and travelling exhibitions of pictures and objets d'art drawn from the extensive collections that make up the National Museum of Wales, and from other sources.

☎ Cardiff (0222) 708870.
Open: Tue-Sat & BH Mons,
11-12.45 & 2-5, Sun 2-5.
(Closed: 24-26 & 31 Dec, 1
Jan, Good Fri & May Day).
Shop ✟

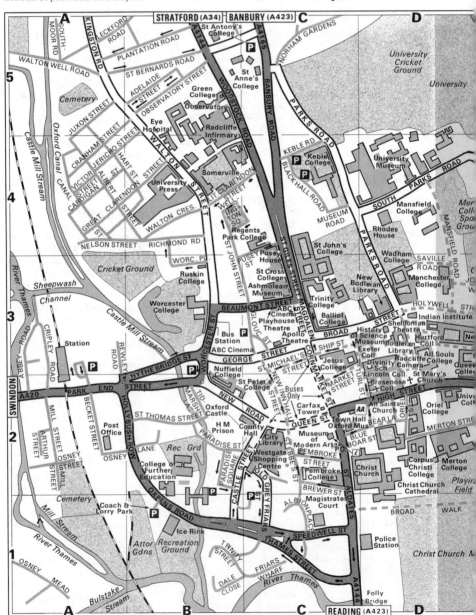

PENARTH FAWR
Gwynedd   *Map 6 SH43.*
(3½m NE of Pwllheli, off A497)
Part of a house whose origins stretch back to the early 15th-century, with hall, buttery and screen.

Open: accessible at all reasonable times.
(AM)

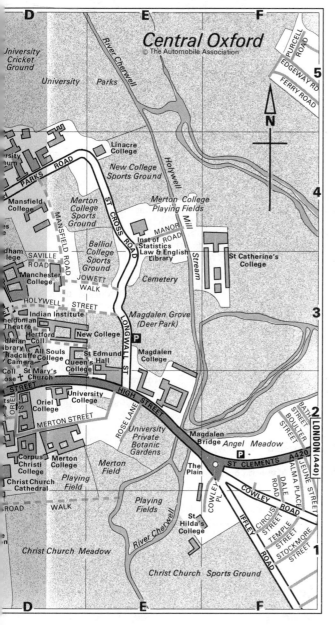

PENMACHNO
Gwynedd   *Map 6 SH75.*
Penmachno Woollen Mill
Records date back to 1650 when the mill started as a Fulling Mill where cloth could be finished by local domestic weavers and flannel shirts for farmers and quarrymen were produced. During the 19th-century power looms were introduced and these still make Welsh tweed today.

☎ Betws-y-Coed (06902) 545.
Open: daily pre Etr-mid Nov 9-5.30. (Closed: Sun am early & late season.)
Shop ✚

PENMON
Gwynedd   *Map 6 SH68.*
Penmon Priory
There has been a religious settlement here since the 6th-century. The Priory church and adjacent ruins date from the 12th century, and have the best Romanesque detail in North Wales. To the north of the church is the holy well where St Seiriol is said to have baptized converts. On the opposite side of the road is a dovecote dating from about 1600 and crowned with an open hexagonal lantern. There are about one thousand nesting holes.

Open: ruins, well, dovecote accessible at all reasonable times.
(AM)

PENZANCE
Cornwall   *Map 2 SW43.*
Penlee House, Penzance and District Museum
Penlee Park
The history and development of the district from earliest man to the 1980s. Exhibition of town paintings.

☎ (0736) 63625.
Open: all year, Mon-Fri 10.30-4.30. Sat 10.30-12.30

(Exhibition of paintings
closed 12.30-2.30) (Closed
BH's). Admission charge
paintings exhibition
Jun-Sep.
& (ground floor only) ✗

PERTH
Tayside (Perthshire)   Map 11 NO12.
**Black Watch Regimental
Museum**
*Balhousie Castle, Hay
Street*
Treasures of the 42nd/73rd
Highland Regiment from 1725
to the present day, including,
paintings, silver, colours and
uniforms.

☎ (0738) 21281 Ext 30.
Open: all year, Mon-Fri
10-4.30 (Winter 3.30); Etr-
Sep also Sun & BH 2-4.30.
(Donations)
Shop ✗

Caithness Glass
Inveralmond Industrial Est
All aspects of glass making
can be seen from the viewing
gallery at this purpose-built
visitor centre.

☎ (0738) 37373.
Open: all year Mon-Sat 9-5,
Sun 1-5. (11-5 Jul & Aug).
⌑ (licensed) & Shop

Dewar's Scotch Whisky
*J Dewar's & Son Ltd,
Inveralmond*
Visitors are given a 1½-hour
tour, showing blending,
bottling, and despatch of
whisky, and coopering of
casks. Whisky sampling may
be available.

☎ (0738) 21231.
Open: guided tours all
year, Mon-Thurs 10.15 and
2.15, Fri 10.15. (Closed
company holidays). Contact
tour organiser in advance.
Children under 14 not
admitted.
✗

Fair Maid's House, Perth

Fair Maid's House
North Port
Situated near the historic
North Inch where the battle of
the Clans was fought in 1396.
In the 14th-century it became
the home of Simon Glover, a
glovemaker whose daughter
Catherine was the heroine of
Sir Walter Scott's 'Fair Maid
of Perth'. The house was a
guildhall for over 150 years. It
was renovated in the 19th-
century and is now a centre
for Scottish crafts. A recently
uncovered wall is said to be
the oldest one visible in Perth.
Changing exhibitions of paintings, sculptures, tapestries
etc.

☎ (0738) 25976.
Open: all year, Mon-Sat
10-5.
& (ground floor only).

**Perth Museum & Art
Gallery**
78 George Street
Purpose-built to house collections of fine and applied art,
social and local history,
natural history and archaeology. Special events
monthly.

☎ (0738) 32488.
Open: Mon-Sat 10-1 & 2-5.
Shop ✗

The Round House
Marshall Place
Built and designed by Dr
Adam Anderson in 1832 the
building was the first water-
works in the city. In 1974 it was
restored by Perth Town
Council and is now the Tourist
Information Centre. There is
a 360° slide programme
showing Perth in sound and
vision.

☎ (0738) 22900/27108.
Open: all year, Mon-Fri 9-7,
Sat 9-6; Jun-Sep also Sun
12-5.

PETERBOROUGH
Cambridgeshire   Map 4 TL19.
**City of Peterborough
Museum and Art Gallery**
Priestgate
Collections include local geology, archaeology, natural
history and articles from
former French prisoners' jail
at Norman Cross. Also paintings and ceramics.

☎ (0733) 43329.
Open: May-Sep Tue-Sat
10-5; Oct-Apr Tue-Sat 12-5.
(Closed: Good Fri & Xmas.)
Shop ✗

PETERHEAD
*Grampian (Aberdeenshire)
                    Map 15 NK14.*
**Arbuthnot Museum and
Art Gallery**
St Peter Street

Dewar's ®

DEWAR'S
AGED 12 YEARS
ANCESTOR

Dewar's
"White Label"

GLENORDIE
SINGLE MALT
DEWAR'S
12 YEARS OLD

FINE SCOTCH WHISKIES

Specialises in local exhibits, particularly those relating to the fishing industry with Arctic and whaling specimens. Also a British coin collection which can be viewed by appointment.

☎ (0779) 77778.
Open: all year, Mon-Sat 10-12 & 2-5. (Closed: PH.) Shop ✕ (ex guide dogs)

PITLOCHRY
Tayside (Perthshire)   Map 14 NN95.
Faskally
(2m NW)
Incorporates woodland and lochside parking with picnic area and forest walk.

☎ (0796) 3437.
Open: daily Apr-Sep, dawn-dusk.
🚗 &

PLYMOUTH
Devon   Map 2 SX45.
City Museum & Art Gallery
Drake Circus
Collections of paintings and drawings, ceramics (especially Plymouth porcelain), silver; archaeology and local history. Cottonian collection of Old Master drawings, engravings and early printed books. Monthly exhibitions.

☎ (0752) 264878.
Open: all year Mon-Fri 10-5.30, Sat 10-5. (Closed: Good Fri & 25, 26 Dec.)
& Shop ✕

Royal Citadel
Magnificent entrance gateway, dated 1670 and designed probably by Sir Thomas Fitz for stronghold, begun by Charles II in 1666. The remaining buildings from the fort include the Guard House, Governor's House and Chapel.

Open: May-Sep. Guided

tours daily 2-6. Winter access by permission of the Ministry of Defence. Enquire at Guardroom. (AM)

PONTEFRACT
West Yorkshire   Map 8 SE42.
Pontefract Museum
Salter Row
Museum of Pontefract history, with temporary exhibitions.

☎ (0977) 797289.
Open: all year, Mon-Sat 10.30-12.30 & 1.30-5. (Closed BH.) & ✕

PONTERWYD
Dyfed   Map 6 SN78.
Bwlch Nant-Yr-Arian Forest Visitor Centre
(3m W)
Situated on a pass, just off the A44 10 miles E of Aberystwyth. Spectacular views over the wooded valleys below and towards the sea. Audio-visual programme explains the landscape, and its industry and wildlife. Forest trail and walks nearby.

☎ (097085) 694 or Crosswood (09743) 404.
Open: daily, Etr-Sep 10-5 ex Sat 12.30-5 (6pm in Jul & Aug). 🚗 & Shop

PONTYPRIDD
Mid Glamorgan   Map 3 ST09.
Welsh Characters
Models of miners, hill farmers, coracle men, as well as sculptured figures from Welsh folklore and amusing Welsh rugby characters and other pieces are made here in an individual, slightly 'primitive' style. Visitors can watch John Hughes (the sculptor) and his team at work.

☎ (0443) 405001.
Open: all year Mon-Fri 9-5, Sat 10-5, Sun 2-4, BH 11-4.30. (Closed Xmas.)

POOLE
Dorset   Map 4 SZ09.
Upton Park Country Park
Upton Road (off A35)
On the north shore of Poole Harbour, 55 acres of parkland meadow and garden, largely the grounds of historic Upton House. After years of neglect the area is being restored in the tradition of a small country estate. The attractive formal gardens are in the style of Humphrey Repton and the parkland's fine trees are a special feature. A combination of natural and manmade landscape provides a good habitat for many different plants and animals.

☎ (0202) 673555.
Open: daily 9-dusk. House open Sun noon-6 only.
🚗 & (ornamental gardens only)

PORTHMADOG
Gwynedd   Map 6 SH53.
Ffestiniog Railway Museum
Located in Harbour Station and includes old four-wheeled hearse converted from quarryman's coach, one of the original steam locos (1863), historic slate wagon, model steam engine (1869), and maps and diagrams illustrating history of the well-known narrow-gauge railway.

☎ (0766) 2340 or 2384.
Open: Feb-Dec every weekend & Mar-Nov when train services operating.
🍴 (licensed) & Shop

PORTSMOUTH
Hampshire   Map 4 SZ69.
HMS Victory
The Hard
Nelson's famous flagship, still in commission, manned by regular serving officers and men of the Royal Navy and Marines, and being restored

The Grogg Shop

Broadway, Pontypridd, Mid-Glam.
Telephone- (0443) 405001.

Opening hours

Weekdays 9–5pm Saturdays 10–5pm
Sundays 2–4pm

to its original appearance before the Battle of Trafalgar in 1805. Navy Days 29-31 Aug.

☎ (0705) 822351 Ext 23111. Open: Mar-Oct, Mon-Sat 10.30-5.30 & Sun 1-5; Nov-Feb Mon-Sat 10.30-4.30 & Sun 1-4.30. (Closed 25 Dec.) ☞ (100 yds) & (Lower Gun Deck) Shop ✗

Round Tower
Broad Street, Old Portsmouth
Dating from the early 15th century, this is the first permanent defensive work to be built in Portsmouth and commands the entrance to the Harbour. It now provides an excellent vantage point.

☎ (0705) 827261.
Open: at all reasonable times.
✗ (ex guide dogs)

Royal Marines Museum
Eastney
A chronological history of the Royal Marines from 1664 to the present day. Specialist displays of uniforms, badges, Royal Marines' bands and medals, including the complete collection of 10 Royal Marines VCs. A display 'The Royal Marines through the 70s into the 80s' opened in 1982 covering Northern Ireland and the 'Arctic' commandos, together with other aspects of Corps activities over the past decade. A 'Falklands' display was added in 1983. Temporary exhibitions are a feature of the museum, which is established in the original Royal Marine Artillery Officers' Mess, a superb example of Victorian architecture retaining original mouldings and fireplaces. 1983 European Museum of the Year Award.

Portsmouth: Nelson model

☎ (0705) 822351 Ext 6133.
Open: daily 10-4.30.
☞ (May-Sep) & (ground floor & gardens only) Shop ✗

PRESCOT
Merseyside   *Map 7 SJ49.*
Prescot Museum of Clock & Watch-Making
34 Church Street
An attractive 18th-century town house containing exhibits about the clock, watch and tool making industry of the area. Display includes a reconstruction of part of a traditional watchmaker's workshop, examples of hand tools and machinery used to make the many intricate parts of watch and clock movements.

☎ 051-430 7787.
Open: all year Tue-Sat & BH Mon, 10-5, Sun 2-5. (Closed: 24-26 Dec, New Year's Day & Good Fri.)
& (ground floor only) Shop ✗

PRESTON
Lancashire   *Map 7 SD52.*
Harris Museum & Art Gallery
Market Square
Impressive neo-classical building containing extensive collections of Fine and Decorative Arts. Includes paintings by the Devis family, the Newsham bequest of 19th-century paintings and sculpture, and the Houghton bequest of ceramics. Also social history and archaeology collections together with regular temporary exhibitions.

☎ (0772) 58248.
Open: all year Mon-Sat 10-5. (Closed BH's.)
☞ (Mon, Wed & Fri 10.30-1.30) & Shop ✗ (ex guide dogs)

PRESTONPANS
Lothian (East Lothian)   Map 11 NT37.
Scottish Mining Museum
Prestongrange
Oldest documented coal mining site in Britain, with 800 years of history. Cornish Beam Engine, Visitor Centre, Exhibition Hall, 16th-century Customs Port, Self-drive Coal Heritage Trail to Lady Victoria Colliery. This is a new independent twin-site museum of coal mining in Scotland.

☎ 031-665 9904.
Visitor centre open: all year Mon-Fri 10-4, Sat & Sun 12-5. Special steam days first Sun of month Apr-Oct.
& (ground floor only) ✗

PRESTWICH
Gt Manchester   Map 7 SD80.
Heaton Hall
Heaton Park (on A665)
The finest house of its period in Lancashire and one of the finest in the country. Designed for Earl of Wilton by James Wyatt in 1772, the house has magnificent decorated interiors and commands panoramic views of Manchester.

☎ 061-236 9422.

Open: Apr-Sep, Mon, Wed-Sat 10-6 also Sun 2-6.
☎ (ground floor only) Shop ✖

QUEEN'S VIEW
Tayside (Perthshire)   Map 14 NN85.
Tummel Forest Centre
Exhibits show changes in the Tummel Valley since Queen Victoria's visit in 1866. Audio-visual programmes, forest walks and information desk.

☎ Pitlochry (0796) 3437.
Open: daily, Etr-mid Oct 9.30-5.30.
☎ Shop ✖

RADCLIFFE
Gt Manchester   Map 7 SD70.
Radcliffe Tower
Tower Street, off Church Street East
Remains of medieval tower once part of a larger hall occupied by the Radcliffe family. Adjacent to medieval parish church.

☎ 061-761 4021 Ext 54 (enquiries to Bury Art Gallery & Museum)
Open: at all reasonable times.
☎ (ground floor & gardens only)

RAMSEY
Cambridgeshire   Map 4 TL28.
Abbey Gatehouse
A 15th-century Benedictine ruin.

Open: daily, Apr-Oct 10-5 (or dusk) (NT)

Ramsey Abbey
House (now a comprehensive school) erected c.1600 on the site of a Benedictine mona-stery, fragments of which still remain. An interesting mix-ture of architectural styles, reflecting its varied history, the house was extended and refurbished by architects, Sir John Soane and Edward Blore in the 19th century.

☎ (0487) 813285.
Open: Sun 2-5, 31 Mar-27 Oct (NT)
✖

RAMSGATE
Kent   Map 5 TR36.
Ramsgate Museum
Ramsgate Library,
Guildford Lawn
A display of objects, pictures and documents illustrating the history of Ramsgate.

☎ Thanet (0843) 593532.
Open: all year Mon-Wed 9.30-6, Thu & Sat 9.30-5 Fri 9.30-8. (Closed BH.)
☎ (ground floor only) ✖
See advert Mad Chef's Bistro Broadstairs, 2m N page 27

RAWTENSTALL
Lancashire   Map 7 SD82.
Rossendale Museum
Whitaker Park, Haslingden Road
Set in pleasant parkland with

moorland views, the museum is housed in a former Victorian mill owner's mansion. Apart from special temporary exhibitions throughout the year, there is a varied collection of permanent exhibits of fine arts and furniture, and industrial and domestic artefacts.

☏ Rossendale (0706) 217777.
Open: all year Mon-Fri, 1-5 (Wed also 6-8; Apr-Sep); Sat 10-12 & 1-5; (Sun, 2-4; Apr-Oct) BH 2-5. (Closed Xmas & New Year.)

READING
Berkshire   Map 4 SU77.
Blake's Lock Museum.
Gasworks Road
This recently opened museum, originally a pumping station, is located in an attractive Victorian building built in 1870. Exhibits mainly relate to the 19th- and 20th-centuries and concentrate on some of the manufacturing products of Reading — biscuits, beer and bulbs. Reconstructions of a barber shop, a bakery and a printer's workshop are on display and among other attractions is a history of the Kennet and Avon Canal which passes alongside the museum.

☏ (0734) 55911 Ext 2242.
Open: all year Wed-Fri 10-5 Sat, Sun 2-5.
 ⅃ ⚲ ✖

Museum & Art Gallery
Blagrave Street
Noted especially for its exceptional collection of exhibits from Roman Silchester, the museum also features finds from the River Thames area, including a splendid Bronze Age torc from Moulsford, and displays of local natural history. Some exhi-

bitions change monthly. See also: Silchester, Calleva Museum.

☏ (0734) 55911 Ext 2242.
Open: all year Mon-Fri 10-5.30 & Sat 10-5. (Closed BHs.)
Shop ✖

Museum of English Rural Life
The University, Whiteknights Park, Shinfield Road entrance.
Collection of highly interesting agricultural, domestic and crafts exhibits.

☏ Reading (0734) 875123 Ext 475.
Open: Tue-Sat 10-1 & 2-4.30. (Closed BHs.)
⚲ Shop

REAY
Highland (Caithness)   Map 14 NC96.
U.K.A.E.A. Dounreay Exhibition
(2m NE)
Information panels, models, participatory displays and charts relating to fast reactors and nuclear energy generally. Housed in a former airfield control tower overlooking the plant which is conspicuous for its 135 ft sphere and the prototype fast reactor.

☏ Thurso (0847) 62121 Ext 656.
Open: daily, May-Sep 9-4.
Exhibition, Public tours of the prototype fast reactor on the hour, starting at 12 noon.
Tickets available from Exhibition or Wick & Thurso Tourist Information Centre.
⚲ ⚲ (ground floor only) ✖

REIGATE
Surrey   Map 4 TQ24.
Priory Museum
Bell Street

Contained in house, originally founded in 1235, and converted into Tudor mansion, of which the hall fireplace is the finest surviving relic. Palladian stucco changed the face of the building in 1779, and the painted staircase by Verrio c1710 is a notable example. House now used as a school and a part is a small museum with changing displays. Special exhibitions throughout the year.

☏ (07372) 45065.
Museum open: Weds only in term time 2-4.30. Conducted tour if requested.
⚲ (ground floor only) Shop ✖

REIGATE HEATH
Surrey   Map 4 TQ25.
Old Windmill
220-year-old mill, converted into a church in 1882. Services (3pm on third Sun of each month between May and Oct.) Restored in 1964.

Open: accessible all year daily, 10-dusk. Key available from Club house. ✖

RICHMOND-UPON-THAMES
Gt London   see page 84.
Richmond Park.
London Plan 2 : 46 B3.
Charles I enclosed the park area as part of a Royal Estate in 1637 and successive monarchs shaped the land to suit their hunting needs. Sometimes described as 'wild countryside' on London's doorstep, it nowadays has large numbers of red and fallow deer roaming unharmed. With other kinds of wildlife in evidence, the park is a favourite haunt for naturalists and tourists alike. The formal gardens at Pembroke Lodge and the various plantations show a wealth of

exotic shrubs and wild flowers. A popular part is the Isabella Plantation, now a woodland garden with rhododendrons, azaleas, and a running brook. 18-acre Pen Ponds have been specially built for angling (a fishing permit is required). Adam's Pond, where the deer are seen to drink, is also used for model sail boats.

☎ 01-948 3209.
Open: dawn-½ hour before dusk. ▱ ♿

ROBERTSBRIDGE
East Sussex   Map 5 TQ72.
Robertsbridge Aeronautical Museum
Bush Barn (1m N off A21)
On display are 29 engines, a Hurricane cockpit section complete with seat, radio, controls, instrument panel and Merlin engine, Lancaster rear turret, many aircraft components, documents, uniforms and associated items. There are at least 60 different types of aircraft represented, dating from the First World War to the present day.

☎ Lamberhurst (0892) 890386.
Open: last Sun of each month (ex Dec) 2.30-5.30. Other times by appointment. (Donations) ▱ Shop ✘ (guide dogs only)

ROCHESTER
Kent   Map 5 TQ76.
Guildhall Museum
High Street
A major portion of the building dates from late 17th-century and has magnificent decorated plaster ceilings. The collections include local history, archaeology, arms and armour, dolls, toys and Victoriana, models of local sailing barges, fishing vessels. Shorts flying boats and Napoleonic prisoner-of-war work. The museum also houses the civic plate, regalia and archives of the city.

☎ Medway (0634) 48717.
Open: daily 10-12.30 & 2-5.30. (Closed: 1 Jan, Good Fri & Xmas.)
♿ (ground floor only) Shop ✘

ROMILEY
Gt Manchester   Map 7 SJ99.
Chadkirk Farm and Chapel
(¾m S, on A627)
Now run by the Metropolitan Borough of Stockport, Chadkirk Farm covers 60 acres in the valley of the River Goyt. In an area rich with alluvial soils, the farm trail enables visitors to see how a small farm operates. A four to five year rotation system is used for crops and there is a milking herd of 25 to 30 cows. At the chapel, which dates

from the late 14th century, there is an exhibition on Britain's agricultural history.

☎ 061-427 6937.
Open: farm trail accessible at all reasonable times. Chapel daily 10-6.
⛫ (✘ on lead only)

ROTHERHAM
South Yorkshire   Map 8 SK49.
Art Gallery
Brian O'Malley Library and Arts Centre, Walker Place
Continuous programme of temporary exhibitions including, at times 19th- and 20th-century paintings from the museum collections, and Rockingham pottery.

☎ (0709) 382121 Ext 3569/3579/3549.
Open: Mon & Wed-Fri 10-6, Sat 10-5. (Closed Sun, Tue, & BH.)
▱ (licensed) ♿ Shop ✘

Museum
Clifton Park
Late 18th-century mansion reputed to be designed by John Carr of York. Contains 18th-century furnished rooms, family portraits, and period kitchen. Displays of Victoriana, local history, local Roman antiquities, numismatics, glass and glassmaking, church silver, and 19th- and 20th-century paintings. Also British

Checking the fermenting process at Glen Grant

which have survived persistent coastal erosion, are dotted around the broch. Nearby is Midhowe Chambered Cairn, considered to be one of the best in Orkney. Its central chamber is almost 75 ft long.

Open: accessible at all reasonable times.

ceramics, including Rockingham, local geology and natural history. Temporary exhibitions.

☎ (0709) 382121 Ext 3519.
Open: Apr-Sep, Mon-Thu & Sat 10-5, Sun 2,30-5; Oct-Mar Mon-Thu & Sat 10-5, Sun 2.30-4.30. (Closed Fri.)
♿ (ground floor only) Shop ✻

ROTHES
Grampian (Moray)   Map 15 NJ24.
Glen Grant Distillery
Established in 1840. The whisky produced here is regarded as one of the best, and is used in many first-class blends as well as being sold as a single Glen Grant Malt in bottles. Traditional malt whisky methods of distillation are used together with the most modern equipment. Reception, shop and Hospitality Bar.

☎ (03403) 494.
Open: Etr-Sep, Mon-Fri 10-4.
Shop ✻

ROTHESAY
Isle of Bute, Strathclyde (Buteshire)   Map 10 NS06.
Ardencraig Gardens
Ardencraig Road, (1½m E off A844)
Overlooking the Firth of Clyde, fine floral displays can be seen in these gardens,

owned by the Royal Burgh of Rothesay. The gardens, which have several ornamental ponds, contain propagation, educational and show units, and an aviary containing a large number of foreign birds.

Open: daily Apr-Sep 10-4.
☞

ROTTINGDEAN
East Sussex   Map 5 TQ30.
Rottingdean Grange Museum & Art Gallery
Early Georgian house, remodelled by Lutyens, now a library, art gallery and museum with Kipling exhibits. It includes part of the National Toy Museum. Frequent temporary exhibitions.

☎ Brighton (0273) 31004.
Open: Mon, Thu & Sat 10-5; Tue & Fri 10-1 & 2-5. (Closed Wed.)
Shop ✻

ROUSAY
Orkney   Map 16 HY33.
Midhowe Broch and Tombs
(5½m W of Island's pier)
Standing on the cliff edge overlooking the small island of Eynhallow, this is a good example of an Iron Age Broch with a walled inclosure cut off by a deep rock-cut ditch. Several secondary buildings,

ROYSTON
Hertfordshire   Map 5 TL34.
Royston Museum
Lower King Street
Former chapel schoolroom, which contains a local history museum with displays depicting the history of the town. Regular temporary exhibitions.

☎ (0763) 42587.
Open: Wed & Sat only 10-5.
♿ (ground floor only) Shop ✻

RUTHWELL
Dumfries and Galloway (Dumfriesshire)   Map 11 NY16.
Duncan Savings Bank Museum
First Savings Bank was founded here in 1810. Interior set in period furnishings around a peat fire and contains many early savings bank documents, four-lock security kist, collection of home savings banks from Great Britain and abroad, International Money Corner etc. Personal pencil drawings and historic papers dealing with the Runic Cross in Ruthwell Church.

☎ Clarencefield (038787) 640.
Open: daily, summer 10-6, winter 10-4. (Closed: for Custodian holidays.) Evenings by arrangement.
♿

Ruthwell Cross
(off B724)
One of Europe's most famous carved crosses resting in the parish church in an apse built specially for it. The date is probably late 7th-century and the 18ft-high cross is richly carved with Runic characters showing the earliest form of English in Northumbrian dialect.

Open: key of church obtainable from the Key Keeper, Kirkyett Cottage, Ruthwell.
(AM)

SAFFRON WALDEN
Essex   Map 5 TL53.
Saffron Walden Museum
Museum Street
Built in 1834, the museum houses collections of local archaeology, natural history, ceramics, glass, costume, furniture, toys, ethnography, geology and local history. Special events include Walden's 750th Anniversary celebrations with special exhibitions and events in grounds Apr-Sep. Reproductions of the Pepys' Mazer Bowl will be available.

☎ (0799) 22494.
Open: Apr-Sep, Mon-Sat 11-5, Sun & BH 2.30-5; Oct-Mar, Mon-Sat 11-4, Sun & BH 2.30-5. (Closed: Good Fri and 24 & 25 Dec.)
& (ground floor & gardens only) Shop ✗

ST ABBS
Borders (Berwickshire) Map 12 NT96.
St Abbs Head (Nature Reserve)
(N from B6438)
This exposed headland north of Eyemouth has fine cliffs rising to 300 ft. It is an important site for cliff nesting seabirds in south east Scotland. Kittiwakes and guillemots are the most numerous with smaller

numbers of fulmars, shags, razorbills, herring gulls and puffins. The headland is a good landfall site for autumn migrants and a number of rarities have been recorded. In 1983 St Abbs Head was declared a National Nature Reserve.

Open: accessible at all reasonable times. (NTS)

ST ALBANS
Hertfordshire   Map 4 TL10.
City Museum
Hatfield Road
Displays collections relating to natural history and geology of south-west Hertfordshire. Salaman collection of craft tools with reconstructed workshops.

☎ (0727) 56679.
Open: Mon-Sat 10-5. (Closed BH.)
Shop ✗

ST ANDREWS
Fife (Fife)   Map 12 NO51.
Crawford Centre for the Arts
93 North Street
Established by the University and named after the late Earl of Crawford and Balcarres (former University Rector). The centre has a programme of changing art exhibitions and theatre which takes place in the galleries and studio.

☎ (0334) 76161.
Open: Mon-Sat 10-5; Sun 2-5.
(Admission charge for theatre performances.)
▯

ST BEES
Cumbria   Map 11 NX91.
St Bees Head (Nature Reserve)
(on public footpath north of car park on seafront)
Sandstone cliffs rising to

almost 300 ft with wide views to the Isle of Man and Dumfries and Galloway. On the headland there is a large seabird colony with guillemots, razorbills and puffins. A cliff path runs between St Bees and Whitehaven.

Open: accessible at all reasonable times.

ST CATHERINE'S POINT
Isle of Wight   Map 4 SZ47.
St Catherine's Lighthouse
Situated at St Catherine's Point, 136 ft above the sea.

☎ Niton (0983) 730284.
Open: Mon-Sat only from 1pm-one hour before dusk, weather and other conditions permitting, at visitors own risk.
Visitors are strongly recommended to telephone the keeper in advance. Cars not allowed within ¼m except on business.
✗

ST DAVID'S
Dyfed   Map 2 SM72.
Cathedral
Centrepiece of the smallest city in Britain is the cathedral which lies in a hollow for protection from invasion. Dating from 12th-14th centuries, it is built of purple sandstone quarried locally. The nave slopes three feet from one end to the other and is noted for its Irish oak roof. The tower rises to 116 ft.

☎ (0437) 720392.
Open: daily 8-6.
(Donations)
&

ST DOGMAELS
Dyfed   Map 2 SN14.
St Dogmaels Abbey
Standing near the centre of the village, the ruinous

Abbey was founded in the 12th century by monks of the French order of Tiron. The north and west walls of the nave still rise to almost their original height.

☏ Cardigan (0239) 613230.
Open: accessible at all reasonable times.
& (AM)

ST HELENS
Merseyside   *Map 7 SJ59.*
Pilkington Glass Museum
(on Prescot Road, A58 1m from town centre)
History of glassmaking from Egyptians to present day, with some of the finest examples of glass in the world. Various temporary exhibitions throughout the year.

☏ (0744) 28882 Ext 2499 or 2014.
Open: all year Mon-Fri 10-5, Sat, Sun & BH 2-4.30; (also open until 9 on Weds, Mar-Oct). (Closed Xmas-New Year.)
& Shop ✻

ST HILARY
South Glamorgan   *Map 3 ST07.*
Old Beaupré Castle
(1m SW)
Ruined manor house, rebuilt in 16th century, with notable Italianate gatehouse and porch. Porch is three-storey and displays Basset arms.

Open: at any reasonable times. (Closed Sun.)

ST IVES
Cambridgeshire   *Map 4 TL37.*
Norris Museum
The Broadway
A comprehensive collection of Huntingdonshire local history, including fossils, archaeology and bygones, water-colours of local features, work in bone and straw by French prisoners at

Norman Cross. Also Huntingdonshire lacemaking.

☏ (0480) 65101.
Open: May-Sep, Tue-Fri 10-1 & 2-5, Sat 10-12 & 2-5, Sun 2-5; Oct-Apr Tue-Fri 10-1 & 2-4, Sat 10-12. (Closed BH weekends.)
Shop

ST NICHOLAS
Dyfed   *Map 2 SM83.*
Tregwynt Woollen Mill
(1½m SW)
Woollen mill in 18th century building where yarns have been made for 200 years. Visitors can see the mill in operation and some of the processes like twisting, cone winding, warping and weaving. Products include tapestry bed covers woven in various designs.

☏ St Nicholas (03485) 225.
Open: Mill, Mon-Sat 9-5 (Sat open but not in operation); mill shop Mon-Sat, 9-5.

ST OLAVES
Norfolk   *Map 5 TM49.*
St Olaves Priory
near Fritton Decoy
Remains of small Augustinian priory. Exceptional early example of brickwork dating from late 13th century or early 14th century.

Open: see page 4 (summer season only.)
& (ground floor & gardens only) (AM)

SALCEY FOREST
Northamptonshire/Buckinghamshire
Map 4 SP85.
(W of B526 on Harlwell road about 8 miles S of Northampton)
Managed by the Forestry Commission, Salcey Forest contains both deciduous and coniferous trees. Planting began in 1847 and now there are a variety of trees growing

separated by rides. The forest contains a rich variety of wildlife including pheasants, woodcocks, owls and deer. Part of the forest has been leased as a nature reserve.

Open: accessible at all reasonable times.
⌂

SALFORD
Gt Manchester   *Map 7 SJ89.*
Museum of Mining
Buile Hill Park, Eccles Old Road
In an attractive Georgian building, the museum has two reproduction coal mines, a large gallery dealing with all aspects of coalmining and its history and a gallery of mining art.

☏ 061-736 1832.
Open: Mon-Fri 10-12.30 & 1.30-5, Sun 2-5. (Closed: Sat 24-26 Dec, 1 Jan & Good Fri.)
Shop ✻ (ex guide dogs)

Ordsall Hall Museum
Taylorson Street
Half-timbered manor house, with later brick-built wing (1639), includes Tudor Great Hall, Star Chamber with 14th-century features and Victorian farmhouse kitchen. On upper floor are local and social history displays.

☏ 061-872 0251
Open: Mon-Fri 10-5, Sun 2-5. (Closed: Good Fri, 25-26 Dec & New Years day.)
& (ground floor only) ✻

Salford Museum & Art Gallery
The Crescent, Peel Park
The ground floor displays a period street scene typical of a northern industrial town at the turn of the century. The first floor art galleries house a large collection of works by

LS Lowry, as well as a regular series of temporary art exhibitions and displays of decorative arts.

☎ 061-736 2649.
Open: Mon-Fri 10-1 & 2-5, Sun 2-5. (Closed: 25-26 Dec, New Years day & Good Fri.)
& ✻

SALTCOATS
Strathclyde (Ayrshire)   Map 10 NS24.
North Ayrshire Museum
A museum in the ancient former parish church, with interesting old churchyard gravestones. Exhibits portray local historical items, and early 19th-century interiors.

☎ (0294) 64174.
Open: summer Mon-Sat, school hols 10-4.30; winter Thu, Fri & Sat 10-4.
& (ground floor & gardens only)

SANDOWN
Isle of Wight   Map 4 SZ58.
Museum of Isle of Wight Geology
Sandown Library, High Street
This museum, situated in the local library, houses a collection of fossils and exhibits of the island's geology.

☎ (0983) 404344.
Open: Mon-Fri 10-5.30, Sat & Sun 10-4.30. (Closed BH's.)
Shop ✻

SAUNDERSFOOT
Dyfed   Map 2 SN10.
Saundersfoot Pottery & Craft Shop
Wogan Street
Hand thrown ceramicware made by Carol Brinton who opened the pottery in 1970. A range of decorative and small colourful pottery is on display and frequent demonstrations of all processes can be seen.

The shop also has one of the best selections of craft goods in the area.

☎ (0834) 812406.
Open: daily, Apr-Sep, 10-5.30; demonstrations on most summer evenings between 8 & 10. Winter months by appointment only.

SCALLOWAY
Shetland   Map 16 HU33.
Scalloway Castle
Erected by Patrick Stewart, Earl of Orkney c.1600, designed on the two-stepped plan.

Open: see page 4, on application to the key keeper.
(AM)

SCUNTHORPE
Humberside   Map 8 SE81.
Borough Museum & Art Gallery
Oswald Road
Exhibits cover prehistoric to recent history, natural history, period rooms and ironstone workers' cottage; continuous programme of temporary exhibitions.

☎ (0724) 843533.
Open: Mon-Sat 10-5, Sun 2-5. (Closed: 25-26 Dec and 1 Jan.)
Admission charge Sat, Sun & BHs.
& (ground floor only) Shop
✻ (ex guide dogs)

SEAFORD
East Sussex   Map 5 TV59.
Seven Sisters Country Park
Exceat (1½m E)
The country park occupies 692 acres of attractive Sussex downlands, chalk cliffs, shingle beach and wet lands beside the Cuckmere River. Wide variety of birds and salt loving plants; the downland is

noted for its orchids and is grazed in the summer by Southdown sheep. At Exceat there is an Information Centre and a nature trail.

☎ Eastbourne (0323) 870280.
Open: country park accessible at all reasonable times, car park — dawn to dusk; Information Centre daily Etr-Oct 11-5.30; Nov-Etr weekends only 11-4.
& ⊓ ✻ (unless on lead)

SEDBERGH
Cumbria   Map 7 SD69.
National Park Centre
72 Main Street
Visitor centre with interpretative display. Maps, walks, guides and local information available.

☎ (0587) 20125.
Open: daily, Apr-Oct, mid morning-late afternoon.

SEDLESCOMBE
East Sussex   Map 5 TQ71.
Nortons Farm Museum & Farm Trail
(4½m NW of Hastings on A21)
Depicts the carthorse era with a fine display of carts, ploughs and handtools. The Farm Trail takes visitors round the fruit and arable farm, where cart horses are still used.

☎ (042487) 471.
Open: daily May-Sep, 9-5.
⊡ ⊓ ✻

SELBORNE
Hampshire   Map 4 SU73.
Selborne Hill
(from car park signed in Selborne village.)
The wooded slopes of Selborne Hill rise steeply to 700 ft to the west of Selborne, home of Gilbert White, the 18th-century naturalist. There are many fine walks through

the beech woods, although care should be taken in wet weather as paths become very slippery and muddy.

Open: accessible at all reasonable times. (NT)

SEVERN BORE
River Severn　　*Map 3 SO71.*
The Severn Bore is a tidal wave that occurs when the moon and the sun exert their maximum influence, causing a difference of 30 to 34 ft between high and low tide in the estuary. This occurs on at least 35 days a year. The tide enters the narrowing estuary at Sharpness and forces its way in a series of waves, until it levels out in the Gloucester area.

The best places to see the Bore are at Stonebench on the east bank, 3 miles SW of

Gloucester, off B4008, and at Minsterworth on the west bank, 5 miles W of Gloucester, on the A48. Full details of times can be obtained from most AA Centres.

SHAP
Cumbria　　*Map 12 NY51.*
Shap Abbey
An abbey of the Premonstratensian order, dedicated to St Mary Magdalene, with buildings dating from 1201-1540, when abbey was dissolved.

Open: at all reasonable times.
& (AM)

SHEFFIELD
South Yorkshire　　*Map 8 SK38.*
City Museum
Weston Park
A regional museum of geology, natural sciences,

archaeology, and Sheffield area trades, including cutlery, plate and ceramics. Educational facilities for schools and colleges.

☎ (0742) 27226.
Open: all year, Mon-Sat 10-5, Sun 11-5; Jun, Jul & Aug 10-8; Sun 11-8. (Closed: 24-26 Dec.)
Shop ✵ (ex guide dogs)

Sheffield Manor
Manor Lane
A ruined manor house which began as a medieval hunting lodge enlarged in the 16th century and between 1406 and 1616 principal seat of the Earls of Shrewsbury. The house fell into disrepair in the 17th century and in the early 1900s the site was cleared of all except the surviving 16th-century structures. Now undergoing restoration and archaeological excavation to

recover information about the house and earlier hunting lodge.

☎ (0742) 734697/27226.
Open: May-Oct, Wed-Sun 10-6.30.
Opening times subject to availability of staff. For visitors safety, access to some parts of the site may be restricted.
♿ (ground floor & gardens only) 🐕 (ex guide dogs)

Shepherd Wheel
Whiteley Woods
An early water-powered cutler's grinding establishment.

☎ (0742) 367731.
Open: all year, Wed-Sat 10-12.30 & 1.30-5, Sun 11-12.30 & 1.30-5. (Nov-Feb 4pm closing.)
♿

SHERE

Surrey — *Map 4 TQ04.*

Silent Pool
(½m W on A25)
Shaded by trees with footpath around, this crystal clear water is formed by a strong spring. Legend states King John watched a local girl bathing here. She drowned herself in a fit of shame. Anybody visiting this quiet water might easily imagine that her spirit lingers here still.

Open: at all reasonable times.

SHOREHAM-BY-SEA

West Sussex — *Map 4 TQ20.*

Marlipins
(Sussex Archaeological Society)
A Norman and later flint building, possibly a warehouse, now a maritime and local history museum.

☎ (07917) 62994.
Open: May-Sep, Mon-Sat 10-1 & 2-5, Sun 2-5. (Donations)
Shop 🐕

SHREWSBURY

Shropshire — *Map 7 SJ41.*

Bear Steps
St Alkmund's Square
Recently restored, timber framed, 14th-century cottage with shops and meeting hall.

☎ (0743) 56511.
Open: all year Mon-Sat 10-5.
Shop 🐕

Clive House Museum
An 18th-century town house occupied by the 1st Lord Clive during his period as Mayor of Shrewsbury in 1762. Now houses fine collections of Shropshire pottery and porcelain, church silver, watercolours, and Museum of the 1st Queen's Dragoon Guards.

☎ (0743) 61196.
Open: all year Mon-Sat 10-5.
Shop 🐕

Quarry Park
On the banks of the River Severn and overlooked by Shrewsbury School. Centrepiece of the park is the Dingle a sunken one-acre garden with lake, woodland garden, rock garden and an annual bedding display of thousands of plants.

☎ (0743) 61411.
Open: daily 8-dusk.
🧺 ♿

SIDMOUTH

Devon — *Map 3 SY18.*

The Donkey Sanctuary
(3m E off A3052)
Visitors can see the many animals taken into care, from geriatrics to the very young. Many donkeys have suffered neglect and ill treatment and the sanctuary's aim is to love and care for them for the rest of their lives.

☎ (03955) 6391.
Open: daily Jun-mid Sep 9-dusk; mid Sep-May 9-4.
♿ ☕ 🧺 🐕 (unless on lead)

SILCHESTER

Hampshire — *Map 4 SU66.*

Calleva Museum
Dealing with the Roman town of Calleva Atrebatum, this small museum includes panels of photographs, maps and other illustrative materials as well as actual objects excavated here, in order to present a brief account of life in the nearby walled Roman town (see Reading Museum).

☎ (0734) 700362 (mid-day, evenings & weekends).
Open: accessible daily 9-sunset. ♿ 🐕

SKENFRITH

Gwent — *Map 3 SO42.*

Skenfrith Castle
(7m NW of Monmouth on B4521)
13th-century Marcher keep within a towered curtain wall, the work of Hubert de Burgh. One of the three 'trilateral' castles at Gwent.

Open: at all reasonable times. (AM & NT)

SKIPTON

North Yorkshire — *Map 7 SD95.*

Craven Museum
Town Hall, High Street
Contains collection dealing especially with the Craven district. There are important exhibits of folk life, lead mining and prehistoric and Roman remains.

☎ (0756) 4079.
Open: Apr-Sep, Mon, Wed-Fri 11-5, Sat 10-12 & 1-5, Sun 2-5; Oct-Mar, Mon, Wed-Fri 2-5, Sat 10-12 & 1.30-4.30. Open some BH & PH, phone to check.

SOUTHAMPTON
Hampshire   *Map 4 SU41.*
Art Gallery
Civic Centre, Commercial Road
18th- to 20th-century English paintings. Continental Old Masters of 14th to 18th century. Modern French paintings. Collection of sculpture and ceramics. Of special interest are paintings and drawings of the 'Camden Town Group'. Particularly good collection of contemporary British painting and sculpture. Temporary exhibitions.

☎ (0703) 223855 Ext 2769.
Open: all year Tue-Fri 10-5, Sat 10-4, Sun 2-5. (Closed: 25-27 & 31 Dec.)
& Shop ✗ (ex guide dogs)

Bargate Guildhall Museum
Above Bar
The medieval North gate of the city. The upper floor, once a guildhall, is used to house displays on special themes.

☎ (0703) 224216.
Open: all year Tue-Fri 10-12 & 1-5, Sat 10-12 & 1-4, Sun 2-5. (Closed: 25-27 & 31 Dec & BH.) Shop ✗

God's House Tower
Winkle Street
Early fortified, sea-defensive, building dating from 1300s. Now a museum of Southampton's archaeology from Bronze Age to medieval times.

☎ (0703) 220007 & 24216.
Open: all year Tue-Fri 10-12 & 1-5, Sat 10-12 & 1-4, Sun 2-5. Shop

Tudor House Museum
Bugle Street, St Michael's Square
A restored, half-timbered 16th-century house, containing a museum of antiquarian and historical interest, social and domestic history, some costume and jewellery. Tudor garden reached through the museum.

☎ (0703) 224216.
Open: all year Tue-Fri 10-5, Sat 10-4; Sun 2-5. (Closed: 25-27 & 31 Dec & BH Mon.)
& (ground floor & garden with help) Shop ✗

Wool House Maritime Museum
Town Quay
This 600-year-old building, once a wool warehouse, has buttressed stone walls and old roof timbering. Houses an interesting maritime museum.

☎ (0703) 223941 & 224216.
Open: all year Tue-Fri 10-1 & 2-5, Sat 10-1 & 2-4, Sun 2-5. (Closed: 25-27 & 31 Dec.)
& (ground floor only) Shop ✗

SOUTH MOLTON
Devon   *Map 3 SS72.*
South Molton Museum
Town Hall, Market Street
Part of the Guildhall, a stone-fronted building of c.1743 entered through open arcaded frontage. Local history, old charters, weights and measures, pewter, old fire engines, giant cider press. Monthly art, craft and educational exhibitions.

☎ (07695) 2951.
Open: Apr-Nov Mon (ex Oct & Nov) Tue, Thu & Fri 10.30-12.30 & 2-4, Wed & Sat 10-12. (Closed BH.)
& Shop ✗
See advert, Rebecca's Great Torrington, 15m W, page 60

SOUTHPORT
Merseyside   *Map 7 SD31.*
Atkinson Art Gallery
Lord Street
19th- and 20th-century oil paintings, watercolours, drawings and prints, 20th-century sculpture. Also visiting exhibition programme.

☎ (0704) 33133 Ext 129.
Open: all year, Mon, Tue, Wed & Fri 10-5, Thu & Sat 10-1.
Shop ✗

Botanic Gardens Museum
Church Town (situated in public park)
Collections of local history, natural history, 18th- and 19th-century china, a display of the local shrimping industry; and a rare example of an early dug-out canoe from the nearby Martin Mere. Also Ainsdale National Nature Reserve display reconstructed. Victorian parlour and Cecily Bate collection of dolls. Several new displays are due to open in July.

☎ (0704) 27547.
Open: all year, Tue-Sat & BH Mon 10-6 (5pm Oct-Apr), & Sun 2-5. (Closed: Mon & Good Fri, also Fri following BH, 25 Dec & 1 Jan.)
⌨ & (ground floor only) Shop ✗

SOUTH SHIELDS
Tyne & Wear   *Map 12 NZ36.*
Arbeia Roman Fort & Museum
Baring Street
Roman fort at the easternmost end of the Hadrianic frontier, displaying fort defences, stone granaries, gateways, headquarters building, tile kilns and latrine. Museum contains site finds and interpretation.

☎ (0632) 561369.
Open: May-Sep, Mon-Fri 10-5.30, Sat 10-4.30 & Sun 2-5; Oct-Apr, Mon-Fri 10-4 & Sat 10-noon. & Shop

South Shields Museum & Art Gallery
Ocean Road
The museum shows the archaeology, history and natural history of South Shields. A maritime display includes a section on the evolvement of the lifeboat and local shipbuilding. The art gallery features a programme of changing exhibitions.

☎ (0632) 568740.
Open: all year Mon-Fri 10-5.30, Sat 10-4.30, Sun 2-5. (Closed: Good Fri, 25 & 26 Dec.)
& Shop ✝

SOUTHWOLD
Suffolk   Map 5 TM57.
Southwold Museum
Bartholomew Green
Formerly known as Dutch Cottage Museum, it contains relics of Southwold light railway and also illustrations of local history.

Open: daily Spring BH-30 Sep. Also Etr Mon & May Day BH, 2.30-4.30. Other times by appointment. (Donations)

SPEY BAY
Grampian, Moray   Map 15 NJ36.
Tugnet Ice House Exhibition
(5m N of Fochabers on B9104)
Located beside the mouth of the River Spey, it is the largest ice house in Scotland and was built in 1830 to store ice for packing salmon. The building has been restored, and now contains an exhibition on the salmon fishing industry and wildlife of the Spey Estuary.

☎ (0343) 45121.
Open: daily Jun-Sep 10-4. Audio visual show on request.
&

STAFFORD
Staffordshire   Map 7 SJ92.
Art Gallery
The Green
Art gallery showing temporary exhibitions of contemporary art, craft and photography. Craft shop selling a wide range of high quality work from British craftsmen.

☎ (0785) 57303.
Open: all year, Tue-Fri 10-5, Sat 10-4.
Shop ✝ (ex guide dogs)

Stafford Castle
Ruined castle dating from 12th century with inner and outer bailey, demolished by Parliamentary forces in 1643. Partly rebuilt c.1800 in Gothic style.

Open: at all reasonable times.

STAPLEHURST
Kent   Map 5 TQ74.
Iden Croft Herbs
Frittenden Road
In quiet country in the heart of Kent, the farm has hundreds of varieties of herbs and plants. Several herb demonstration gardens, an aromatic garden and other growing areas.

☎ (0580) 891432.
Open: daily Apr-Oct, 9-5; Nov-Mar, Mon-Sat 11-5.
⌑ &

STEVENAGE
Hertfordshire   Map 4 TL22.
Stevenage Museum
St George's Way
This museum, in the undercroft of the parish church of St George, tells the story of Stevenage from the earliest times to the present day. Temporary exhibitions.

☎ (0438) 354292.
Open: all year, Mon-Sat

10-5. (Closed BH.)
& Shop ✝

STINCHCOMBE
Gloucestershire   Map 3 ST79.
Cider Mill Gallery
(1m E of A38) Blanchworth Farm
Traditional farmhouse cider making, seasonally made (around October) using old horse-drawn mill and press. Pictures around the mill show the processes. Art gallery, craft shop and Victorian dolls house.

☎ Dursley (0453) 2352.
Open: Jun-Aug, Tue-Sun, 11-5; Apr, May, Sep-Dec, Tue-Sat 11-5. Other times by appointment.
& Shop

STIRLING
Central (Stirlingshire) Map 11 NS79.
Mar's Wark
Broad Street
A partly ruined Renaissance mansion with a gatehouse enriched by sculptures. Built by the Regent Mar in 1570.

Open: at all reasonable times.
(AM)

Stirling Smith Art Gallery & Museum
40 Albert Place, Dumbarton Road
Stirling's story — a permanent display of the history of Stirling from William Wallace to the present day. Lively programme of exhibitions throughout the year.

☎ (0786) 71917.
Open: all year Wed-Sun 2-5 (10.30-5 Sat)
& Shop ✝

STOCKTON-ON-TEES
Cleveland   Map 8 NZ41.
Preston Hall Museum
Yarm Road (2m S on A19)
Museum illustrates Victorian

social history, and collections include costume, arms, armour and period rooms. Also 19th-century reconstructed street with working blacksmiths and farrier.

☎ (0642) 602474 (weekends: 781184). Open: all year, Mon-Sat 9.30-5.30, Sun 2-5.30. Last admission 5pm.
☞ ⊟ & (ground floor & gardens only) Shop ✖ (ex guide dogs)

STOKE-ON-TRENT
Staffordshire   Map 7 SJ84.
City Museum & Art Gallery
Bethesda, Hanley
Exhibits include one of the largest and finest collections of ceramics, with the emphasis on Staffordshire pottery and porcelain. There is also a programme of temporary exhibitions.

☎ (0782) 29611 Ext 2173. Open: all year Mon-Sat 10.30-5, Sun 2-5. (Closed: Xmas week & Good Fri.)
☞ (licensed) & Shop ✖

Coalport Craft Centre
Park Street, Fenton
World famous for its fine bone china tableware, figurines, floral studies, cottages and hand painted collector's pieces. The company was established in 1750 in Shropshire and moved to Stoke-on-Trent in 1926, becoming a member of the Wedgwood Group in 1967. The craft centre provides an opportunity to see the making and hand painting of fine bone china.

☎ (0782) 45274. Open: Mon-Thu 9.30-4.30, Fri 9.30-12.30 & BH except Xmas. Factory tours are chargeable & by appointment only.

Ford Green Hall
Ford Green Road, Smallthorne.
A timber-framed farmhouse built in about 1580 for the Ford family. Brick wings were added in the early 1700s. Furnished with items and utensils used by a farming family from the 16th to the 19th century. Guided tours only (45 mins).

☎ (0782) 534771. Open: all year Mon, Wed, Thu & Sat 10-12.30 & 2-5, Sun 2-5. (Closed: Xmas & New Year.) Last admission 45 mins before closing.
⊟ & (ground floor only) Shop ✖

Minton Museum
London Road
Founded in 1793 by Thomas Minton who gave his name to the business, makers of the 'worlds most beautiful china'. The museum displays examples of Minton ware from 1800 to the present day.

☎ Stoke-on-Trent (0750) 20954. Open: Mon-Fri, 9-12.30 & 2-4.30.

The Sir Henry Doulton Gallery
A tribute to Sir Henry Doulton, the gallery contains pottery treasures and artistry representing over 150 years. Nearly 300 figures, some rare and some very early pieces. Displays by outstanding artists, experimental ceramics and exhibits demonstrate the variety of the Royal Doulton tradition, accompanied by archive material, sketches and pattern books.

☎ (0782) 85747. Open: all year Mon-Fri 9-12.30 & 1.30-4.15. (Closed factory holidays.)
Shop ✖

Stoke-on-Trent: decorating a Coalport China figure

STOKE-SUB-HAMDON
Somerset   Map 3 ST41.
Stoke-sub-Hamdon Priory
A 15th-century Ham-Hill stone house, once a chantry and retaining original screens and part of great hall.

Open: daily 10-6. (NT)

STONEHAVEN
Grampian (Kincardineshire)   Map 15 NO88.
Stonehaven Tolbooth
Old Pier, The Harbour
Once a 16th-century storehouse of the Earls Marischal, later used as a prison. Now a fishing and local history museum.

☎ Peterhead (0779) 77778. Open: Jun-Sep, Mon, Thu, Fri & Sat 10-12 & 2-5, Wed & Sun 2-5.
& (ground floor only) Shop ✖ (ex guide dogs)

STOURBRIDGE
West Midlands   Map 7 SO98.
Thomas Webb Crystal
Dennis Hall, King William Street, Amblecote
The museum is housed in one of the largest rooms of 18th-

century Dennis Hall and contains a fascinating variety of glassware, including superb examples of the work of artists and craftsmen such as George and Thomas Woodall, William Fritsche, Jules Barbe, John Thomas Fereday and many others. There are also numerous interesting documents which are reminders of the long and illustrious history of Thomas Webb Crystal. During the conducted factory tour visitors will see many of the traditional glassmaking and hand cutting techniques used for almost 150 years.

☎ (0384) 392521.
Open: all year Mon-Fri 10-4 (last factory tour 3pm). (Closed BH.)
⌨ Shop ✗

STRANRAER
Dumfries & Galloway (Wigtownshire)
Map 10 NX06.
Wigtown District Museum
London Road
Permanent displays on geology, natural history, archaeology and social history of the district with special exhibits on dairy farming and material relating to Sir John Ross, the Arctic explorer.

☎ (0776) 5088.
Open: Mon-Fri 10-5, Sat 10-1 & 2-5.

STREET
Somerset
Map 3 ST43.
The Shoe Museum (C & J Clark Ltd)
High Street
The museum is housed in the oldest part of the factory and contains shoes from Roman times to the present Georgian shoe buckles, caricatures and engravings of shoemakers, costume illustrations and fashion plates, shoe machinery, hand tools, advertising material, and 19th-century documents and photographs illustrating the early history of the firm from the founding in 1825 by Cyrus Clark.

☎ (0458) 43131.
Open: Etr Mon-Oct, Mon-Sat 10-4.45. Winter months by appointment only.
& (main floor only) Shop ✗

STROMNESS
Orkney
Map 16 HY20.
Pier Arts Centre
Collection housed in warehouse building on its own stone pier. Also galleries for visiting exhibitions and children's work. Arts library and reading room in adjacent house.

☎ (0856) 850209.
Open: all year Tue-Sat 10.30-12.30 & 1.30-5; Jul & Aug also Sun & Mon 2-5.
& (ground floor only) ✗

STROUD
Gloucestershire
Map 3 SO80.
Stroud District (Cowle) Museum
Lansdown
The exhibits cover geology, archaeology, local crafts, industrial archaeology (including local mills and houses), and farmhouse household equipment. A full-length model of the dinosaur Megalosaurus is on display.

☎ (04536) 3394.
Open: all year Mon-Sat 10.30-1 & 2-5. (Closed: BH's & other days, possibly Tue/Wed following BH's.)
& Shop ✗

SUNDERLAND
Tyne and Wear
Map 12 NZ35.
Grindon Close Museum
Grindon Lane
Edwardian period rooms, including chemist's shop and dentist's surgery.

☎ (0783) 284042.
Open: all year Mon-Wed & Fri 9.30-12.30 & 1.30-6 (5pm Tue), Sat 9.30-12.15 & 1.15-4; Jun-Sep also Sun 2-5. (Closed: 1 Jan, 5-8 Apr, 4 & 6 May, 24 & 26 Aug, 25 & 26 Dec.)
Shop ✗

Museum & Art Gallery
Borough Road
On display are examples of local pottery and glass. Local

archaeology, history, regional natural history and geology. 15th- to 19th-century
silver models of Sunderland-
built ships.

☎ (0783) 41235.
Open: all year Mon-Fri
10-5.30, Sat 10-4, Sun 2-5, BH
Mon 10-5. (Closed: New
Year's day, Good Fri, May
Day BH & Xmas.)
🖙 (10-4.45 Mon-Fri, 10-12
Sat) & Shop ✗

**Monkwearmouth Station
Museum**
North Bridge Street
Land transport museum in
station built in 1848. The
booking office, platform
areas and footbridge have all
been restored and there is
also rolling stock. Displays
inside the museum deal with
transport in north-east
England with a display
showing the evolution of
steam locomotives.

☎ (0783) 77075.
Open: all year Mon-Fri &
BH 10-5.30, Sat 10-4.30, Sun
2-5. (Closed: Good Fri, 25 &
26 Dec & 1 Jan.)
& Shop ✗

SWANSEA
West Glamorgan   Map 3 SS69.
**Maritime & Industrial
Museum**
South Dock
Contains complete working

woollen mill in continuous
production. Displays relating
to the industry and the Port of
Swansea and its environment.
Transport exhibits, steam
locomotives which run on
some Saturdays throughout
the season.

☎ (0792) 50351.
Open: daily 10.30-5.30.
(Closed: 25, 26 Dec & 1 Jan.)
& Shop ✗

SWARTHMOOR
Cumbria   Map 7 SD27.
Swarthmoor Hall
Elizabethan and later, the former home of George Fox,
founder of the Quakers. The
house is now administered by
the Society of Friends.

☎ Ulverston (0229) 53204.
Open: mid Mar-mid Oct,
Mon-Wed & Sat 10-12 & 2-5,
Thu & Sun by arrangement
only; mid Oct-mid Mar by
appointment only.
& (ground floor only) ✗

SWINDON
Wiltshire   Map 4 SU18.
Museum & Art Gallery
Bath Road
Contains a small collection of
items of local interest and an
art gallery. Visiting
exhibitions alternate with
pictures by 20th-century
artists.

☎ (0793) 24161 Ext 3129.

Open: all year Mon-Sat 10-6,
Sun 2-5. (Closed: Good Fri,
25 & 26 Dec.)
Shop ✗

Richard Jefferies Museum
Coate Farm (off A345)
Birthplace in 1848 of Richard
Jefferies, the nature writer,
and now a museum exhibiting
literature relating to local
wildlife written by Jefferies
and Alfred Owen Williams.

☎ (0793) 26161 Ext 3130.
Open: all year, Wed, Sat &
Sun 2-5 (Closed Xmas.)
Shop ✗

TARDEBIGGE
*Hereford &
Worcester   Map 7 SO96.*
Tardebigge Locks
*(Between Tardebigge and
Stoke Pound)*
Tardebigge Locks on the
Worcester and Birmingham
Canal were built by John
Woodhouse between 1812
and 1815 and are the largest
flight of locks in the country.
In a little over two miles the
canal is raised 217ft. The top
lock is much deeper than the
rest because in 1808 an experimental boat lift was installed, however it was soon
decided that it would not
stand up to constant rough
treatment. A deep lock was
constructed in its place. A
towpath runs along the eastern bank of the canal.

Open: accessible at all reasonalble times on towpath.

TAUNTON
Somerset   *Map 3 ST22.*
Hestercombe Gardens
(3m N of Taunton off A361 near Cheddon Fltzpaine)
Late 19th-century house, now the headquarters of the Somerset Fire Brigade. The superb gardens, originally planned in 1905 by Sir Edwin Lutyens and Gertrude Jekyll, are at present being restored to their original condition.

☎ (0823) 87222.
Open: all year Tue-Thu 2-5, also 25 May, 29 Jun & 27 Jul.
Donations.
☞ (Only served on Suns and Jun & Jul)

Sheppy's
Three Bridges (3½m SW, A38)
A traditional farm cider makers which has been commercially producing cider sice 1925. Today the farm has 20 acres of standard and 22 acres of bush orchards; there is also an excellent farm and cider museum.

☎ (082346) 233.
Open: all year Mon-Sat 8.30-dusk; Etr-Xmas also Sun 12-2.
& (ground floor only) Shop

Making farmhouse cider at Sheppy's, near Taunton

TENBY
Dyfed   *Map 2 SN10.*
Tenby Pottery
Upper Frog Street
All processes of pottery making can be seen from the showroom; throwing, firing, decorating, glazing and kiln-packing. Everything is hand thrown and individually decorated, ranging from thimbles to large plant pots.

☎ (0834) 2890.
Open: Mon-Fri 10.15-1 & 2.15-5.30, Sat 10.15-1.

TEWKESBURY
Gloucestershire   *Map 3 SO83.*
Tewkesbury Abbey
The impressive Abbey Church dates from Norman times and in the 12th century formed part of a Benedictine Monastery. The tower is 132ft high and dates from about 1150. The interior has some fine Romanesque and Gothic architecture; monuments to historic families. During the Dissolution of the Mona-steries, the Abbey was saved from distruction when the towns people bought it for £453.

☎ (0684) 292896.
Open: daily Apr-Sep 8.30-6; Oct-Mar 8.30-5.
Donations.
& ✟ Shop

THETFORD
Norfolk   *Map 5 TL88.*
Thetford Castle
One of the original motte and bailey castles, at 80ft, perhaps the largest still in existence. This represents the earliest form of castle, before masonery was added.

Open: accessible at all reasonable times.

Thetford Priory
Extensive remains of Cluniac monastery founded at beginning of 12th century. The 14th-century gatehouse of priory stands to its full height.

Open: at all reasonable times.
& (AM)

Warren Lodge
(2m NW of town, on B1107)
Remains of a two-storey hunting lodge in 15th-century flint with stone dressings.

Open: at all reasonable times.
& (AM)

THETFORD FOREST
Norfolk   *Map 5 TL88.*
Covering a vast area extending both sides of the Norfolk and Suffolk border, Thetford Forest's varied landscape and wildlife can be explored along the many rides, tracks and waymarked walks.

☎ Thetford (0842) 810271.
Open: forest all year; Information Centre at Santon Downham 2m E of Brandon Mon-Fri.
☖

THORNHAM MAGNA
Suffolk   *Map 5 TM17.*
Thornham Magna Herb Garden
An 18th-century walled herb garden with herb knot garden and astrological garden;

hundreds of spices, wild flowers and herbs. Woodland walks.

☎ Mellis (037983) 510.
Open: daily, 9.30-6.
☐ ☖

TILBURY
Essex   *Map 5 TQ67.*
Thurrock Riverside Museum
Civic Square
Illustrates the history of the River Thames and the people of its riverside. Ship and barge models, photographs, etc.

☎ (03752) 79216.
Open: all year Tue-Fri 10-1 & 2-5.30, Sat 10-1 & 2-5.
(Closed: Sun & BHs.)
Advisable to telephone beforehand.
& ✟

TITCHWELL MARSH
Norfolk   *Map 9 TF74.*
(6m E of Hunstanton off A149)
An area where not only is the birdlife protected but new habitat is created. Nesting-ground to the ringed plover, oystercatcher, common and little tern; wading birds forage on the exposed muds between autumn and spring. Hides on the reserve provide the opportunity to view the birds at close range.

☎ Brancaster (0485) 210432.
Open: public footpath all year. Visitor centre and hides Apr-Oct, 10-5.
☖

TIVERTON
Devon   *Map 3 SS91.*
Tiverton Museum
St Andrew Street, near Town Hall. (Entrance from public car park)
Museum housed in a restored 19th-century school containing numerous local exhi-

bits; a Victorian laundry, two water-wheels, costume gallery, industrial gallery covering the Grand Western Canal and local trades, natural history and wartime rooms. Heathcoat Lace gallery featuring 19th-century lace making machine and other relics of Heathcoat Lace Making Factory. Agricultural section includes a collection of farm wagons and a complete smithy. A large railway gallery houses the GWR locomotive No 1442, and other railway relics.

☎ (0884) 256295.
Open: Mon-Sat 10.30-4.30.
(Closed: BH & 23 Dec-1 Feb.)
& (ground floor only) Shop
✟ (ex guide dogs)

TOMATIN
Highland (Inverness-shire)
    Map 14 NH82.
Tomatin Distillery
Visitors can see the process of whisky making, which relies on traditional skills and techniques, at the largest malt whisky distillery in Scotland.

☎ (08082) 234.
Open: tours by arrangement at 3pm Mon-Fri.

TOMINTOUL
Grampian (Banffshire)   *Map 15 NJ11.*
Tomintoul Museum
The Square
Reconstructed farm kitchen and blacksmith's shop, Harness displays, local landscape and wildlife displays. Exhibition 'Scotland's Disappearing Wildlife' for one month in summer.

☎ Forres (0309) 73701.
Open: Apr, May & Oct, Mon-Sat 9-5.30; Jun & Sep, Mon-Sat 9-6, Sun 2-6; Jul & Aug, Mon-Sat 9-7, Sun 11-7.
& Shop ✟

TOMNAVOULIN
Grampian (Banffshire)   Map 15 NJ22.
Tamnavoulin-Glenlivet Distillery
(on B9008 6½m N of Tomintoul)
A video presentation is followed by a tour where visitors will see the process of whisky making, followed by whisky sampling in the hospitality lounge. Picnic area by the River Livet.

☎ Glenlivet (08073) 442.
Open: Etr-Oct, tours 9.30-4.
ℝ

TONDU
Mid Glamorgan   Map 3 SS88.
Glamorgan Nature Centre
(1m W)
A small nature reserve in open countryside, headquarters of Glamorgan Trust for Nature Conservation. Exhibition area in centre building, giving an introduction to the wildlife of the county and the work of the Trust. Waymarked trail.

☎ Aberkenfig (0656) 724100.
Open: most weekends Etr-Sep, pm only. ℝ

TONGLAND
Dumfries and Galloway (Kirkcudbrightshire)   Map 11 NX65.
Tongland Tour
Tour of SSEB Galloway hydro-electricity scheme. It includes video presentation and a visit to the dam and power station at Tongland. A fish ladder is an added attraction.

☎ Kirkcudbright (0557) 30114.
Open: May-Sep, Mon-Sat Tours 10, 11.30, 2, 3.30, by telephone appointment. Visitors taken to power station from Kirkcudbright by minibus.
✗ (ex at discretion of guides)

TOPSHAM
Devon   Map 3 SX98.
Topsham Museum
25 The Strand
Small museum, located in the sail-loft of a beautiful old Dutch-gabled 17th-century house, depicting its history and trade through the centuries.

☎ Exeter (0392) 56724.
Open: all year, Mon, Wed & Sat 2-5.

TORQUAY
Devon   Map 3 SX96.
Pepe & Son
Kingskerswell Road, off Newton Road
Production of French and German wines, matured in traditional casks giving them their characteristic flavour. A selection of wine making implements and various manufacturing processes is explained in the winery here. A vineyard, planted in 1981, can also be seen.

☎ (0803) 62166.
Open: daily, 11-6. Free tasting.

TREFRIW
Gwynedd   Map 6 SH76.
Trefriw Woollen Mill
Woollen mill dating from 1859. All stages of woollen manufacture can be seen, including blending, carding, spinning, dyeing, warping, weaving and tailoring, also hydro-electric turbines. Large shop selling own products. Demonstration of hand spinning, weaving and machine knitting Jun-Sep.

☎ Llanrwst (0492) 640462.
Open: Mon-Fri 9-5.30. Shop also open Sat 10-4. (Mill closed BH & 2 weeks Xmas.)
⌕ (Jun-Sep) ᵬ (shop only) shop ✗ (in mill)

TREWINT
Cornwall   Map 2 SX28.
Wesley's Cottage
(near Altarnun)
Small 18th-century Methodist shrine, well-restored in 1950. John Wesley came here six times between 1744 and 1762. Annual Wesley Day service is held. Also Sun services in summer. Interesting testaments and period furnishings are on display. Wesley Day celebrations 24 May.

☎ Pipers Pool (056686) 572.
Open: all year, daily, 9-dusk.
ᵬ (ground floor only) ✗

TRING
Hertfordshire   Map 4 SP91.
The Zoological Museum
Akeman Street
A branch of the British Museum (Natural History) specialising in mounted specimens of mammals, birds and insects from the Zoological collections of the second Baron Rothschild who opened the museum in 1892.

☎ (044282) 4181.
Open: all year, Mon-Sat 10-5, Sun 2-5. (Closed: 24-26 Dec, 1 Jan, Good Fri & May Day.)
ᵬ (ground floor only) Shop ✗ (ex guide dogs)

TRURO
Cornwall   Map 2 SW84.
County Museum & Art Gallery
River Street
Interesting display illustrating the history of the county. The mineral collection is world-famous. Collections of pottery, pewter, old-master drawings, Japanese ivories and lacquer-work.

☎ (0872) 72205.
Open: all year Mon-Sat, Library closes 1-2. (Closed BH's.) Shop ✗

TUNBRIDGE WELLS

Kent   Map 5 TQ53.

Tunbridge Wells Museum & Art Gallery

Civic Centre

Local and natural history, and Tunbridge ware. Collections of toys, dolls and domestic bygones.

☎ (0892) 26121 Ext 171.
Open: all year Mon-Fri 10-5.30 & Sat 9.30-5.
(Closed: Sun, BH & Tue after spring & summer BH's and Etr Sat.)
✠

TWICKENHAM

Gt London   see page 84.

Marble Hill House

Marble Hill Park, Richmond Road.   London Plan 2 : **44 B2.**

An example of English Palladian school of architecture standing in a wooded park near the River Thames. Built 1724-9 for Henrietta Howard, mistress of George II and later Countess of Suffolk. Today it contains Georgian paintings and furniture; there are notable Italian paintings by G P Panini in the Great Room.

☎ 01-892 5115.
Open: all year Mon-Thu, Sat & Sun 10-5 (4pm Nov-Jan).
(Closed 24 & 25 Dec.)
🖵 (Apr-Sep) ♿ (ground floor & gardens only Shop ✠

Orleans House Gallery

Riverside   London Plan 2 : **45 B2.**

Survivor of Orleans House, in which Louis Phillippe, Duc d'Orléans, King of the French 1830-48, lived in exile in the early 19th century. It was demolished in 1927. Surviving octagonal room, designed by James Gibbs in c.1720, has exquisite plasterwork.

☎ 01-892 0221.
Open: all year Tue-Sat 1-5.30 (4.30pm Oct-Mar) Sun & BH 2-5.30 (Oct-Mar 2-4.30).
(Closed: 25 & 26 Dec and Good Fri.)
Woodland gardens open all year, daily 9-dusk.
♿ (ground floor only) ✠

UFFINGTON

Oxfordshire   Map 4 SU28.

Uffington White Horse & Castle

(1¾m S off B4507)

Measuring 374 ft, this chalk figure overlooks the Vale of the White Hors. Its origins are uncertain but it is thought it may of been cut by Iron Age Celts or in Saxon times to commemorate King Alfred's victory over the Danes. The summit of Whitehorse Hill (856 ft) is crowned by Uffington Castle, an Iron Age camp.

Open: accessible at all reasonable times.
(AM)

UPMINSTER

Gt London   Map 5 TQ58.

Tithe Barn Agricultural & Folk Museum

Hall Lane

15th-century thatched timber building contains large selection of old agricultural implements, craft and farm tools, domestic bygones and items of local interest, over 2,000 exhibits in all.

☎ Hornchurch (04024) 47535.
Open: 1.30-6 on 5 & 6 Apr; 3 & 4 May, 7 & 8 Jun; 5 & 6 Jul; 2 & 3 Aug; 6 & 7 Sep; 4 & 5 Oct.
♿ Shop ✠

VENTNOR

Isle of Wight   Map 4 SZ57.

Botanic Gardens

One of Britain's younger botanic gardens, but already acclaimed by horticulturalists for fine range of plants, palms, trees and exotic shrubs.

☎ Shanklin (098 386) 2942.
Open: all year daily 10-5 (Museum, Etr-Sep).
🖵 ♿

WAKEFIELD

West Yorkshire   Map 8 SE32.

Wakefield Art Gallery

Wentworth Terrace

Good collection of modern paintings and sculpture including works by Henry

Moore, Barbara Hepworth,
Jacob Epstein, Graham
Sutherland, Ben Nicholson
etc. Temporary exhibitions.

☎ (0924) 370211 Ext 8031.
(After 5 & Sat (0924) 375402)
Open: all year, Mon-Sat
10.30-12.30 & 1.30-5. (Closed
BH.)
✗

Wakefield Museum
Wood Street
Archaeology, social history
displays. Waterton Collection of natural history specimens. Temporary exhibi-
tions.

☎ (0924) 370211 Ext 7190.
(After 5 & Sat (0924) 361767)
Open: all year Mon-Sat
10.30-12.30 & 1.30-5. (Closed
BH.) ✗

WALSALL
W Midlands   Map 7 SP09.
**Jerome K Jerome
Birthplace Museum**
*Belsize House, Bradford
Street*
Birthplace of Jerome K
Jerome, now restored as a
museum, housing documents
and memorabilia of the
author. One room is a recon-
struction of an 1850's parlour.

☎ (0922) 21244 Ext 3115.
Open: all year Tue-Sat 10-5.
(Closed: Sun, Mon & BH.)
Shop ✗

Museum & Art Gallery
*Central Library, Lichfield
Street*
Garman Ryan collection
including important works by
Blake, Degas, Van Gogh and
Epstein. Regular loan exhi-
bitions. Local history
museum.

☎ (0922) 21244 Ext 3124.
Open: all year Mon-Fri 10-6
& Sat 10-4.45. (Closed: Sun
& BH.)
₺ Shop ✗

Botanic Gardens, Ventnor

WALTHAM ABBEY
Essex   Map 5 TL30.
**Waltham Abbey
Gatehouse, Bridge &
entrance to Cloisters**
14th-century gatehouse with
separate carriage and
pedestrian entrances.
Harold's Bridge is also 14th-
century. Cloister entrance
dates from 12th-century. In
the historic Norman and later
Abbey Church nearby is an

undercroft museum.

Open: at any reasonable
time.
(AM)

WANDLEBURY RING
Cambridgeshire   *Map 5 TL45.*
*(4m SE of Cambridge off
A1307)*
On the summit of the low Gog
Magog Hills, the remains of
an Iron-Age hill fort which
once comprised a double
rampart and ditch, 1,000 ft in
diameter; about 110 acres of
the hills have been protected
by the Cambridge Preser-
vation Society.

Open: daily.
(Donations welcome)
Run for dogs Shop

WANTAGE
Oxfordshire   *Map 4 SU48.*
**Vale & Downland Museum
Centre**
*The Old Surgery, Church
Street*
A lively museum centre with
displays on the geology,
archaeology and local history
of the Vale of the White Horse
and the town of Wantage.
Temporary exhibitions and
local craft demonstrations
occasionally.

☏ (02357) 66838.
Open: all year Tue-Sat
10.30-4.30 & Sun 2-5.
⌨ 큐 ⅙ (with assistance)
Shop

WARRINGTON
Cheshire   *Map 7 SJ68.*
**South Lancashire
Regiment (PWV)
Regimental Museum**
Peninsula Barracks, Orford
Military museum of South
Lancashire Regiment from
1717 onwards.

☏ (0925) 33563.
Open: all year, Mon-Fri 9-3,
also for parties evenings &

weekends by arrangement.
✝

WARWICK
Warwickshire   *Map 4 SP26.*
St John's House
*Coten End (Junction of A429
& A445 E of town)*
Fine 17th-century house rebuilt by the Stoughton family
on the site of an old hospital.
It is now a branch of the
County Museum (domestic
scenes, costume, and musical
instruments),   Victorian
schoolroom. Includes the
museum of the Royal War-
wickshire Regiment on the
first floor.

☏ Leamington Spa (0926)
493431 Ext 2021. For
Regimental Museum (0926)
491653.
Open: all year Tue-Sat & BH
10-12.30 & 1.30-5.30; May-
Sep also Sun 2.30-5.
⅙ (ground floor only) Shop

Warwickshire Museum
Market Place
17th-century Market Hall now
a museum displaying the geology, history and natural
history of Warwickshire.
Notable for the Sheldon
tapestry map of Warwick-
shire, habitat displays and
giant fossil plesiosaur. Temporary exhibitions throughout
the year and children's holiday activities during the summer and Christmas. 150th
Anniversary Celebration including special exhibition
summer.

☏ (0926) 493431 Ext 2500.
Open: all year Mon-Sat
10-5.30; May-Sep also Sun
2.30-5. ✝ Shop

**Warwickshire Yeomanry
Museum**
*The Court House, Jury
Street*
Display of military exhibits,
includes uniforms, medals,

militaria and weapons dating
from 1794 to 1945. Also selec-
ted items of silver from the
Regimental collection. There
is a very fine display of
paintings and pictures covering the same period.

☏ (0926) 492212.
Open: Good Fri-Sep, Fri,
Sat, Sun & BH 10-4. Shop

WASHINGTON
West Sussex   *Map 4 TQ11.*
Chanctonbury Ring
*(1½m SE) Reached by
footpath (South Downs Way)*
Situated on the crest of the
South Downs, Chanctonbury
Ring consists of a clump of
beech trees standing within
the remains of an Iron Age
fort. The trees were planted
in 1760 by Charles Goring.
Excavations at the fort have
revealed remains of two
Roman buildings and prehistoric barrows. There are
good views from the summit.

Open: accessible at all
reasonable times.

WATFORD
Hertfordshire   *Map 4 TQ19.*
Watford Museum
194 High Street
The history of the Watford
area from earliest times to the
present day. There are
special features on brewing
and printing together with a
display of wartime Watford
based on the 'Dad's Army'
series written by Jimmy Perry
from his Watford experience.
A good art gallery and a constantly changing programme
of exhibits.

☏ (0923) 32297.
Open: all year Mon-Sat 10-5.
(Closed: Xmas & New
Year's Day.)
⅙ Shop ✝ (ex guide dogs)
*See advert Chequers
Restaurant Rickmansworth,
3m W page 121.*

WAYLAND'S SMITHY

Oxfordshire *Map 4 SU28.*

(1m S off the B4507 Compton Beauchamp turning near end of unclass road)

A well preserved megalithic long barrow in a copse close to the Ridgeway path. The long barrow was excavated in 1919-1920 and revealed eight-stone age skeletons. Wayland the Smith figures in Scandinavian mythology as a maker of invincible weapons.

Open: accessible at all reasonable times.
(AM)

WEETING

Norfolk *Map 5 TL78.*

Weeting Castle

A ruined 11th-century fortified manor house, situated in a rectangular enclosure and preserving slight remains of a three storeyed cross-wing.

Open: at all reasonable times.
(AM)

WELSHPOOL

Powys *Map 7 SJ20.*

Cockpit

New Street

During the 18th century cockfighting was a keenly followed sport and this grade II listed cockpit has been recently restored to original state

Open: Apr-Sep, Mon-Fri 10-4
♿

Oriel Gallery

High Street

The largest collection of original prints in mid-Wales are contained in this gallery which also shows all the print processes of lithography, woodcraft and screen printing. Every month there are changing exhibitions with a wide range of subjects from

West Bretton: 'Knife Edge' sculpture by Henry Moore

sculpture and photography to textiles and painting.

Open: all year Mon-Sat 11-5.

Powysland Museum

Salop Road

Museum of archaeology and local history.

☎ (0938) 4759.
Open: all year Mon-Fri 11-1 & 2-5, Sat 2-4.30. (Closed: Wed in winter.) Shop 🐕

WEST BRETTON

West Yorkshire *Map 8 SE21.*

Yorkshire Sculpture Park

Bretton Hall College

Set in beautiful grounds, this park is the country's leading outdoor exhibition centre of contemporary sculpture, including works by Henry Moore and Barbara Hepworth. There is a programme of changing exhibitions, educational activities and events.

☎ (092485) 302.
Open: daily, summer 10-6; winter 10-4. ♿ ⛩

See advertisement on page 137

WEST BROMWICH

West Midlands *Map 7 SP09.*

Oak House

Oak Road

Half-timbered 16th-century house, the result of three separate building phases. The rooms display superb period furnishings and furniture. An Elizabethan garden is at the front of the house.

☎ 021-553 0759.
Open: Apr-Sep, Mon-Sat 10-8 (ex Thu 10-1 & Sun 2.30-8); Oct-Mar, Mon-Sat 10-4 (ex Thu 10-1).
♿ (ground floor & gardens only) 🐕

WEST MALLING

Kent *Map 5 TQ65*

St Leonard's Tower

The surviving part of the former castle or fortified manor house belonging to Bishop Gundulph.

Open: at all reasonable times.
♿ (grounds only) (AM)

WESTON-SUPER-MARE

Avon *Map 3 ST36.*

Woodspring Museum

Burlington Street

The museum is housed in the old workshops of the Edwardian Gaslight Company. Around a central courtyard are displays of the Victorian Seaside Holiday, an old chemist's shop, a dairy, a lion fountain with Victorian pavement mosaic and a gallery of wildlife in the district. Other exhibits include Mendip minerals and mining, transport from penny farthing to Weston Autogyro, cameras, a display of Peggy Nisbet dolls and the Dentist in 1900. There is also a display featuring "The Weston-super-Mare Story", and various changing exhibitions are held in the Art Gallery.

☎ (0934) 21028.
Open: all year Mon-Sat, 10-5 (ex Nov-Feb closed 1-2). (Closed: Good Fri, Xmas & New Year.)
🚻 ♿ (ground floor only)
Shop ✗

WESTRAY
Orkney   *Map 16 HY44.*
Noltland Castle
Late 16th-century ruined castle which was never completed. It has a fine hall, vaulted kitchen and a notable winding staircase.

Open: at all reasonable times on application to Key Keeper.
(AM)

WEYMOUTH
Dorset   *Map 3 SY67.*
Radipole Lake and Lodmoor
(Radipole W of Weymouth, Lodmoor on A353 1m NE)
Two RSPB nature reserves

close to the centre of large seaside town. Despite their proximity to this hubbub both have retained a natural feeling and a wealth of wildlife is attracted. At Radipole a large reserve overlooks the lake.

☎ (03057) 773519.
Open: reserve daily, dawn-dusk; information centre daily 10-5.
🚻 🪑 ♿ ✗

WHITEHAVEN
Cumbria   *Map 11 NX91.*
Whitehaven Museum & Art Gallery
Market Place
Lower gallery devoted to

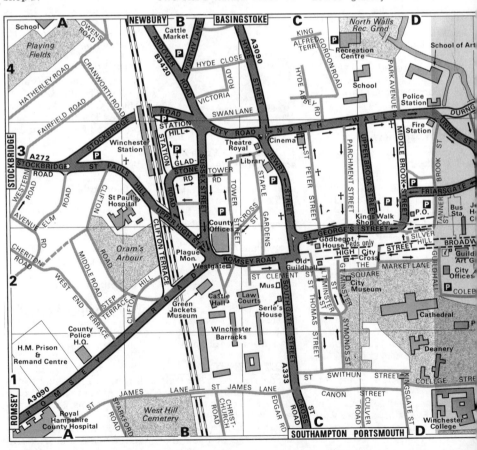

approximately 20 exhibitions per year. The upper gallery features local history and Whitehaven-made pottery. Slide/tape shows usually featured in upper gallery.

☎ (0946) 3111 Ext 307.
Open: all year Mon, Tue & Thu-Sat 10-5. (Closed BH.)
& (ground floor only) Shop
✟ (ex guide dogs)

WHITTINGTON
Staffordshire   Map 7 SK10.
Whittington Barracks, Staffordshire Regiment Museum
An interesting museum displaying details of the Regiment's battle honours; cap-

tured trophies, weapons old and new, uniforms past and present, and a special display of medals.

☎ (0543) 433333 Ext 229.
Open: all year Mon-Fri 8.30-4.30; Sat, Sun & BH by appointment only.
& Shop ✟

WICK
Highland (Caithness)   Map 15 ND35.
Caithness Glass
Harrow Hill
All aspects of glass blowing on view. There is also a factory seconds shop.

☎ (0955) 2286.
Open: all year Mon-Fri 9-5,

Sat 9-1 (4.30 May-Sep).
⛴ & Shop ✟ (ex shop)

Castle of Old Wick
A four storeyed ruined square tower, known also as Castle Oliphant, probably of 12th century.

Open: accessible except when adjoining rifle range is in use.
(AM)

Castle Sinclair and Castle Girnigoe
(½m W of Noss Head Lighthouse)
Perched on the cliff edge on this bleak coastline the castles are reached along the coast from Noss Head Lighthouse. Little remains of Castle Girnigoe, built late in the 15th century but there are impressive remains of Castle Sinclair (1606-7). Both castles were strongholds of the Sinclairs but clan battles in the latter part of the 17th century left them in ruins.

Open: accessible at all reasonable times.

WILLENHALL
West Midlands   Map 7 SO99.
Lock Museum
Willenhall Library, Walsall Street.
The aim of the museum is to interpret all aspects of the locksmith's trade and the people who are employed in it, from the earliest times to the present day and from all over the world. There are locks on display to demonstrate the main developments over the years of lock mechanisms and these range from padlocks no bigger than a finger nail to 32lb heavyweights, and from mechanisms which resemble fine ornaments to the harsh, unmistakably functional prison asylum lock.

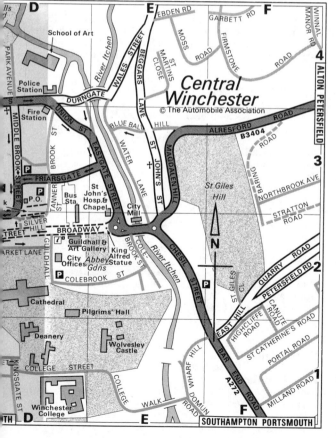

☏ Walsall (0922) 21244 Ext 3115.
Open: all year Mon, Tue, Thu & Fri 9.30-6, Sat 9.30-12.30 & 2-4.30. (Closed BH.)
Shop ✗

WILMINGTON

East Sussex *Map 5 TQ50.*

The Long Man

(½m S on footpath)

The exact date of this 231 ft chalk cut figure on Windover Hill is unknown. It is thought that it may date from the 6th century. The figure holds an upright staff in each hand. During the 19th century the figure was renovated, having been almost lost from sight.

Open: accessible at all reasonable times.

WINCHESTER

Hampshire *Map 4 SU42.*

Guildhall Gallery

Broadway Plan : **D2.**

On show are local topographical views. Temporary exhibitions.

☏ (0962) 68166 Ext 296.
Open: during exhibitions, Tue-Sat 10-5, Sun & Mon 2-5. (Closed Mon in winter.) Subject to alteration.
☕ ♿ Shop ✗

Pilgrims' Hall (School)

The Close Plan : **D2.**

Its name is derived from the pilgrims who came to the shrine of St Swithun of Winchester (Bishop 852-862). Its most notable feature is the 14th-century hammerbeam roof. Today the hall is used by the Cathedral choir school.

☏ (0962) 54189.
Open: daily 9-6 (except when in use by the school for concerts, examinations etc.)

Royal Green Jackets Museum

Peninsula Barracks, Romsey Road Plan : **B2.**

This interesting display illustrates the history of the Royal Green Jackets and the three regiments from which they were formed, the Rifle Brigade, the King's Royal Rifle Corps and the Oxfordshire and Buckinghamshire Light Infantry.

☏ (0962) 61781 Ext 288.
Open: Apr-Sep, Mon-Fri 10-12.30 & 2-4.30, Sat 2.30-4.30; Oct-Mar, Mon-Fri 10.30-12.30 & 2-4. (Closed: 25 Dec-2 Jan & BH.) ✗

Serle's House

Southgate Street Plan : **C2.**

A fine Baroque-style 18th century house, now incorporating the Royal Hampshire Regiment museum and memorial garden.

☏ (0962) 61781 Ext 261.
Open: all year Mon-Fri 10-12.30 & 2-4. (Closed BH.)
♿ (ground floor only) ✗

The Great Hall of Winchester Castle

Castle Avenue, off High Street Plan : **B2.**

The only surviving portion of the castle is the notable great hall of 1235 with Purbeck marble columns. At the west end is the legendary Round Table of King Arthur.

☏ (0962) 54411 Ext 366.
Open: all year daily 10-5. (Closed: Good Fri & Xmas.) (Donations)
♿ Shop ✗

WINDSOR

Berkshire *Map 4 SU97.*

Household Cavalry Museum

Combermere Barracks, St Leonards Road

One of the finest military museums in Britain. Uniforms, weapons, horse furniture and armour of the Household Cavalry from 1660 to the present.

☏ (07535) 68222 Ext 203.
Open: all year Mon-Fri (ex BH) 10-1 & 2-5; 2nd weekend in May-1st weekend Sep also Suns 10-1 & 2-4 (ex BH Suns).
♿ Shop ✗

Windsor Castle

A restored Norman royal castle with 19th century additions for George IV by Wyattville.

☏ (07535) 68286.
Castle precinct open: daily Jan-31 Mar 10-4.15; Apr 10-5.15; May-Aug 10-7.15. (Closed 17 Jun); Sep-26 Oct 10-5.15; 27 Oct-Dec 10-4.15. Always subject to closure, sometimes at very short notice.
♿ Shop ✗

WINSTER

Derbyshire *Map 8 SK26.*

Market House

Stone-built 17th- or 18th-century market house in main street of village.

Open: Apr-Sep, Sat, Sun & BH Mon 2-6 (or sunset)
Shop ✗ (NT)

WIRRAL COUNTRY PARK

Cheshire/Merseyside Map 7 SJ28/37.

The park follows a former railway line and includes the 'Wirral Way', a 12-mile footpath from West Kirby to Neston, the line runs along the Dee Estuary with access to the beach at various points: the haunt of vast congregations of ducks and wading birds outside the breeding season. Beyond Neston the track turns inland to Hadlow Road Station, near Willaston, where the booking hall is laid out as in the 1930's.

☎ 051-648 4371 (Visitor centre, Thurstaston). Open: park at all reasonable times; Visitor Centre and Hadlow Road Station, daily Nov-Mar, 10.30-3.30 (Station 10.30-4); Apr-May, Sep-Oct, 10.30-5; Jun-Aug 10.30-8. (Station 10.30-5). (Closed Xmas.) ﾖ (Visitor Centre) ﾋ Thurstaston, Caldy, Heswall, Parkgate, Neston, Willaston

WISBECH
Cambridgeshire   Map 5 TF40.
Wisbech and Fenland Museum
Contains fine collection of ceramics, objets d'art, archaeology, natural history and articles which illustrate Fenland life.

☎ (0945) 583817. Open: all year Tue-Sat 10-5 (4pm Oct-Mar). (Closed BH.) Museum library and archives available by appointment only. Shop ﾒ

WITCOMBE, GREAT
Gloucestershire   Map 3 SO91.
Witcombe Roman Villa
A large courtyard Roman Villa in which a hypocaust and several mosaic pavements are presented.

Open: at all reasonable times. (Keys at farmhouse adjoining.) (AM)

WOLVERHAMPTON
West Midlands   Map 7 SO99.
Bantock House Museum
Bantock Park, Bradmore Road
This 19th-century house contains important collections of English enamels, japanned tin and papier-maché products of the Midlands. Also shown are early Worcester porcelain, pottery, English and foreign dolls and toys.

☎ (0902) 24548. Open: all year Mon-Fri 10-7, Sat 10-6 & Sun 2-5, BH Mon & Tue 2-5. (Closed: Good Fri, Etr Sun, Xmas & New Years day.) ﾋ (ground floor only) ﾒ

Bilston Museum & Art Gallery
Mount Pleasant, Bilston
Houses a large collection of fine English painted and transfer printed enamels from 18th and 19th centuries. Also iron and steel artefacts relating to the industrial history of the area. Staffordshire pottery is on display and there are frequently held ex-

Wirral Country Park, Port Sunlight Village, Ness Gardens and the Ellesmere Port Boat Museum are just a few of the host of attractions in Wirral. They are set in a wealth of magnificent scenery amidst rolling countryside and picturesque villages with unsurpassed sea views and easy access to Chester, Liverpool and North Wales.

For more information and your free colour brochure contact:
WIRRAL TOURIST INFORMATION Dept.AA
Marine Promenade, New Brighton L45 2JU. Tel: 051-638 7144

hibitions of contemporary
interest.

☎ (0902) 49143.
Open: all year Mon-Sat 10-5.
(Closed BH.)
✕

Central Art Gallery
Lichfield Street
18th- and 19th-century
English water colours and oil
paintings. Modern paintings,
sculpture and prints. Fine
Oriental collections and full
programme of temporary exhibitions including Chinese
Art 8 Mar-19 Apr. Artists in
Industry 14 Jun-12 Jul.

☎ (0902) 24549.
Open: all year Mon-Sat 10-6.
(Closed BH.)
& (ground floor only) ✕

WOODHENGE
Wiltshire   Map 4 SU14.
(1m N of Amesbury)
Consisted formerly of six
concentric rings of timber
posts within a ditch. Positions
of the posts are marked by
concrete pillars. Discovered
accidentally by aerial recon-
naissance in 1925.

Open: accessible at all
reasonable times.
& (AM)

WORCESTER
Hereford and Worcester Map 3 SO85.
**City Museum & Art
Gallery**
Foregate Street
Temporary art exhibitions
from local and national
sources. Natural history and
geology displays. 19th-cen-
tury chemists shop. Also
collections of Worcestershire
Regiment and Worcester-
shire Yeomanry Cavalry.

☎ (0905) 25371.
Open: all year Mon, Tue,
Wed & Fri 9.30-6, Sat 9.30-5.
Shop ✕

**Dyson Perrins Museum of
Worcester Porcelain**
Severn Street
The finest collection of
Worcester china in the world,
with an unrivalled display of
pieces dating from 1751 to the
present day.

☎ (0905) 23221.
Open: all year Mon-Fri 9-5;
Apr-Sep also Sat 10-5.
(Tours of works Mon-Fri by
prior arrangement, charge.)
⌂ & Shop ✕

Guildhall
High Street
The Guildhall has a fine early
Georgian frontage and from
June will become a major
Heritage Centre. Wor-
cester's history and
personalities are vividly
portrayed in sight and sound,
with a very varied display
featuring such people and
places as Edward Elgar,
Woodbine Willie, Vesta
Tilley and the Music Halls.
Also shown are the seven
ages of Worcester.

☎ (0905) 23471.
Open: all year Mon-Fri
9.30-5 & occasional Sat in
summer. (Closed BH.)
& (ground floor only) ✕

Tudor House
Friar Street
500-year-old timber-framed
house, with a squint and an ornate plaster ceiling. Now a
museum of local life featuring
social and domestic history,
including children's room,
Edwardian bathroom and
World War II Home Front
Displays. Large agricultural
exhibits are displayed in yard
at rear.

☎ (0905) 25371.
Open: all year Mon-Wed &
Fri-Sat 10.30-5.
& (ground floor only) Shop
✕

WORDSLEY
West Midlands   Map 7 SO88.
Stuart Crystal
Red House Glassworks
The Redhouse Cone and
Museum opened Easter 1984
representing 200 years of
glassmaking history. The factory tour enables the visitor to
see at close hand the glassmaking process from raw
materials to finished items.

☎ Brierley Hill (0384) 71161.
Redhouse Cone & Museum
Open: daily 9-5; Factory
Tours Mon-Fri 10-11.15 &
1.30-3.15; (Fri closed
2.30pm). (Closed for tours
26-31 May & 28 Jul-8 Aug; all
facilities closed 23-27 Dec &
1 Jan.) ⌂ & Shop ✕

WORKINGTON
Cumbria   Map 11 NY02.
**Helena Thompson
Museum**
Park End Road
Costume, furniture and other
decorative art in 18th-century
house. Temporary exhi-
bitions in former stable block.

☎ (0900) 62598.
Open: all year Mon-Sat 11-3.
& (ground floor & garden
only) Shop ✕

WORKSOP
Nottinghamshire   Map 8 SK57.
**Worksop Priory Church &
Gatehouse**
Church has unique Norman
west front with twin towers
and 12th-century Transitional
nave, with 20th-century
additions, 14th-century scroll
ironwork on doors in south
porch. Remarkable 14th-
century double archway with
large upper room which from
1623 housed earliest
elementary school in county.
Elaborate façade with
statues, and 15th-century
wayside shrine and chapel.

☎ (0909) 472180.

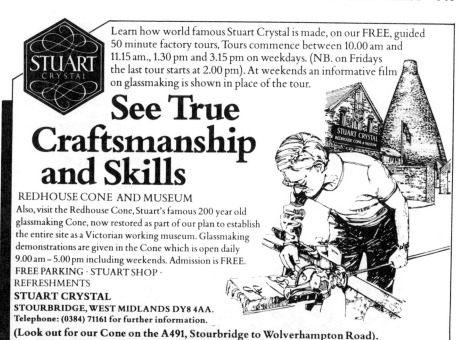
Church open: daily 7.30-12 & 1.30-4.30; gatehouse Mon-Wed 9.30-1 & 2-4. ⑤ (ground floor only) Shop ☒

WORTHING
West Sussex   *Map 4 TQ10.*
Worthing Museum & Art Gallery
Chapel Road
Archaeology, geology, history of Worthing, pictures and pottery. Large costume collection. Frequent exhibitions.

☎ (0903) 39999 Ext 121. Sat only (0903) 204229.
Open: Mon-Sat 10-6 (summer), 10-5 (winter). ⑤ Shop ☒

WRAXALL
Somerset   *Map 3 ST63.*
Wraxall Vineyards
Set on the foothills of the Mendips, this 10-acre vineyard was founded in 1973 by the Holmes family. The two

main vines are the German Müller Thurgau and the French hybrid Seyval. Visitors are welcome to look round unaccompanied and wines may be purchased from the shop.

☎ Ditcheat (074 986) 486 or 331.
Open: daily at all reasonable times. Shop

WREXHAM
Clywd   *Map 7 SJ35.*
Bersham Industrial Heritage
Bersham (2m SW)
An interpretative centre housed in a Victorian school building which is situated along an eight-mile industrial history trail. Exhibitions on John Wilkinson, the Bersham iron-works, the Davies Brothers, gatesmiths of Croes Foel and a reconstructed forge.

☎ (0978) 261529.
Open: Etr-Oct, Tue-Sat & BH 10-12.30 & 1.30-4, Sun 2-4; Nov-Etr, Tue-Fri 10-12.30 & 1.30-4, Sat 12.30-3.30. ⑤ Shop ☒

WYRE FOREST
Herefs & Worcs/Shropshire
        Map 7 SO77.
Ranking alongside the New Forest and the Forest of Dean nearly 1,000 acres of the forest is now a National Nature Reserve. Special features are the numerous old meadows and orchards around the fringes, and Dowles Brook and its tributaries. These various habitats make it a good place for the naturalist.

Open: accessible at all reasonable times. Car park closes at dusk. Location W of Bewdley. Information centre on A456.

YARMOUTH
Isle of Wight   *Map 4 SZ38.*
Fort Victoria Country Park
Sconce Point (½m W)
Remains of fort built in 1852-3 to protect the western approach to Portsmouth. Now being developed as a Country Park with free guided walks, exhibition, picnic and barbecue facilities. Spectacular views of the Solent are among the pleasures of the park's nature trail.

☎ (0983) 760860 or Newport (0983) 524031 Ext 162.
Open: daily. Guided tours from 17 Apr.
🖵 🍴 ♿ (ground floor & grounds only)

YARMOUTH, GREAT
Norfolk   *Map 5 TG50.*
Museum Exhibition Galleries
Central Library, Tolhouse Street
Travelling and local art exhibitions.

☎ (0493) 858900.
Open: all year Mon-Sat 9.30-5.30. (Closed: 5-8 Apr, 6 & 25-27 May, 24-26 Aug, 25-28 Dec & 1 Jan.)
🍴

Tolhouse Museum
Tolhouse Street
Late 13th-century building with old dungeons and exhibits on local history. Brass rubbing centre with wide range of replica brasses.

☎ (0493) 858900.
Open: all year Mon-Fri 10-1 & 2-5.30; (Sun Jun-Sep). (Closed: Good Fri, Xmas & New Year.)
Charge for brass rubbing
Shop 🍴

YELVERTON
Devon   *Map 2 SX56.*
Paperweight Centre
4 Buckland Terrace, Leg O'Mutton
Exhibition of over 800 beautiful antique and modern glass paperweights. Millefiori, faceted, diamond-cut dated and signed 'invest-

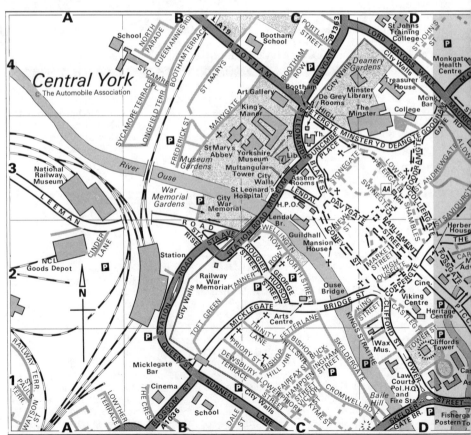

ment' paperweights, many for sale (from £3-£300).

☎ (0822) 854250.
Open: week before Etr-Oct, Mon-Sat 10-5; winter opening Wed 1-5.
&. (ground floor only) Shop

YEOVIL
Somerset   *Map 3 ST51.*
Yeovil Museum
Hendford Manor Hall
Local history and archaeology and specialised collections of costumes and firearms.

☎ Mon-Fri (0935) 75171 Sat (0935) 24774.
Open: all year Mon-Wed,

Fri & Sat 9.30-1 & 2-5.
Shop

YORK
North Yorkshire   *Map 8 SE65.*
Borthwick Institute of Historical Research
St Anthony's Hall,
Peasholme Green   *Plan : E3.*
Originally a late 15th-century Guildhall, it has served in turn as poor-house, hospital, armoury, and Blue-Coat school. Now the Borthwick Institute of Historical Research, part of York University, with a collection of ecclesiastical archives. Exhibition of documents.

☎ (0904) 642315.

Hall open: all year Mon-Fri 9.30-1 & 2-5. (Closed: Xmas, Etr. Search rooms closed week of Aug BH & preceeding week.)
&. (ground floor & gardens only) ✗

Guildhall
off Coney Street   *Plan : C2.*
A 15th-century building, restored after severe war damage. Hall with notable timbered roof. Underground passage leading to the river.

☎ (0904) 59881 Ext 208.
Open: May-Oct, Mon-Thu 9-5, Fri 9-4.30, Sat 10-5, Sun 2.30-4.30; Nov-Apr, Mon-Thu 9-5, Fri 9-4.30. (Closed: Good Fri, 25 & 26 Dec & 1 Jan.)
&. (ground floor only) ✗

King's Manor
Exhibition Square   *Plan : C4.*
Former home of Abbot of St Mary's Abbey, later stopping place of James VI of Scotland on way to become James I of England, and of Charles I at time of Civil War. Much altered in early 17th century, and fully restored to become part of university in 1964.

☎ (0904) 59861.
Courtyards open: daily 9-5 (ex 25 Dec). Principal rooms open on certain days only during spring & summer. Check with porter.
🚻 (ex PH) &. (gardens only)

Museum Gardens   *Plan : B3.*
Botanical gardens in which stand the ruins of St Marys Abbey with multangular tower nearby.

Open: daylight hours.

National Railway Museum
Leeman Road   *Plan : A3.*
Illustrates the history and de-

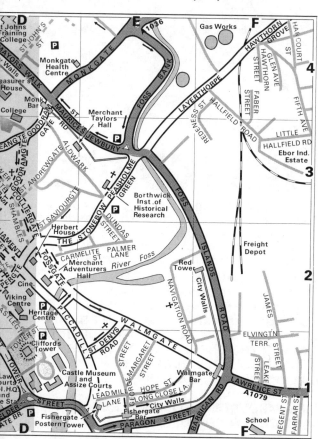

velopment of British railway engineering including social aspects. Collection contains some 25 locomotives and about 20 items of rolling stock as well as signalling equipment etc. Small exhibits feature models of locomotives (many working) and rolling stock. Also variety of railway equipment and material, plus collections of paintings, posters, drawings and films. Reference library service by appointment. Lecture theatre seating 80, is incorporated in the building and an education programme is available. Please apply for details.

☎ (0904) 21261.

Open: all year, Mon-Sat 10-6, Sun 2.30-6. (Closed: Good Fri, May Day BH, Xmas eve, Xmas day, Boxing day & 1 Jan and some other public holidays: contact Museum for details.)
⊓ & Shop ✘ (ex guide dogs)

York: Railway Museum

AA Viewpoints

A full list of AA Viewpoints, which provide excellent panoramas of the surrounding countryside, is given below. They are also shown in the atlas section of this book and can be located by using the map references given with each Viewpoint's name.

ENGLAND

Avon, **Portishead** 1 mile W of Portishead Map Ref 3 ST47.

Cornwall, **Pendennis Head** 1 mile SE of Falmouth Map Ref 2 SW83.

Derbyshire, **Highoredish** 3 miles E of Matlock Map Ref 8 SK35.

Dorset, **Bulbarrow** 5 miles S of Sturminster Newton Map Ref 3 ST70.

Essex, **One Tree Hill** ¼ mile NW of A13/B1420 junction 1½ miles S of Basildon Map Ref 5 TL68.

Gloucestershire, **Robinswood Hill** 2 miles S of City Centre in Robinswood Hill Country Park Map Ref 3 SO81. **Symonds Yat** 3 miles N of Coleford off B4432 Map Ref 3 SO51.

Hampshire, **Portsdown Hill** 1 mile N of Cosham Map Ref 4 SU60.

Hereford & Worcester, **Clent Hills** S of A456, 2 miles SW of Halesowen Map Ref 7 SO98. **Windmill Hill** Waseley Country Park 3½ miles S of Halesowen Map Ref 7 SO97.

Isle of Wight, **Bembridge Down** 2 miles ENE of Sandown Map Ref 4 SZ68.

Kent, **Farthing Corner** on Farthing Corner service area M2 Map Ref 5 TQ86.

Leicestershire, **Beacon Hill** 2 miles SW of Loughborough Map Ref 8 SK51.

Oxfordshire, **Wittenham Clumps** 1½ miles off A4130 Nr Brightwell Map Ref 4 SU59.

Shropshire, **Clee Hills** 6 miles E of Ludlow Map Ref 7 SO67.

Somerset, **Dunkery Beacon** between Luccombe and Wheddon Cross Map Ref 3 SS84. **Wellington Monument** 2½ miles S of Wellington Map Ref 3 ST11.

Staffordshire, **Central Forest Park** Stoke-on-Trent. Part of City Centre reclamation scheme. Map Ref 7 SJ84.

W Sussex, **Duncton Hill** 5 miles SW of Petworth Map Ref 4 SU91.

Warwickshire, **Magpie Hill** in Burton Dassett Hills Country Park between Gaydon and Warmington Map Ref 4 SP35.

Wiltshire, **Barbury Castle** in country park 5 miles S of Swindon Map Ref 4 SU17.

N Yorkshire, **Sutton Bank** 5 miles E of Thirsk Map Ref 8 SE58.

W Yorkshire, **Holme Moss** 1 mile SW of Holme to East of A6024 Map Ref 7 SK00.

WALES

Anglesey, **South Stack** in South Stack reserve (RSPB) 3 miles W of Holyhead Map Ref 6 SH28.

Dyfed, **Foel Eryr** 13 miles NE of Haverfordwest ½ mile W of B4329 Map Ref 2 SN03.

Gwent, **Sugar Loaf** 3 miles NW of Abergavenny Map Ref 3 SO21.

Gwynedd, **Great Orme's Head** on top of Great Orme, Llandudno Map Ref 6 SH78.

Powys, **Montgomery Town Hill** ½ mile SW of Montgomery, off B4385 via unclassified road Map Ref 7 SO29.

SCOTLAND

Borders, **Scott's View** 3 miles E of Melrose Map Ref 12 NT53.

Central, **David Marshall Lodge** 1 mile N of Aberfoyle Map Ref 11 NN50. **Queen's View, Auchineden** 6 miles N of Bearsden Map Ref 11 NS58.

Highland, **Bealach Na Ba'** *(Pass of the Cattle)* 5 miles SE of Applecross Map Ref 14 NG74. **Glen Garry** On A87 7¼ miles from A82 at Invergarry Map Ref 14 NH20. **Knockan Cliff** 8 miles NE of Ullapool Map Ref 14 NC20. **Struie Hill** 6 miles SE of Bonar Bridge Map Ref 14 NH68.

Lothian, **Cockleroy** Beecraigs Country Park, 2 miles S of Linlithgow Map Ref 11 NS97.

Strathclyde, **Lyle Hill** 2 miles E of Greenock, midway between A78 & A770 Map Ref 10 NS27.

Tayside, **Queen's View** 6 miles E of Tummel Bridge on B8019 Map Ref 14 NN85.

INDEX

158

160

ORDNANCE SURVEY
Leisure Guides

LAKE DISTRICT

Voted the award of best new publication about
the area in 1984, this superb guide describes the
topography and traditions of the area and offers
scenic drives, walks, and masses of information
about what to see and where to stay, linked to
large-scale Ordnance Survey maps, and illustrated throughout in colour.

NEW FOREST

Walks, drives, places to see, things to do, where
to stay, all linked to large-scale Ordnance Survey
mapping, with useful background information to
the area. Illustrated throughout with superb
colour photography.

YORKSHIRE DALES

Descriptions of scenery, history, customs and 'a
day in the life of a dalesman' evoke the
atmosphere of this remote and beautiful region
and introduce the walks, drives and directory of
places of interest. Large-scale Ordnance Survey
maps and a wealth of colour photography make
this guide a must for tourist and walker alike.

All available in hard or paperback; forthcoming titles include
Scottish Highlands, Cotswolds.

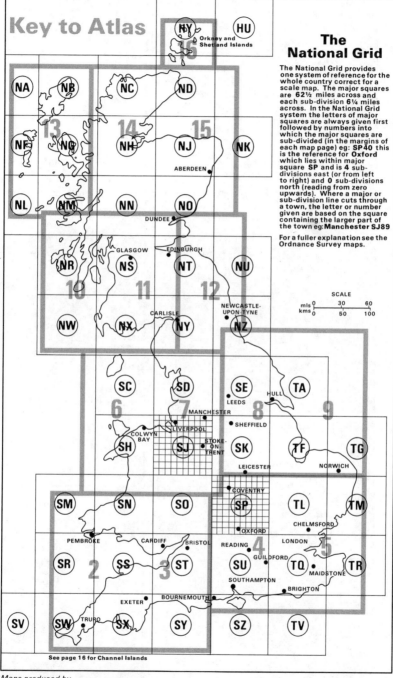

Key to Atlas

Orkney and Shetland Islands

The National Grid

The National Grid provides one system of reference for the whole country correct for a scale map. The major squares are 62½ miles across and each sub-division 6¼ miles across. In the National Grid system the letters of major squares are always given first followed by numbers into which the major squares are sub-divided (in the margins of each map page) eg: **SP40** this is the reference for **Oxford** which lies within major square **SP** and is 4 sub-divisions east (or from left to right) and 0 sub-divisions north (reading from zero upwards). Where a major or sub-division line cuts through a town, the letter or number given are based on the square containing the larger part of the town eg: **Manchester SJ89**

For a fuller explanation see the Ordnance Survey maps.

SCALE

See page 16 for Channel Islands

Maps produced by

The AA Cartographic Department
(Publications Division), Fanum House,
Basingstoke, Hampshire RG21 2EA

This atlas is for location purposes only: see Members' Handbook for current road and AA road services information.

162

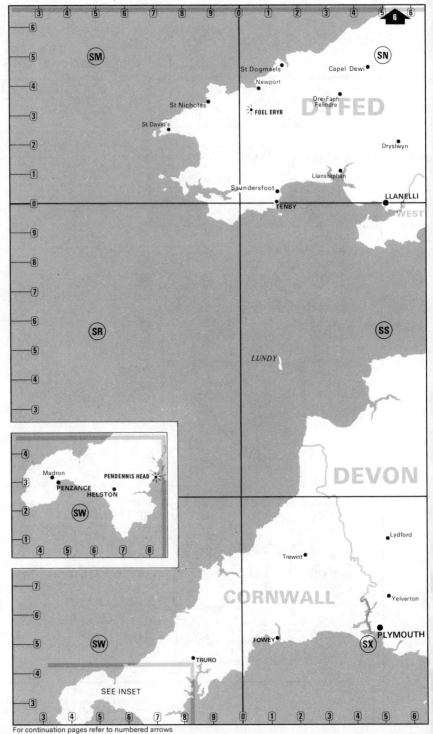

For continuation pages refer to numbered arrows

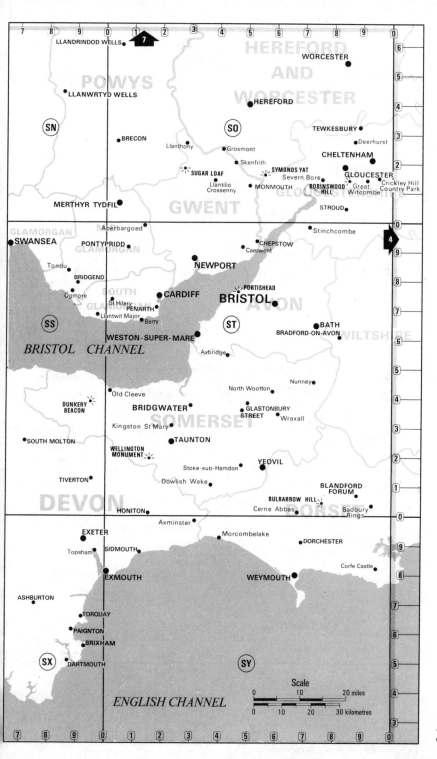

ENGLISH CHANNEL

Scale
0   10   20 miles
0   10   20   30 kilometres

3

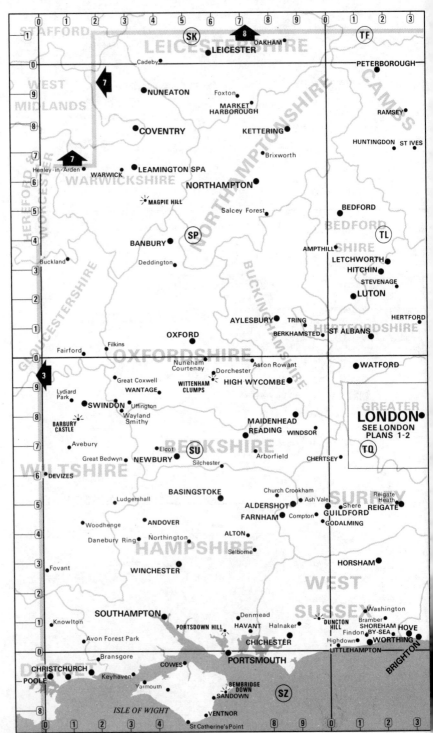

4

For continuation pages refer to numbered arrows

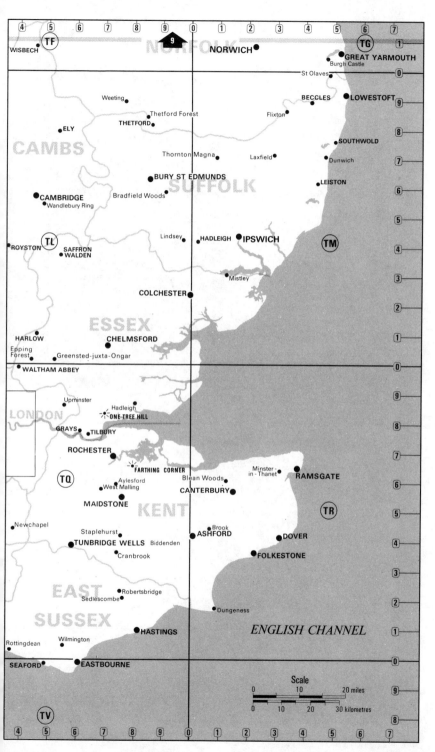

ENGLISH CHANNEL

Scale

0 .... 10 .... 20 miles

0 .... 10 .... 20 .... 30 kilometres

5

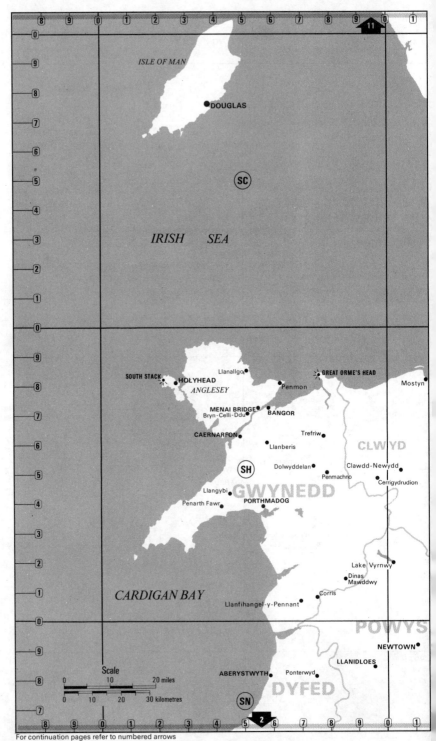

ISLE OF MAN

●DOUGLAS

(SC)

IRISH   SEA

SOUTH STACK
HOLYHEAD
ANGLESEY

Llanallgo●

●Penmon

☀GREAT ORME'S HEAD

Mostyn●

MENAI BRIDGE●
Bryn-Celli-Ddu●

●BANGOR

CLWYD

CAERNARFON●

Trefriw●

Llanberis●

Dolwyddelan●

Penmachno●

Clawdd-Newydd●

(SH)

●Cerrigydrudion

Llangybi●

GWYNEDD

Penarth Fawr●

●PORTHMADOG

Lake Vyrnwy●

Dinas
Mawddwy●

CARDIGAN BAY

Corris●

Llanfihangel-y-Pennant●

POWYS

NEWTOWN●

LLANIDLOES●

Scale

0   10   20 miles

0   10   20   30 kilometres

ABERYSTWYTH●

Ponterwyd●

DYFED

(SN)

11

2

6

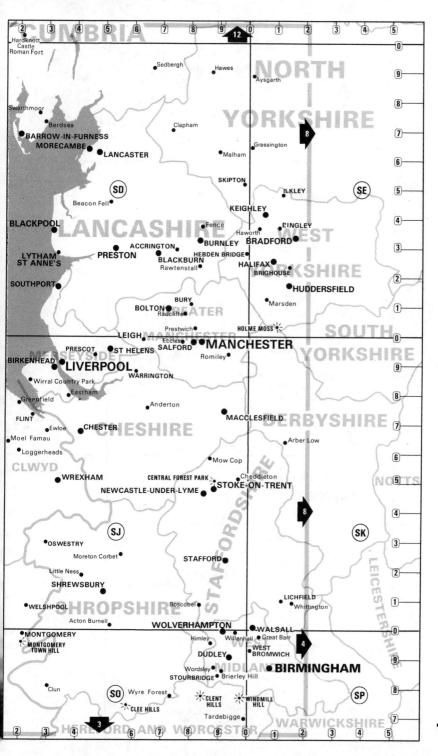

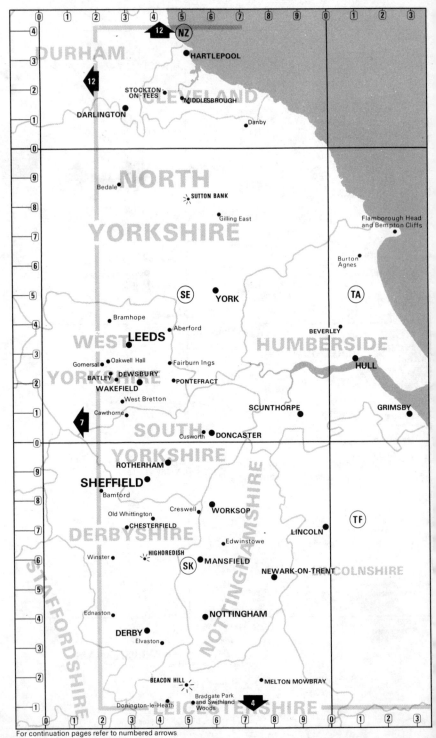

For continuation pages refer to numbered arrows

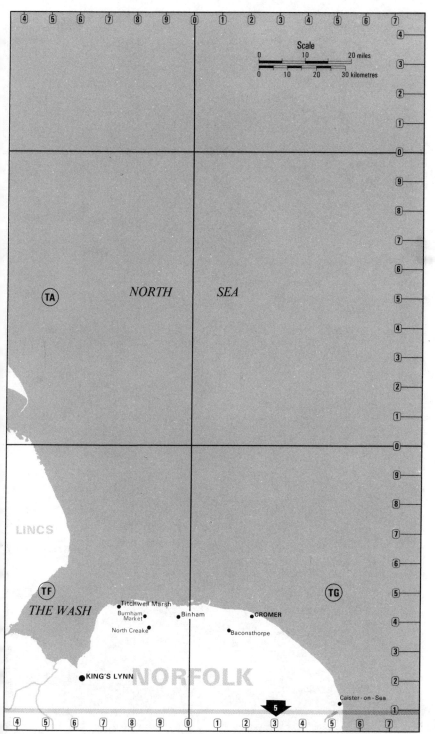

Scale

0   10   20 miles

0   10   20   30 kilometres

TA

NORTH   *SEA*

LINCS

TF

THE WASH

TG

• Titchwell Marsh

Burnham
Market •
• Binham

• North Creake

• CROMER

• Baconsthorpe

• KING'S LYNN   NORFOLK

Caister - on - Sea •

5

9

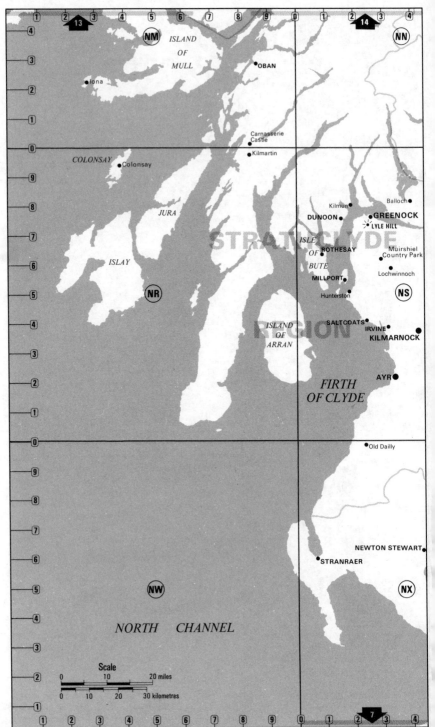

Scale
0 — 10 — 20 miles
0 — 10 — 20 — 30 kilometres

For continuation pages refer to numbered arrows

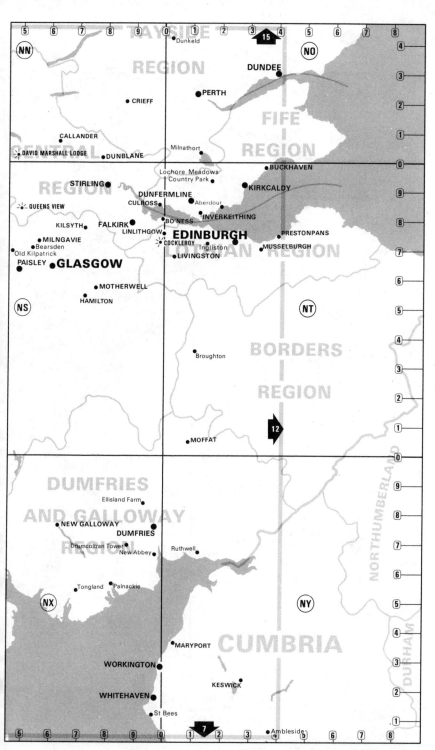

11

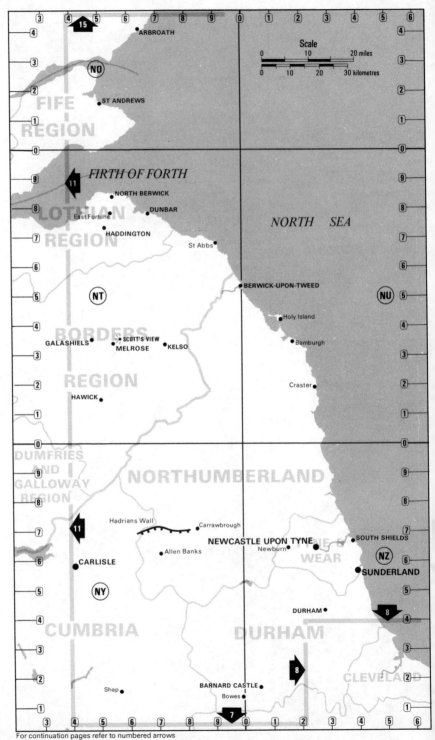

Scale

0 — 10 — 20 miles

0 — 10 — 20 — 30 kilometres

ARBROATH

NO

FIFE REGION

ST ANDREWS

FIRTH OF FORTH

NORTH BERWICK

DUNBAR

East Fortune

LOTHIAN

HADDINGTON

REGION

St Abbs

NORTH SEA

NT

BORDERS

BERWICK-UPON-TWEED

NU

Holy Island

Bamburgh

GALASHIELS

SCOTT'S VIEW

MELROSE

KELSO

REGION

Craster

HAWICK

DUMFRIES AND GALLOWAY REGION

NORTHUMBERLAND

Hadrians Wall

Carrawbrough

NEWCASTLE UPON TYNE

SOUTH SHIELDS

Allen Banks

Newburn

WEAR

NZ

CARLISLE

SUNDERLAND

NY

DURHAM

CUMBRIA

DURHAM

CLEVELAND

Shap

BARNARD CASTLE

Bowes

12

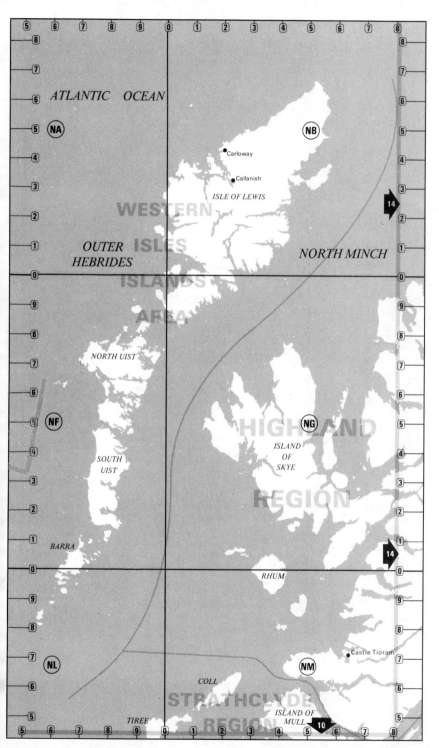

ATLANTIC OCEAN

NA

NB

Carloway

Callanish

ISLE OF LEWIS

WESTERN

OUTER ISLES

HEBRIDES

ISLANDS

AREA

NORTH MINCH

NORTH UIST

NF

HIGHLAND

NG

ISLAND OF SKYE

REGION

SOUTH UIST

BARRA

RHUM

NL

COLL

Castle Tioram

NM

STRATHCLYDE

TIREE

REGION

ISLAND OF MULL

13

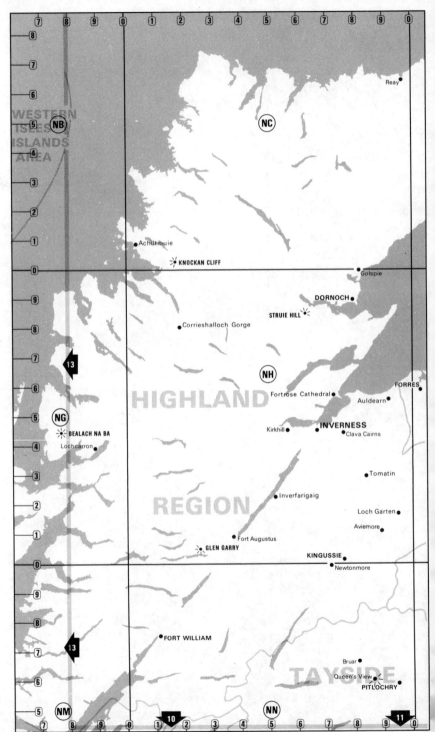

For continuation pages refer to numbered arrows

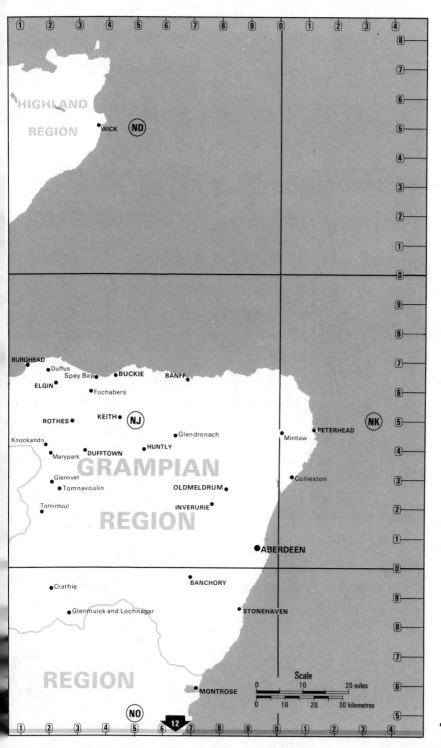

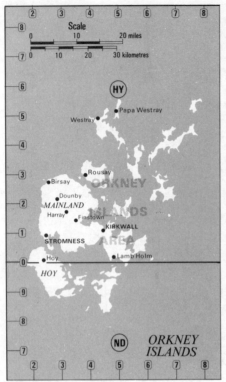

Scale
0   10   20 miles
0   10   20   30 kilometres

HY

● Papa Westray
Westray ●
Rousay ●
Birsay ●
Dounby ●
MAINLAND
Harray ● Finstown ●
KIRKWALL ●
STROMNESS ●
Hoy ●   ● Lamb Holm
HOY

ORKNEY
ISLANDS
AREA

ND

ORKNEY
ISLANDS

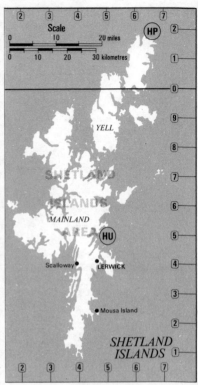

Scale
0   10   20 miles
0   10   20   30 kilometres

HP

YELL

SHETLAND
ISLANDS
AREA

MAINLAND

HU

Scalloway ●   ● LERWICK

● Mousa Island

SHETLAND
ISLANDS

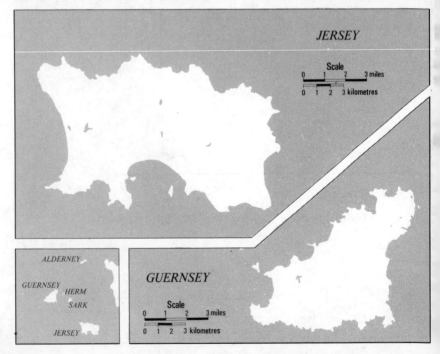

JERSEY

Scale
0   1   2   3 miles
0   1   2   3 kilometres

ALDERNEY

GUERNSEY   HERM
SARK

JERSEY

GUERNSEY

Scale
0   1   2   3 miles
0   1   2   3 kilometres

16